CRIMES AND PUNISHMENT

VOLUME
3

Crimes and Punishment takes a hard and objective look at crime and criminals—their ways and methods and the means by which they are caught and punished. This authoritative edition combines material from *Murder Casebook, Science Against Crime,* and *Crimes and Punishment* which were originally published in the United Kingdom. This new compilation casts a penetrating eye upon the violence around us with which we must live.

CRIMES AND PUNISHMENT

The *Illustrated* CRIME ENCYCLOPEDIA

VOLUME
3

H. S. STUTTMAN, INC. *publishers* Westport, CT 06889

CONTENTS

Charles Manson was a cult leader who completely dominated his followers. In August 1969, he led his "family" into Los Angeles, from their desert commune, where they massacred Hollywood star Sharon Tate and six others.

Published by H. S. STUTTMAN INC.
Westport, Connecticut 06880

PRINTED IN THE UNITED STATES OF AMERICA

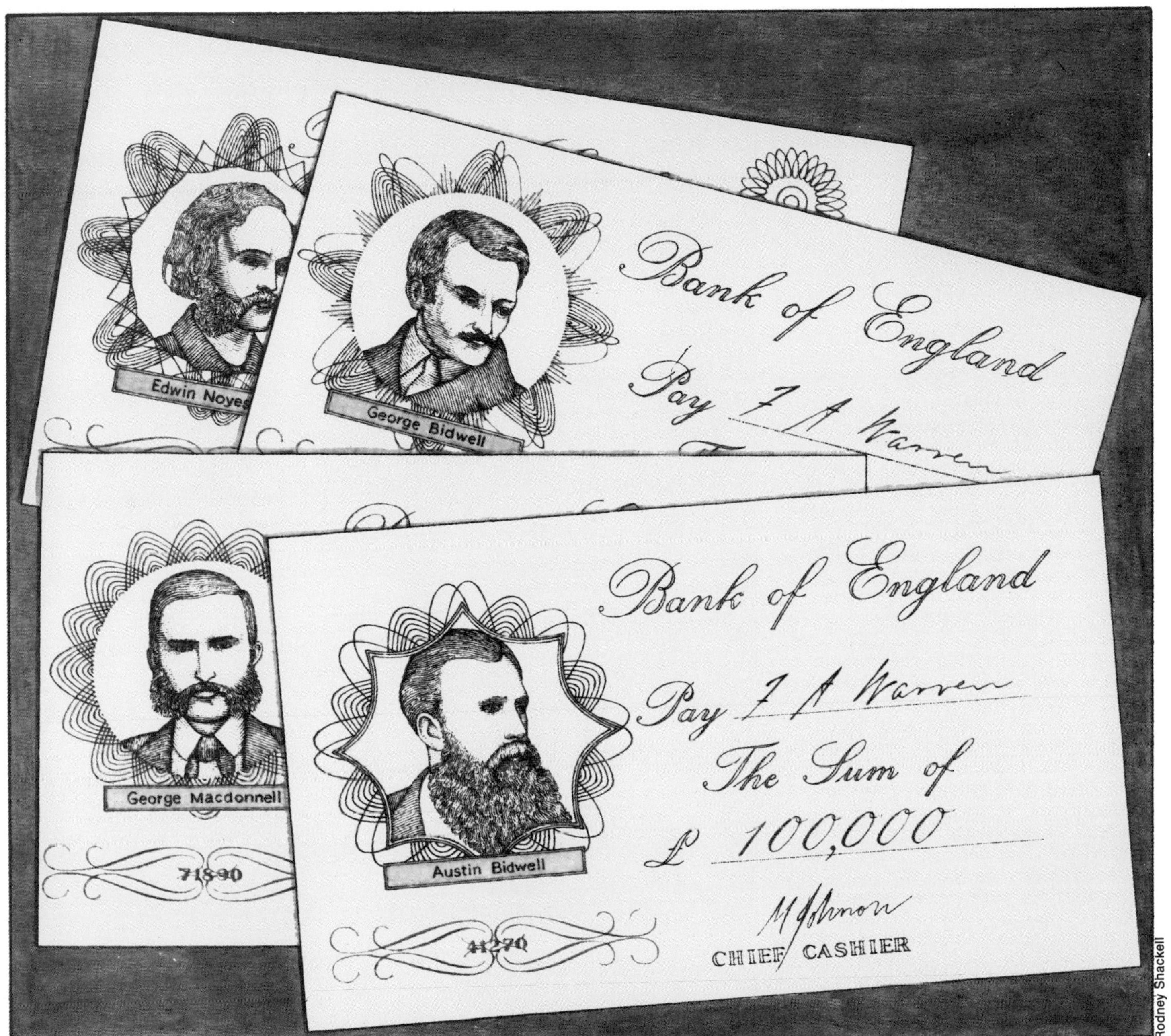

Rodney Shackell

THEY SWINDLED THE BANK OF ENGLAND...

From the shadier side of Wall Street, they came with an audacious plan to make themselves richer by £100,000. The Old Lady of Threadneedle Street was to be rudely conned. A wealthy American customer would turn out to be nothing better than a disgusting foreigner. He would commit an affront to a Great British institution famed for its impregnability . . .

IT WAS with a routine flourish that Colonel Peregrine Madgwick Francis, manager of London's Western Branch of the Bank of England, signed the note to his wealthy American customer, Mr. Warren. After all, the note was purely routine; just an acknowledgement of another satisfactory piece of business with a gentleman of substance. The message itself had been penned in immaculate copperplate by one of his senior clerks:

"Your favour of the 21st enclosing £4,250 in bills for discount is received and the proceeds of same passed to your credit as requested."

An hour or so later, that January day in 1873, the note was on its way to the flourishing Midlands city of Birmingham, where busy Mr. Warren was so clearly making commendable progress in selling some of the new Pullman's Palace Sleeping Cars to British railway companies. Since Mr. Warren was a typical go-getting American, with no time to have a permanent residence in Britain, it was addressed, as ordered, care of the Central Post Office, Birmingham.

Pure invention

So far as Colonel Francis was concerned, the acknowledgment in the note meant simply that the Bank of England had promptly and properly honoured payment on bills of exchange issued by no less a merchant bank than the illustrious House of Rothschild in Paris—furthermore, Mr. Lionel Rothschild was one of the Bank of England's 24 directors.

But Colonel Francis would not have turned with contentment to the other business of the day if he had known the alarming truth about his "impressive" customer. For Mr. Warren and his bills of exchange were both phoney. The name Warren was fictitious, the story of the Pullman business trip to Britain was pure invention.

Worst of all for the Colonel, however, was the fact that the Rothschild bills were brilliant but worthless forgeries, and the "impregnable" 179-year-old Bank of England had been neatly swindled, and would soon be swindled again.

The following morning, January 23, a cabdriver, taking two passengers from Birmingham's Queen's Hotel to New Street railway station was ordered to stop on the way at the Post Office and collect any mail addressed to Mr. Warren. There was just one letter. The cabbie took it and duly handed it to his passengers, who leapt from the cab at the station and sprinted to catch the London train.

Only when they were certain that they

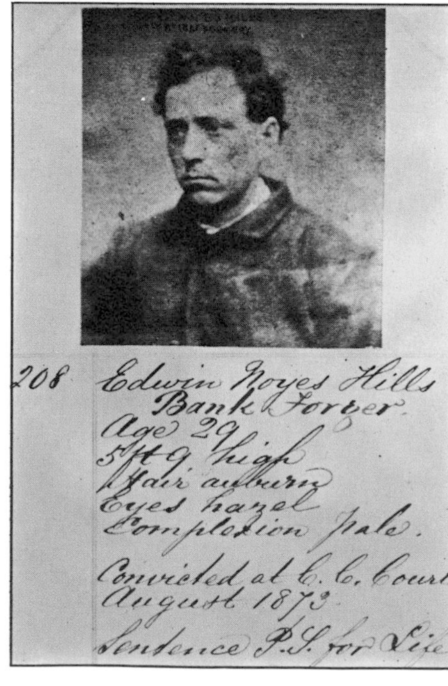

TEEMING with activity, as it is today, the bank (right in the big picture) was given even more to think about by the four cunning men on the right.

Mansell

Commissioner of the City of London Police

were alone in the compartment, and the train was pulling out, did one of the men, George Bidwell, rip open the envelope and greedily read through the enclosed note.

Then, eyes shining with triumph, he handed it to his companion, Edwin Noyes, stabbing his finger as he did so at the signature: "Yours faithfully, P. M. Francis". Noyes gave a gasp of relief and excitement. "My God, George," he cried, "we're rich men!"

Rich indeed, it seemed, were Bidwell and Noyes. And not only themselves but George Bidwell's brother, Austin (alias Mr. Warren) and a fourth man, George Macdonnell. For with that note from Colonel Francis the four Americans had succeeded in the first phase of an audacious plan to rob the "Old Lady of Threadneedle Street" by forgery, and to go on to an ultimate target that would overshadow any other recent fraud – a staggering target of £100,000.

Swollen with pride

George Bidwell and Noyes could hardly wait to rejoin their fellow conspirators in London, and pass on their tremendous news. They were swollen with pride at the thought of how much their crooked syndicate had achieved in so short a time.

The Bidwell brothers and Macdonnell had arrived in England in April of the previous year, 1872, with the specific intention of "taking" the Bank – but with no fixed idea of how to set about the coup.

Both the Bidwells, George, then 33, and Austin, 25, had dabbled for some years in shady Wall Street finance, and were fascinated by the Bank of England's much-vaunted reputation for total security. They were sure that, somehow, they could change all that, and so they had invited the 26-year-old Macdonnell to join them.

To them, Macdonnell was a highly attractive proposition. The son of wealthy Bostonians, he had turned his back on family respectability and enrolled as the talented "apprentice" to a forger named George Engels – whose highly damaging and spurious financial documents had earned him the nickname of "The Terror of Wall Street"

Each man had put up £400 in sterling as working capital to finance the enterprise – a substantial total, and one that would allow them to present a "cover" as well-heeled gentlemen. Their manners suited their pocket books. They had engaging personalities, were elegantly polite, and there was a certain romanticism about their strong American accents which might – and did – disarm the most stolid and cautious of English bankers.

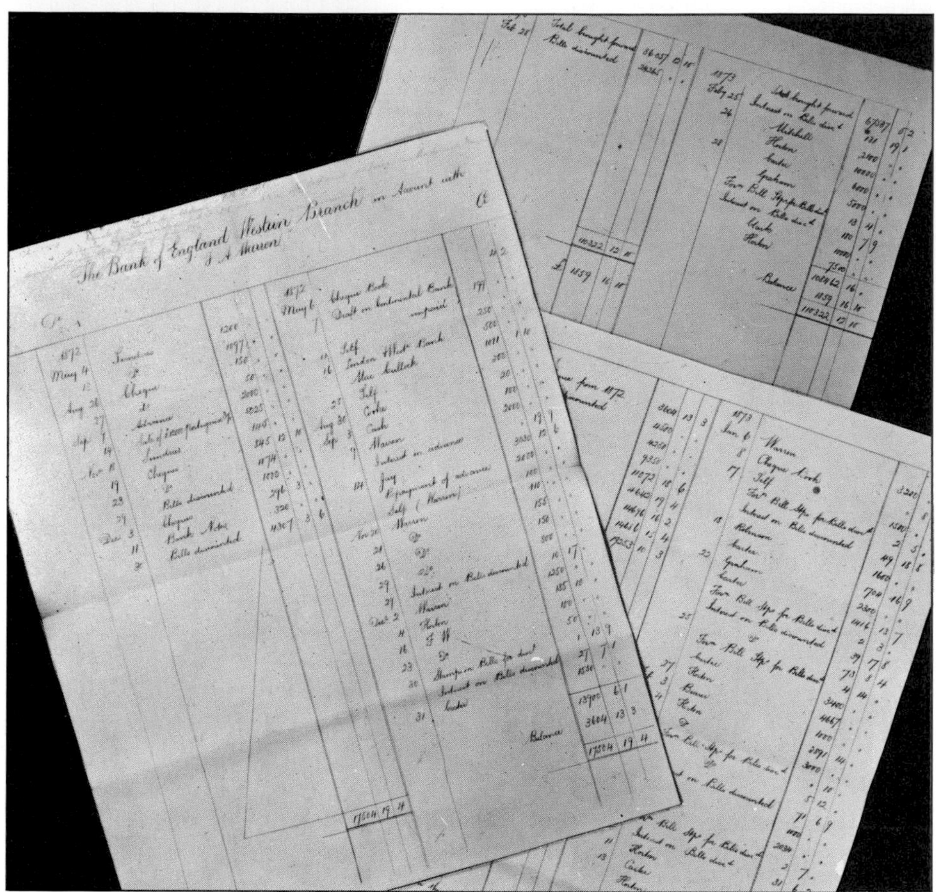
The Bank of England Western Branch in Account with F. A. Warren

Courtesy of The Bank of England

STATEMENTS OF ACCOUNT . . . Little by little, the forged bills of exchange were paid in, and accepted. It was greed that betrayed the gang.

As soon as they reached London they took modest lodgings in the anonymous North London suburb of Haggerston. They selected Austin Bidwell as the syndicate member who would become the Bank of England's "customer", and booked him a room at the respectable Golden Cross Hotel at Charing Cross—which, from then on, he would use purely as an accommodation address.

Austin was the most experienced and travelled man of the three. Only a few years before he had visited Europe, as courier for a criminal organization, and had successfully disposed of a batch of stolen bonds for a "commission" of $13,000.

Opulent district

The prospects for the Bank of England job looked good from the start. The trio found that, for the convenience of businessmen living or working in the opulent district of Mayfair, the bank had opened its Western Branch in Burlington Gardens, just off Piccadilly. From there, they reasoned, it should be easier to make a "sound impression", and build up close financial contacts, than in the more impersonal headquarters of the bank in Threadneedle Street.

It only remained for the three to keep watch on the Western Branch, follow some of the customers back to their business premises, and decide who could best "assist" Austin Bidwell with an introduction to the manager. The choice fell upon a certain Mr. Green.

Edward Hamilton Green was, at the age of 55, one of London's most fashionable tailors. He had a business at 35 Savile Row, and his ears were acutely tuned to the voices of lavish spenders. It was not surprising, therefore, that one morning strong American tones drew him from his office into his dim, gaslit store. There, for the first time, he saw the six-foot form of Austin Bidwell, adorned with a large Stetson hat and a choice Havana cigar.

"I require a fashionable city suit," Austin demanded, and Mr. Green was eagerly helpful. "Allow me to suggest this large-pattern worsted," he purred, unrolling a length of cloth. Graciously Austin accepted his recommendation and, to the tailor's delight, nonchalantly ordered five suits and two formal frock coats.

Mr. Green reached across the counter and opened a large leather-bound volume. "If you would fill in the customers' signature book, please," he said, "there is room for your references beneath."

As Austin Bidwell took the tailor's proferred pen, and scribbled "Frederick Albert Warren, Golden Cross Hotel, London," he thought swiftly about the problem of references. "There is no need for an account," he said, airily. "I shall pay cash for everything. I am not a resident." Mr. Green bowed, arranged the dates for "Mr. Warren's" fittings, and sent an assistant scuttling to summon a cab for his impressive new customer.

During the fittings over the next few weeks, Austin built up a close and confidential relationship with Mr. Green, and on May 4 he arrived to collect his impeccably tailored clothes. While they were being placed in his leather travelling case—ostentatiously marked with the initials "F.A.W."—he flourished a £500 banknote and told Mr. Green:

"I would like to settle my account now, if you please." His bill came to £150, and he was therefore invited into the office while the tailor found the change in his safe.

Delighted to oblige

The safe apparently impressed "Mr. Warren", who remarked: "How advantageous! I have more money than I care to carry. Perhaps I could leave it with you?" Mr. Green was delighted to oblige—until he observed that his customer was counting out a series of notes of large denominations, and had still not stopped when he reached a total of £1000.

This sum was too great a responsibility even for a wealthy tailor. A bank, he suggested, would be a safer place. "Mr. Warren" hesitated, then confided: "I have no bank account here." Mr. Green smiled. "I'm sure we can attend to that Mr. Warren. I will be delighted to introduce you to my bank. It is just at the end of the street!"

True to his word, Mr. Green made the personal introduction to Mr. Fenwick, the assistant manager of the Western Branch, and Bidwell duly deposited £1200, describing himself, after the signature "F. A. Warren", as "Commission Agent".

Mr. Fenwick could not have been more helpful. He said not a word about written references, and added the encouraging information: "You may now make remittances and withdrawals as you wish." He handed "Mr. Warren" a book of 50 Bank of England cheques.

So far, it appeared, so good. But just how was the big "killing" to be worked? Forged letters of credit might succeed in some foreign banks. But surely they would not pass undetected through the mighty Bank of England? The crucial questions seemed unanswerable until everything was suddenly solved by a most happy accident.

While Austin had been busy with Mr. Green, George Bidwell and Macdonnell had slipped across to the Continent to

Central Criminal Court
August Sessions 1873
The Queen on the Prosecution of
The Governor and Company of The Bank of England
against
Austin Biron Bidwell George Bidwell George Macdonnell and
Edwin Noyes Hills — For Felony

Statement as to Investments &c.

Both courtesy of The Bank of England

raise more capital. In Rotterdam Macdonnell had converted some foreign currency into a perfectly legitimate bill of exchange drawn on Baring Brothers, the famous city of London merchant banking firm.

Back in London he presented it to the London and Westminster Bank, where he expected to be told it would be honoured after it had been checked. But, unbelievably, the money was paid out there and then, at the counter, with no questions asked.

Fortune's gates

Bills of exchange are a special system of transferring money between different countries, which came into popular use in Western Europe in the Middle Ages. In the earliest days they worked accordingly: a trader in one country ordering large consignments of goods which took a long time to deliver would give his supplier in the other country a note promising payment three or four months later.

As time passed the "bills of exchange" came to be accepted as legal tender, like banknotes. If a person to whom the bill was made out presented it *before* the stated settlement date, the bank would hand over the face value, less a discount for early payment.

Then, when the date arrived, the bank would reclaim the full amount from the banking house or individual who accepted

STATEMENT OF PROSECUTION . . . It was a unique trial. Incredibly, for Britain, the judge was armed. He talked of "a blow to confidence in this country".

Peter Jackson Collection

responsibility for the bill – the "Acceptor", in financial language.

This, to the Bidwell group, seemed like the opening of fortune's gates. Clearly, unlike United States banks, British banks made no check with "acceptors" before making early payment on bills. All the syndicate had to do, therefore, was to produce authentic-looking forgeries dated for settlement at least three months ahead.

They would then present these, collect immediate payment, and be out of the country before the bills eventually found their way back to the acceptors.

Blank bills of exchange, printed in a variety of languages, were not difficult to obtain. With these, some wood block engravings, and his mastery in copying signatures, Macdonnell produced documents in which, even after intensive scrutiny, the Bidwell brothers could detect no differences from genuine bills. First of all, however, a little more caution was needed. They had to be absolutely sure that the Bank of England was as trusting as the other banks.

Reputable firm

On November 29, "Mr. Warren" went to the Western Branch, met his manager, Colonel Francis, and handed him two perfectly legal bills bearing the name of the reputable City of London firm of Suse and Sibeth as acceptors. They were dated for settlement on February 3, 1873 – nearly three months hence.

When he looked at them Colonel Francis was disconcerted. "Ah, but Mr. Warren," he apologized, "we never accept bills of exchange for discount at the Western Branch." Mr. Warren was visibly annoyed. Could the Bank of England question the credentials of Suse and Sibeth? Colonel Francis was loath to fail this very businesslike American. He would make personal inquiries at the bank's headquarters. "Perhaps," he said hopefully, "they will make an exception in this case."

An exception *was* made, and the next day the money was credited to "Mr. Warren's" account. The Bidwell syndicate realized it had succeeded beyond its most avaricious hopes. After that incident, Colonel Francis would never dream of questioning any of "Mr. Warren's" future demands. It remained now only to tie up one or two minor ends in the scheme.

"We can now syphon funds from the Bank of England into a new account at another bank on cheques from Mr. Warren," George Bidwell proposed. "But we must have a fourth man to withdraw cash from this new account. We'll send for Edwin Noyes."

Noyes, from Hartford, Connecticut, was an old friend of the Bidwells, a minor-league criminal who had dabbled in forgery and served time in the New Jersey State Penitentiary. He had a simple faith in the Bidwell brothers, and an unfailing readiness to share in any easy money wherever it might be found. He welcomed his invitation and accordingly arrived in London on December 17.

By then, Austin Bidwell had opened an account at the Continental Bank in Lombard Street in the name of Charles Johnson Horton, and Noyes was "appointed" his confidential clerk. The final act of the drama was about to unfold. Austin, as "Mr. Warren", would regularly convert forged bills into credit at the Western branch, and then transfer that money, sum by sum, to "Mr. Horton" at the Continental.

From the Continental, Noyes, acting on "Mr. Horton's" instructions, would draw the money in cash. All four syndicate members would then share it out, take it back to the States and live richly ever after.

Syndicate delighted

Still with an eye to caution, the syndicate decided it would be safer for Austin Bidwell not to hand forged bills to Colonel Francis in person. Consequently, he explained to the manager that he would be in Birmingham "on Pullman's business", and that any forthcoming bills from European customers should be forwarded to the bank by registered letter. Colonel Francis accepted the arrangement and the syndicate was delighted when a first receipt for credit of £4250 reached Birmingham.

George Bidwell spent a busy time as "postman", hurrying every few days from London to Birmingham to dispatch the bills on which Macdonnell had worked with loving care. So "Mr. Warren's" credit gradually mounted. One day's batch of bills totalled £9850, another day's £11,072. Before long the "income" from the forgeries had reached £45,000, and was still rising.

"Mr. Horton" did well, too. Cheques to his credit flowed in a steady stream from the Bank of England to the Continental Bank, and poor Noyes, the cash-collecting courier, began to feel the strain. At one point he complained:

"I have carried 400 lbs. of gold from the Bank of England, 40 times I have visited the Continental Bank under threat of awkward questions or even sudden arrest and I have been buying U.S. bonds in thicker and thicker bundles!"

By Wednesday, February 26, the syndicate had cashed close to £100,000, and the time had come to burn all the evidence and vanish. Everything went into the fire in their lodgings—Mr. Warren's cheque books, Mr. Horton's credit slips, wood engraving blocks.

George Bidwell, however, felt dissatisfied. He was unwilling to wind up the coup when they had not quite reached the magical target figure. "Are these bills good enough to send in, Mac?" he asked, fondling a batch of paper about to be tossed into the flames. "We've only the details to fill in," Macdonnell replied. "Right then, fill them in," Bidwell commanded.

Working rapidly Macdonnell completed three bills which reached Colonel Francis on Friday morning, February 28. With only a cursory glance, the manager handed them to his discount clerk. But an hour later the clerk returned, looking puzzled. "Excuse me, sir," he said, "the dates of issue on these bills seem to be missing."

Colonel Francis examined the items and agreed. Obviously, he supposed, it was an oversight on the part of the banking house whose name appeared as the acceptors, B. W. Blydenstein and Company. It was a matter easily rectified. "Send them down to Blydenstein's for correction," he instructed.

Later that day Colonel Francis received the most appalling shock of his life. He had completely dismissed the minor problem of the bills from his mind, when a messenger gave him an envelope marked "Urgent and Confidential". Inside it were the bills and a single sheet of paper, bearing a brief message of doom from Blydenstein and Company:

"We have no record of these bills and can only assume they are forgeries.—William Henry Trumpler, Member."

The unfortunate Colonel, sick with anxiety, took a close look at "Mr. Warren's" file, sped to Threadneedle Street and panted out his dreadful news to Mr. May, the Bank's deputy chief cashier. Mr. May seemed most shocked that the fraudulent customer was a foreigner, an American.

"Disgusting!" he gasped, and went off personally to make inquiries at Rothschild's, and at the Continental Bank where "Mr. Warren" had passed so many cheques.

Excited headlines

Next day the machinery of the law began to move. Edwin Noyes, arriving with an order to collect the last batch of cash for "Mr. Horton" was arrested at the Continental Bank. The other members of the syndicate were warned by the excited headlines in the newspapers and, too late, they learned that the greedy haste of those final, incomplete bills had brought their "perfect" plan crumbling about them. Panic-stricken, they split up and fled.

In New York the Pinkerton Detective Agency went immediately to work. It produced a list of 20 forgers known to deal in financial documents, eliminated 16 and noted the name of Austin Bidwell among the remaining four. It was an important lead and a finely-meshed net was spread, into which Macdonnell was the first man to walk—as he prepared to land in New York on a liner from France.

He was extradited to England and was followed, a few weeks later, by Austin Bidwell who had been arrested in Havana, Cuba. Only George Bidwell was unaccounted for. He had a long run, dodging across first to Ireland, where close watch on the ports prevented him from boarding a ship, and thence to Scotland. Finally he was captured in Edinburgh.

At the swindlers' trial at London's Old Bailey, in August 1873, there were fears of an escape plot. Armed guards surrounded the court, and even the judge himself carried a gun in his pocket.

There was little hope for the unrepentant prisoners. Even so, the sentence—penal servitude for life—came as a shock to many people in the United States and Britain. No doubt the affront to the Bank of England added to the severity for the judge told the four men:

"It is not the least atrocious part of your crime that you have given a severe blow to the confidence which has been so long maintained in this country."

As it turned out, Austin Bidwell served 17 years and Noyes and Macdonnell 18 years. The strangest and most stubborn of the prisoners was George Bidwell. He refused to undertake any work in the fortress prison of Dartmoor, took to his cell bed and stayed there for 14 long years. All attempts to make him walk failed. He wasted away until he was reduced almost to a skeleton, and was hardly able to use his legs. The prison governor felt certain he could not last long. In July, 1887, George Bidwell was released on the grounds that he was close to death. He returned to the States, recovered his health and made a comfortable living out of lecturing on the evils of crime.

KILLER UNKNOWN

From the top of her raven-tressed head to the tip of her black patent shoes, her sombre sexiness was indelibly blazoned on the soul of any man who knew her. Miss Elizabeth Short knew a lot of men. At least one man too many.

ON the chill, blustery morning of January 15, 1947, a sobbing, hysterical woman frantically flagged down a passing police patrol car in a suburb of Los Angeles, California, and screeched out an incoherent stream of words. When the patrol car crew had managed to calm her a little she pointed with shaking fingers to a nearby, garbage-strewn vacant lot. The police car leapt forward, turned on to the lot, and there the officers immediately understood the woman's behaviour.

What she had seen, and what the policemen now saw for themselves, were the nude halves of the corpse of a young woman. The body had been crudely cut in two at the waist, and each half tied with ropes. Deep into one thigh the killer had carved the initials "BD".

It was a sickening sight, but the repulsion which the hardened police officers felt was deepened when pathologists examined the body in detail and found that it had been revoltingly mutilated. What was even more hideous was the fact that most of the injuries had been inflicted before death—probably while the victim was suspended, head down, by ropes or wires. She might, indeed, have been still living when her murderer began the incisions to sever her body.

A SICKENING SIGHT met the horrified gaze of the police: Elizabeth Short's hideously mutilated body. Her injuries had obviously been inflicted while she was still alive. Her mother (below) had often been unable to cope with her young family. . . .

It was clear that the girl had not been long dead when the passing woman came across the dismembered corpse. The immediate theory was that she had been killed somewhere nearby, and the remains tipped on to the lot from a car. The police were puzzled by the incised initials "BD", and there were no obvious clues to identification. But, as a matter of routine, the police took fingerprints from the few fingers that had escaped mutilation. These were sent to the Federal Bureau of Investigation in Washington, D.C., for checking against the millions on file.

The Los Angeles police knew only too well that the print check was an outside chance. To their satisfaction, a message came back from the F.B.I. within hours stating that the prints matched those on file for 22-year-old Elizabeth Short, born in the small town of Medford, Massachusetts, who had a police record as a juvenile delinquent.

Her mother, Mrs. Phoebe Short—who was separated from her husband—was then traced. She had the task of trying to identify the body. So thoroughly had the killer carried out his work that she was

All photos UPI

La Times

THE TIDE TURNED in Elizabeth Short's life when she met Army Air Force Major Matt M. Gordon Jr. (above). But he was killed in action . . . and the Black Dahlia was born. Many men felt driven to confess to the spectacular murder; one, Joseph Dumais (bottom far right), was arrested, but released to a psychiatrist.

unable positively to say that what she looked upon had once been her daughter. But she *was* able to produce a letter which Elizabeth had written to her a few weeks before from San Diego. Detectives went immediately to the address and learnt that Elizabeth Short had left there six days before the discovery of her body. Since she had taken no luggage with her, it seemed as though she had intended to return, and had gone to Los Angeles for no more than a brief visit.

Slowly the police built up a picture of Elizabeth Short, her life and her background. One fact was beyond any doubt and dominated all others: she had been tall, graceful, and exceedingly beautiful, with milk-white skin and a mass of raven hair. She was the kind of girl upon whom all men's eyes focused when she walked into a room; if ever any girl was instantly desirable, that girl was Elizabeth.

Great Depression

However, there was little of beauty in her background. She had grown up in an unhappy home and was only six when, in 1931, her parents separated and her father moved to California. He took one child of the family with him, and left his wife to look after Elizabeth and their other three children.

It was the period of the Great Depression, and Phoebe Short often found herself unequal to both making a living and bringing up the youngsters.

Often alone and miserable, without much close contact with her mother, Elizabeth's one main ambition began to grow into an obsession: the moment she was old enough she would leave home and make a new and independent life for herself.

The opportunity came in 1942, when she was not yet 17. With the United States engulfed by world war there were plenty of job opportunities for young women. Elizabeth decided to seize one of those opportunities for herself—but as far away and as different from Medford as she could make it. She chose Miami.

It seemed to her that the "sun city" was tailor-made for her ambitions. She was already well aware of her physical appeal; there was an air base near Miami, and at week-ends there was no shortage of young servicemen enjoying their brief leaves on the Florida beaches.

The only information the police could obtain about her life in Miami was sketchy—but it was enough to show that it had finally added to her unhappiness and loneliness. She had taken a job as a waitress. For a time it seemed that she had found her hoped-for young lover. But the romance languished when the man went off to the war. Then, while she worked and counted the days to his return, he died on a distant battlefield.

It was a blow from which Elizabeth Short did not recover. She took to drink, and she took to men—any men. She became so promiscuous that word of her readiness to go to bed with anyone who would buy her drinks and a meal swiftly spread around the Miami bars.

Eventually, almost inevitably, the police caught up with her, and, found drinking with soldiers in a café, she was arrested as a juvenile delinquent. The authorities decided that, since she was in need of care and protection, she should be sent home to her mother. They gave her a rail ticket to Medford and a small amount of subsistence money and put her on a train.

She stayed aboard the train as far as Santa Barbara, and there she got off and found herself another job as a waitress. In the distraction of war no one had checked to see if she had reached home and the custody of her mother, and Elizabeth stayed in Santa Barbara until 1944. But once more, as though she were singled out to be one of nature's chosen victims, the fates were unmerciful to her.

Having got over her first sad love affair, she formed an attachment for an Army Air Force major. It seemed like the turning of the disastrous tide of her life, and, as though to confirm her own good intentions, she returned, in 1944, to her mother in Medford, to await the major's homecoming from the Far East and the marriage which was to follow.

Home was no happier than it had been in the past, but this time, at least, she could look forward to settling down to a new life with a husband to whom she could devote herself. On the morning of August 22, 1946, when it seemed so certain that her major would soon be back from the war, the front-door bell rang and Elizabeth answered it. A taciturn postal messenger handed her a telegram addressed to herself. Excitedly she tore it open. The message inside was from the mother of the major. Cryptically, it said: "Have received notification from War Department my son, Matt, killed in air crash."

Zombie-like trance

In a zombie-like trance, Elizabeth screwed the telegram into a tight-knit ball of paper, tossed it aside and went straight to the nearest bar. There she drank until her lovely grey-green eyes were cloudy with alcohol and her tall, elegant frame sagged over the edge of the bar. The barman became embarrassed by her tipsy monologue in which she declared: "Some people have a hex on them, y'know what I mean? Some people can't never get the breaks, and nuthin' they can do will give 'em the breaks. Y'listenin' me, now? Why'd things happen to me, this way?"

The next day she decided that there was nothing to keep her in Medford any longer, and she set out for California, this time to the place for which her

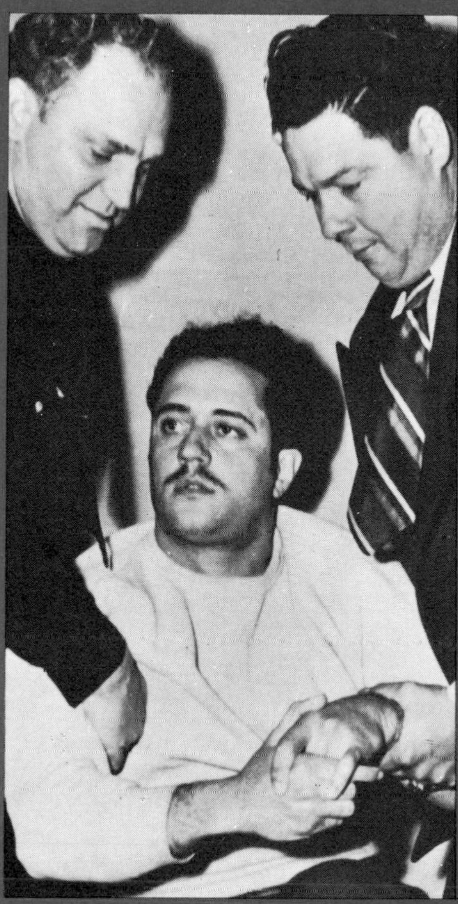

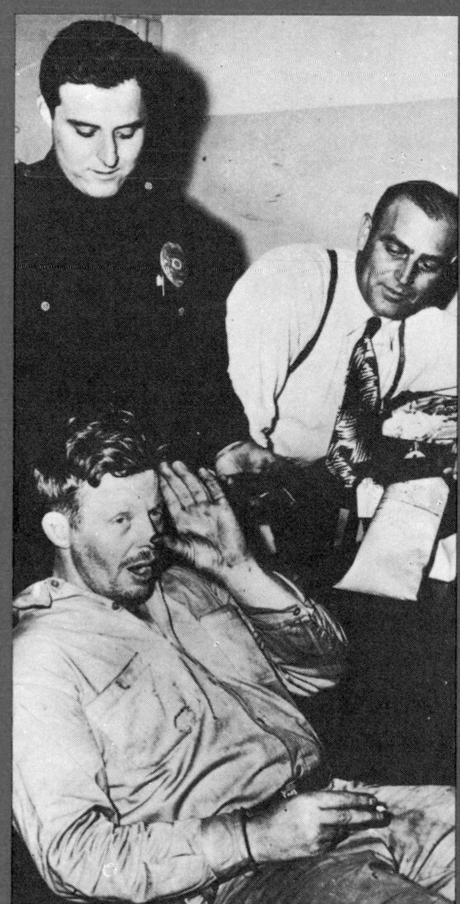

All photos UPI

poise and stunning looks seemed to be so perfectly fitted: Hollywood. The major studios had not yet been overtaken by the TV revolution, and the feeling in the movie capital was that business would be as it always had been, booming. Every day there were calls for "extras", and Elizabeth Short joined the casting lines successfully. For her there was regular and reasonably well-paid work.

She had heard that there were producers and casting directors who were prepared to give a photogenic girl a chance in pictures, for "a consideration". Elizabeth was only too ready to oblige, especially when she was sufficiently anaesthetized with liquor, and she devoted her spare time to going to bed with almost all men who invited her, even though most had no more than tenuous associations with the studios.

Black stockings

She had learned that in Hollywood it was as well to establish some kind of particular identity. Her method was to match her raven hair by dressing totally in black: black sheath dresses, black stockings and underwear, black shoes, even a jet black ring. In its own strange way the ploy worked, and someone named her the "Black Dahlia". The title stuck, she used it herself, and few men who passed in and out of her life were unaware of it.

She took, and discarded, lovers the way most women accept and discard clothing fashions. Some of them she lived with for brief periods. With one man she formed something more than a passing attachment, for in the few effects found after her death was a note addressed to her which read: "I might be gone before you arrive. You say in your letter that you want us to be good friends. But from your wire you seemed to want more than that. Are you really sure what you want? Why not pause and consider just what your

coming out here would amount to? You've got to be more practical these days."

No one would ever discover where "out here" was, and certainly one thing that the Black Dahlia seemed incapable of achieving was practical behaviour. In any case, as the Hollywood movie empire declined into an era of uncertainty it was clear that stardom was not waiting around the corner for Elizabeth Short, and, no longer earning anything like a regular income, she drifted south to San Diego and resumed her career as a waitress.

Her drinking continued unabated, and men pursued her as readily as ever. One man with whom she established a brief liaison was tall and red-haired and reported as having been seen with the Black Dahlia in a San Diego bus station a few days before her dismembered body was discovered. The man was traced by the police and admitted that he had been with the girl. He declared that he went on a drunken binge with her, took her afterwards to a motel and then drove her to the Biltmore Hotel in Los Angeles.

"She said she was going to meet her sister at the hotel," the man told detectives. "I left her there. That was the last time I saw her, and I have no idea what happened to her afterwards or where she went." The police accepted his story; in any case, the man was able to prove that, at the time when the Black Dahlia must have been murdered, he and his wife were visiting friends.

For the authorities the trail set by Elizabeth Short ended at the front entrance to the Biltmore Hotel. She had become lost in the city sprawl; somewhere she met the man who was to so brutally slay her. Her clothing had totally disappeared, and extensive searches—including examinations of drains and sewers—failed to produce any garment that could be traced to her.

From the moment that the news of the severed corpse discovery appeared in the newspapers the police were overwhelmed by supposed "confessions" and reports of suspects. The anxiety of so many men to "confess" to such a deed said a great deal about individual mental states, but told the police nothing that was relevant to their inquiries. One man, at least, had an unusual motive for presenting himself as the killer. His wife, he said, had deserted him. He hoped that if he could make himself notorious, and have his picture in the papers, she might return.

Hysterical cases

One person sent the police a message, composed of pasted-up letters cut from a magazine, offering to meet them and provide them with information. He signed himself "Black Dahlia Avenger". Detectives waited at the proposed rendezvous but no one turned up. One woman walked into a police station and announced: "The Black Dahlia stole my man, so I killed her and cut her up."

Tired-eyed but patient officers chatted to the eager woman, and discreetly mentioned one or two facts about the murdered girl's corpse that could only have been known to the killer. From the woman's response, it was clear that she was no more than another hysterical case.

In the midst of such confessions there was one curious and baffling event. A Los Angeles newspaper received a note which read: "Here are Dahlia's belongings. Letter will follow." Enclosed with the note were Elizabeth Short's birth certificate, address book, and social security card. No letter followed and fingerprints, clearly visible on the envelope and note, were forwarded to the F.B.I.—but they matched none on file. Detectives spent long days searching out men named in the address book, but none of the interviews produced a positive murder lead.

Calls promising information were made to the Los Angeles police from all parts of the United States, and some of the

CURIOUS AND BAFFLING, this note (and the package with it) was never followed up. The killer had made a gesture and turned away—perhaps to new victims.

UPI

callers were asked to appear in person. But officers discovered nothing of value.

One development, however, looked promising. U.S. army investigators arrested a 29-year-old corporal, just back from 42 days' leave, who had talked loudly and convincingly about having known the Black Dahlia, and having been with her a few days before her body was found. There were bloodstains on his clothing and, in his locker, newspaper clippings about the murder. He seemed to possess a lot of circumstantial evidence about some of the injuries to the body, and he insisted: "When I get drunk I get rough with women." However, on closer examination, he, too, was found to be an unbalanced personality and recommended for psychiatric treatment.

The gory facts

Despite all the time and energy that the police spent on such confessions, they were helped by one important factor in the case: some of the mutilations of the body were so foul that no newspaper had written about them in any detail. This served in eliminating false confessions, since it was clear that none of the would-be "murderers" knew the full, gory facts.

As a variation on the theme of most of the confessions, one man later came forward and announced that, although he had not murdered the girl, he *had* helped to dismember her body. The murderer, he said, was a friend of his. He did not, or could not, identify him—and, as in other offers of "information", his statements did not conform to the facts known only to the police.

THE MYSTERY surrounding her death has helped keep alive the memory of the Black Dahlia: this beautiful young victim who seemed so destined for suffering.

Almost certainly someone, somewhere in Los Angeles, knew the identity of the killer. The police considered it hardly credible that he could have committed such an atrocious crime without leaving some clues behind. The killing and mutilation might have taken place in a deserted warehouse, or some remote building—and yet there was no evidence of the girl being seen with a man just before her death. It seemed unlikely that she might have gone to meet her end, in a place conveniently designed for it, without even being observed by a passer by.

In fact two bartenders reported having served her with drinks, two or three days before her death, when she was in the company of a woman. These reports gave rise to rumours that she had been murdered by a lesbian acquaintance. But there was neither direct evidence nor even remote indications to suggest that she was homosexual.

Then there were those who claimed that the murder was the work of a madman driven by motives similar to those of Jack the Ripper—the unidentified nineteenth-century killer who disposed of prostitutes in the East End of London. Perhaps, they argued, the Black Dahlia murder was a case of a man wishing to rid the world of a woman of easy virtue.

The bald fact was that the killer was never found, and his motives, therefore, remain undisclosed. For some time the police inquiries continued and—for a long time after—the "confessions" flowed in.

These—and the nickname she was given—have kept alive the memory of the young victim who seemed so destined for suffering. The most important is that her murderer knew her, and had probably been out with her several times before.

From the address book, sent anonymously to the local newspaper, one page was missing. It had apparently been removed because it contained the name and address of the Black Dahlia's "friend", who turned out to be her murderer. Was the person who posted that book to the newspaper the killer himself? The odds are that it was. And that, having made his "gesture", he turned his attention to other women—and perhaps other victims.

THE PEASANT POISONER

The charge was grotesque: that Marie Besnard had poisoned no less than 30 people, including her mother and two husbands. But few crimes could have been stranger than the trial itself, which took more than a decade to separate fact from rumour. . . .

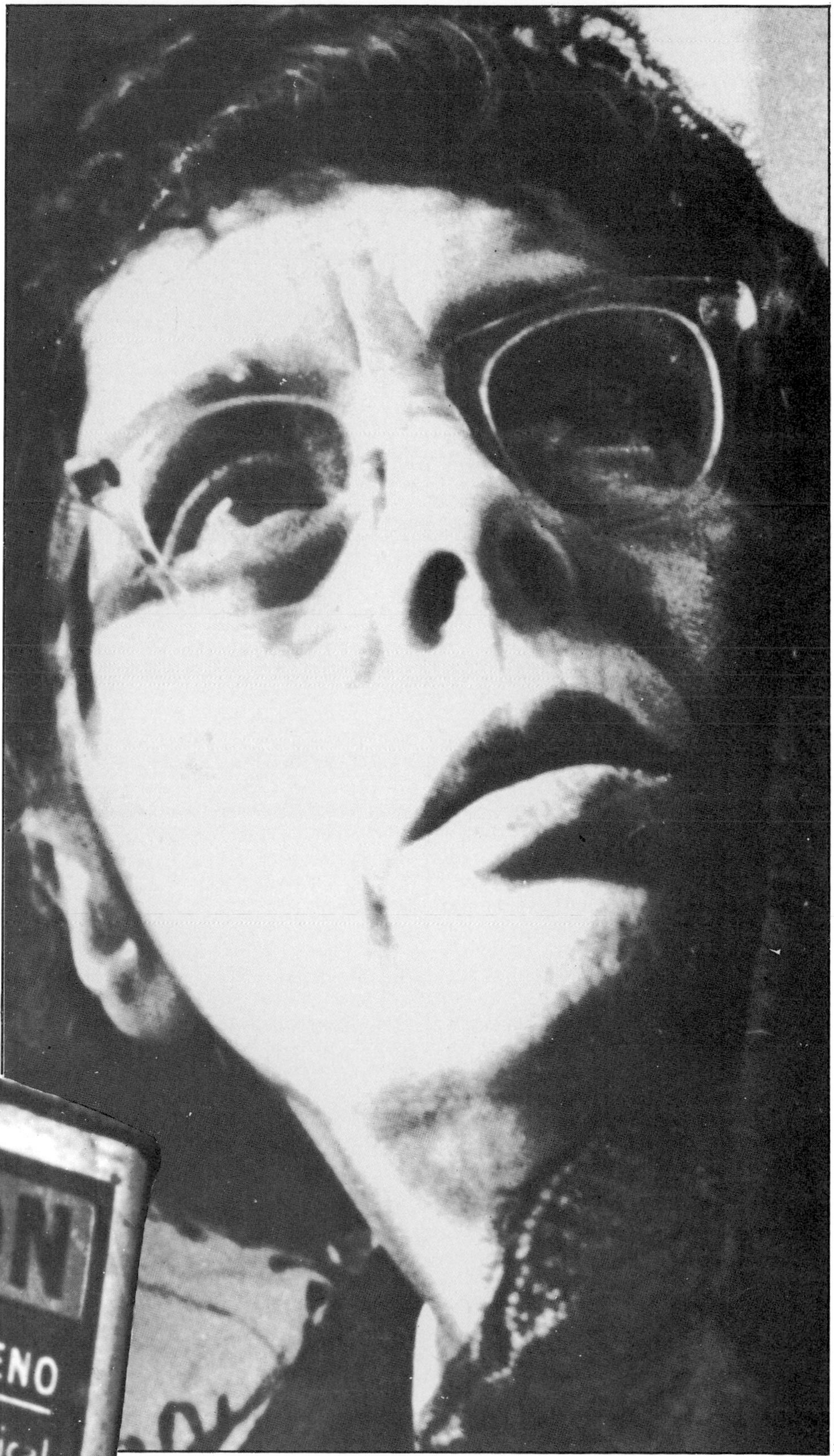

Keystone

HYSTERIA burst forth like the sudden releasing of a champagne cork, that February day in the little courtroom of the French town of Poitiers. A horde of stampeding press photographers fought each other with thrusting elbows and screamed curses at rivals who pushed in front of their lenses. The flaring of flash bulbs dazzled the lawyers' eyes, and people in the public seats leapt up and down in their anxiety for a better view and jabbered with excitement. "The Black Widow!" some of them shouted. "When do we see the Black Widow?"

Then, as suddenly as it had started, the hubbub in the room ceased. A side door opened and into the court stepped a 55-year-old countrywoman, Marie Besnard. As she moved forward to a seat facing the public benches, she looked around with bewildered eyes, her sturdy body twitching as the photographers, brought to attention like a disciplined firing-squad, stood still in their ranks and clicked their shutters at her.

Dignity and intelligence

Marie Besnard appeared hypnotized by the array of crimson just above the level of her head—the crimson of the court president, the judges and the Avocat Général, the prosecuting counsel. Some of the spectators, as they stared at her, seemed uncomfortably disturbed and disappointed. For this was the Black Widow, of whom the newspapers wrote and all France spoke about. This was the woman said to be a mass poisoner. Yet she seemed a homely woman of typical French peasant stock; a woman, one could see at a glance, who had been pretty in her youth and who now bore herself with a certain dignity and intelligence.

However, this impression was immediately countered by the monotonous voice of the clerk of the court who began to read the deposition of the examining judge who, in the tradition of French law, had spent long weeks before the trial in a person-to-person interrogation of the accused. Now the report that he had prepared brought Marie Besnard to this moment in Poitiers to hear the formal charge against her: that she, by arsenical poisoning, had murdered no fewer than 13 people, including her mother and two husbands.

As the clerk read it to the hushed court, the examining judge's report sounded distinctly more like the entries in a private diary than a legal document upon which a woman's life might depend. In accordance with French law it even altered her identity, referring to her throughout by her maiden name.

"Your name is Marie Joséphine Philippine Davaillaud and you were born on August 15, 1896," it said. "You had a hard youth, though you bore it patiently . . . Information about you is contradictory. Some depict you as a gentle, obliging and respectable woman. Others say that you have the reputation of being vicious, a liar, a flatterer and of easy morals. . . ."

In 1919, the court heard, she had married her cousin. He died in 1927 and two years after that, in August 1929, she married Léon Besnard, who owned a rope shop in Loudun—the French town which, in the seventeenth century, had gained lasting notoriety as a supposed centre of witchcraft. In October 1947, Léon Besnard died—from a heart attack, according to his doctor—and it was then, as the examining judge recorded, that Marie's troubles began.

"An inquiry was made into the death of your husband as a result of a letter sent to the public prosecutor. . . ." The clerk droned on and there was a flutter of whispering among the spectators. This, then, they seemed to be saying, was how it had all begun; a tittle-tattle letter, of a type not common merely to French villages, which passes on half-digested gossip or is designed to cause harm to a neighbour.

The court was told how Léon Besnard's body was exhumed from its grave—and here Marie Besnard, the focus of all eyes, lowered her head. Some thought it was a gesture of guilt, others that the grim details were too much for her to bear. The clerk continued reading: "Specimens of Léon Besnard's internal organs were taken by Dr. Guillon, and Dr. Béroud, who examined them, discovered an abnormal quantity of arsenic. He thinks that the dose employed might quite well have been poured into a soup plate, and he adds that it is easily procured as arsenic is sold for agricultural purposes."

AGIP

SWOLLEN with pride, good neighbour and prosecution witness Madame Pintou (above) was soon punctured. Could "tainted soup" have killed the Black Widow's two husbands (inset: Auguste Antigny, right, and Léon Besnard)?

Then, for the first time, those in the courtroom realized that this was not a hopeless, simple peasant woman with whom they were dealing. For the judge's report, still in its style of a not-so-friendly letter to the accused, went on: "When I informed you of Dr. Béroud's report you asked me to have a second expert examination carried out. I replied that I could not accede to this request, in view of Dr. Béroud's competence.

Broad-shouldered confidence

If there was any one man who would be the central figure in the case he would be Dr. Béroud—and the drama began to open up when he—broad-shouldered, dark, confident—was called to the witness-stand. It was clear that he exercised a great fascination for the onlookers for, as it soon emerged, he had examined a whole series of exhumed bodies and found arsenic in them. All of them were bodies of people Marie Besnard had known, from her own father and mother, to Léon Besnard's father and beyond the family circle to a Loudun pastrycook and his wife.

Both AFP

There are no greater difficulties for lawyers than examining experts in murder trials, and Marie's two defence counsel, Maître Hayot and Maître Gautrat, at first proceeded cautiously and politely. Maître Gautrat asked about the methods Dr. Béroud had used to analyze the organs taken from the exhumed bodies. He spoke in quiet conversational tones, as one professional man discussing routine business with an equal.

In each case the organs had been put into jars and sent to Marseilles for examination, had they? Yes, that was so, answered the doctor, adjusting his bright yellow scarf with outspread fingers. "I see," said the lawyer, thoughtfully, and produced a typed list, copies of which he handed to the judges and the scribbling newspaper reporters.

"Now you will notice," the lawyer went on, addressing the judges, "that the record shows that there were always more jars of specimens arriving at Marseilles than had been taken from the bodies. This suggests only two hypotheses—that either someone intervened during the journey to Marseilles, or jars had been added in the Marseilles laboratory."

The president of the court peered at his copy of the list and nodded his head as if in agreement. But from Dr. Béroud there burst a snort of outrage. Maître Gautrat retained his air of politeness. "Calm yourself, doctor," he said. "It can happen in a big laboratory like yours, for you are the expert for all the courts and you receive many jars every day."

Dr. Béroud shot the lawyer a sharp, questioning glance as though there had been something in the tone of voice that contained a double meaning. But Gautrat pressed on: "And as these jars are put on the shelves they may get muddled. That must often happen because of the staff, but if you received the remains of muscles and not intestines, and if you wrote in your report that you found arsenic in the intestines, then you must have analyzed the intestines of a body unconnected with the Besnard case."

The doctor sat in angry silence and made no response. The photographers, seeing this as a moment of confrontation, leaped forward and fired their flash bulbs full in his face. Dr. Béroud flushed and Gautrat hurriedly added, as if to compliment him, "Of course, we know you are a great expert, a great chemist and toxicologist."

The witness stirred in his chair with impatience and looked towards the judges as though asking for protection. None was forthcoming and Gautrat extracted more documents from his file.

"These," he said, "are letters you wrote to the examining judge, saying you could clearly distinguish by eye the antimony rings and the arsenic rings in the Marsh tube." He then plunged into a reading of the letters whose scientific significance was certainly above the heads of most of those in the court, but which meant a great deal to Gautrat and the doctor. For a moment Marie Besnard almost beamed, as though in admiration of a lawyer who had done such excellent research into clinical matters.

Yes, yes, Dr. Béroud snapped, of course he had written those letters. Then his eyes widened as Maître Gautrat, like a Christmas party conjurer, reached into the wide sleeves of his lawyer's gown and whisked out six small test-tubes. Holding them aloft, and allowing a moment for the photographers to immortalize them on film, he demanded of Dr. Béroud: "There now, tell the court, if you please, which of these contain arsenic."

A court official received the tubes from the lawyer and handed them to the doctor. In absolute silence Dr. Béroud took each one and held it up to the light. He turned each in his hand and studied it with mouth-tightened concentration. As everyone had by now guessed, he was looking for ring markings, for that was what the lawyer was so interested in: rings that would testify either to the presence of the metallic substance, antimony, or of arsenic.

Finally, and evidently annoyed by the calculated drama, the doctor handed

POISON-PEN letters helped prolong Madame Besnard's ordeal—and poison rings deposited in the intestines of the "victims" sparked a years-long conflict of expert testimony. (Defence counsel Hayot wields some grisly evidence, far right.) Dr. Béroud (below) was one of the first professional casualties when the defence trapped him into confusing arsenic and antimony. But Prosecutor Girault (inset top) was undeterred.

AGIP

three of the tubes back to the court official. "These three," he said, "contain arsenic." Maître Gautrat swooped upon the court official in triumph. He snatched the three test-tubes from his hand and passed them to the Avocat Général.

In strident tones, contrasting vividly to his conversational cross-examination, he declared: "I wish these tubes to be admitted as exhibits. For here"—he flung out his arm towards the doctor—"is a proof that Dr. Béroud is an expert who deserves his great fame! Dr. Béroud, I owe it to you to tell you, but don't repeat it, that not one—no, not one—of those tubes contained arsenic. All the rings you saw were antimony rings!" Then reaching for yet another document and waving that aloft, too, Gautrat shouted: "Here is the guarantee of the laboratory that gave them to me!"

There was a brief hush and then the whole court seemed to be convulsed with laughter and cheering and counter-cheering. Spectators leapt to their feet and even Marie Besnard, her face suddenly alive with hope, rose and looked about her in astonishment. One of the judges allowed himself a frosty smile and a voice shouted: "Dr. Béroud, you have been judged." But in the midst of the tumult were voices that did not approve of

AP

AGIP

prisoners scoring off distinguished experts. "Dr. Béroud for ever," one voice cried, and another, jabbing a finger towards Maître Gautrat, demanded: "Back to Paris with the Paris lawyer!"

To the journalists, rushing to their telephones, it seemed that this might well be the end of the case against Marie Besnard. One was so confident that he called to her, over his shoulder, "Bravo, Marie, you're winning!" But this was February 1952, and Marie had been arrested in July 1949. Ahead of her were years of further ordeal.

A few days later she was brought back to court to hear expert defence witnesses argue that Dr. Béroud's methods of detecting arsenic were unsatisfactory. And there was one witness, a Professor Perperot, who had something of importance to say but who was given scant attention. Yes, he stated, you might dig up many bodies from many cemeteries in Marie Besnard's home territory and find them filled with enough arsenic to decimate a regiment of men—for the very good reason that the soil was steeped in arsenic.

But the court decided that fresh expert advice should be sought, and a panel of three pharmacists and toxicologists was appointed for the task. As a bizarre turn of events in the apparently all-embracing trial, Marie was found guilty of forging a postal order—even though there was strong evidence to show that the forged signature bore no relationship to her own handwriting. However, the verdict enabled the authorities to hold her and, in addition to a fine of 50,000 francs, she was sentenced to two years' imprisonment.

Eight months later, in October 1952, Marie was once more called upon to stand trial for murder—but by now six indictments against her had been withdrawn. The hearing made no progress and it was adjourned—again, not merely for months, but until March 1954. This time the hearing was moved to Bordeaux.

Despite the obvious importance of the scientific evidence, much of this trial was devoted to a regurgitation of village rumour, some of which had a distinctly farcical flavour. Marie sat silent and anxious while the court bubbled with hilarity at the evidence offered by a large,

All AGIP

"VICIOUS liar" or "gentle woman"? From local gravedigger to village gossip, none missed a chance to air their opinion of the accused (pictured in her flat, left).

bumbling farmhand, whose total inability to understand what the proceedings were about did the prosecution no good.

"Who wore the trousers in the Besnard household?" he was asked, and the spectators rolled in helpless mirth as he answered: "I dunno. I never saw hers." Yes, the desperate prosecutor insisted, "But who gave the orders?" The bewildered peasant knitted his leathery brows, as though in a monumental effort of recollection, and replied: "Well, Monsieur Besnard, when he was alive and Mme Besnard after he was dead." This was too much for the French reporters, who did not regard their role in the trial as entirely passive. "Sit down, sit down!" they chorused and the farmhand duly sat. "No, no, stand up!" the court president commanded.

Exchanges of this kind set the pattern for the trial, and there was little dignity remaining when the prosecution brought on one of its chief witnesses – a Madame Pintou, who had written one of the original letters to the authorities casting suspicion on Marie Besnard. According to Madame Pintou, who had been a frequent visitor to the Besnards, Léon Besnard had told her shortly before his death that Marie had served him with "tainted" soup.

Maître Gautrat, as energetic as ever for the defence, made the most of his opportunities in cross-examining the woman. "When Léon was alive and you would come and relax in the Besnard house in the evening, were you happy?" he asked. "Yes," she replied. "And the day of Léon's funeral, didn't you take Marie in your arms and didn't you and your son both say she was like one of the family and you could easily comfort her in her great grief?" Madame Pintou visibly swelled with pride that her good neighbourliness should be so publicly paraded. "Oh, yes, yes!" she exclaimed.

Such noble feelings

Stone-faced, Maître Gautrat stood poised for the fatal blow. His voice raced on. "And the day after the funeral you again comforted your friend, Marie Besnard, and there was no end to your praises of her?" Madame Pintou answered instantly, "Oh, yes." Gautrat added, with a touch of irony, "It was noble of you," and then went on: "Certainly this shows you have noble feelings. But would you have had this attitude to Marie Besnard if you had believed she was a criminal and had poisoned Léon?"

Madame Pintou was now positively anxious not to let her noble image appear tarnished. "Oh, no!" she cried. "I didn't believe it." Ah, Gautrat responded, swiftly, in that case did she *now* believe that her friend, Marie, was guilty? Madame Pintou looked up sharply with surprise, as though realizing the significance of the questioning at last. "No," she answered in a voice so low that only the sudden silence in the court made it audible. "No, I don't believe it."

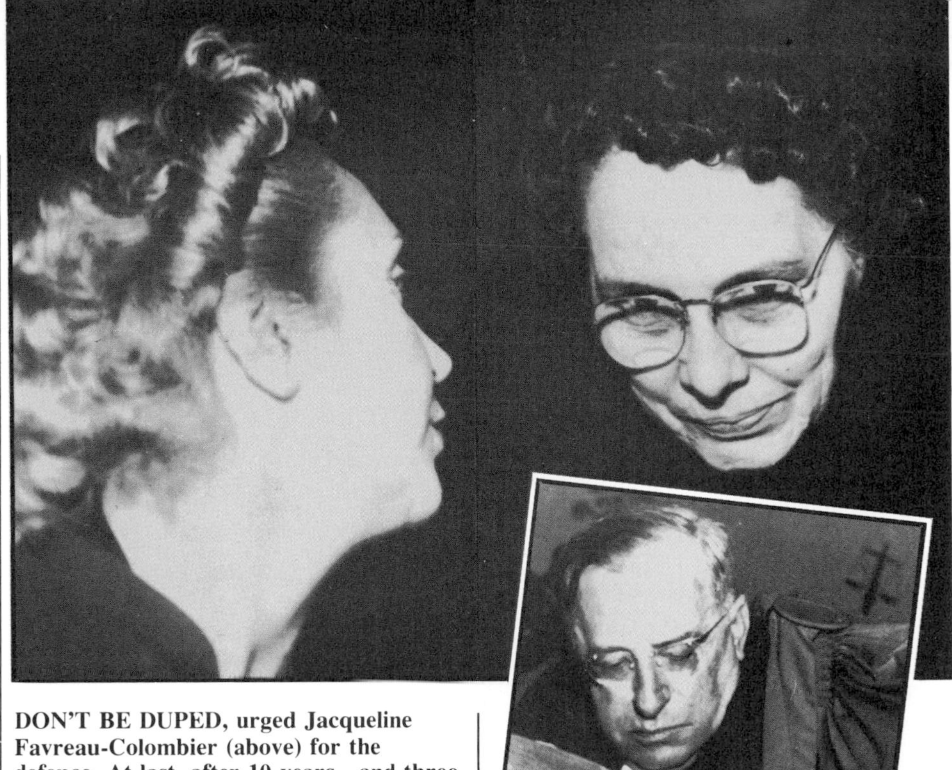

AP

DON'T BE DUPED, urged Jacqueline Favreau-Colombier (above) for the defence. At last, after 10 years – and three judges (right) – the end was in sight.

ACIP

Maître Gautrat spun around to face the prosecuting counsel and demanded, with a flourish: "Do you not have the impression that the accusation against Marie Besnard has crumbled?" But the prosecution was far from being ready to concede, however much its case had been devastated by a leading witness. Once more it sought for salvation through its expert scientific witnesses.

These included the men who had been assigned in the earlier trial to re-examine the toxicological evidence, and whose inquiries had involved exhuming the allegedly murdered bodies for a second time. Those spectators who had come to court in gleeful anticipation of yet another vitriolic battle between experts were not to be disappointed.

The verbal fisticuffs began almost immediately, with the disclosure that one of the experts – who, by using a Geiger counter, had reaffirmed the presence of arsenic in the bodies – had produced mathematical inaccuracies in his findings. When this was put to him the scientist turned crimson with anger and shouted to the defence lawyers: "Ah, yes, I found arsenic and you don't like that, do you?"

His analysis results, one of the defence lawyers told the witness, had been sent for checking to experts at the British Atomic Authority, "and they have found an error of 80 per cent in them". The witness flailed his arms like a man driven beyond all realms of patience. "Aaaah!" he shouted. "The English don't know how to use an atomic pile!" Low whistles of incredulity were heard from the lawyers' benches.

Maître Gautrat snapped in return: "Well, you had better go over there and give them some lessons. In return they'll show you that a straight line that you show in your analysis is really a curve, and that you don't know how to calculate a conic surface." There were few people in court who knew what that meant, but some applauded – and the witness shook with rage and shouted that his "honour" was being impugned.

This tortured case

The defence called its own scientific experts, who refuted the findings of the prosecution's witnesses, insisting that the calculations had been slip-shod and once more advancing the opinion that arsenic in the bodies had been absorbed from the soil. A blackboard had been brought into court so that any scientific witness could demonstrate his evidence in mathematical form.

What was clear in this tortured case was that no two groups of scientists were ever going to agree. Through it all, with a quietly resigned air, sat Marie Besnard.

She reminded some international criminologists of the British woman, Ruth Ellis, who had sat through her own murder trial with the same apparent imperturbability.

In his summing-up speech, Maître Gautrat concentrated upon the conflict between the experts—placing special emphasis on the errors of which, he declared, the prosecution witnesses were plainly guilty. He pressed home the point that no prisoner ought to be convicted on such highly doubtful evidence, and ended with a plea to the jury: "And now, gentlemen, you can make the order that will restore hope to this poor woman. The hope that wipes out all past sufferings and bears in its hand that rare flower promised to all, justice."

Subdued weeping

But incredible as it seemed, particularly to some of the visiting British and American journalists, the case of Marie Besnard was still to be denied a verdict. After the judges had deliberated for an hour, and Marie Besnard had at last allowed herself the luxury of subdued weeping during the adjournment, the president of the court announced:

"As things stand at present, the court and the jury have not sufficient data to pronounce judgment. Corroborative information is necessary." Three more investigating scientists would be appointed, he added.

Madame Besnard looked crushed—but then came a further announcement by the president which brought her some relief from her misery: she was to be freed from custody on a bail of 1,200,000 francs. For the first time in four years and nine months, the widow Besnard, caught up in this interminable French legalistic web, was to be allowed out of prison.

Within two weeks she was back in Loudun, with her bail provided partly by her second cousins, and partly by a Paris bank which had generously responded to appeals by her lawyers. There was one aspect of her good fortune that mocked the "justice" of her two years' imprisonment on the theft charge. The relatives who put up 210,000 francs of the bail were members of the very family she was supposed to have swindled by the so-called forged postal order.

But Marie Besnard—who was still officially "the accused"—once more had not weeks nor months to wait, but years. To be precise she had, unbelievably, seven more years and eight months to bear her twilight life as the suspect Black Widow. Postponement followed postponement, and it was not until November 20, 1961, that she was again called to stand trial at Bordeaux.

Marie was now in her mid-sixties, and she had to endure a long cross-examination on her life with her husband and other events which happened even further back than the 12 years since her arrest. Among them were allegations, based on poison-pen letters, that during the war she had had a love affair with a German prisoner-of-war assigned to work for her husband in his rope shop. But despite the energy it had devoted to assembling such "evidence", even the prosecution was unable to corroborate it.

Keystone

A FREE WOMAN at last, the Black Widow of Loudun set out to rebuild her life as best she could at the age of 65. Proceeds from her "Memoires" helped. . . .

Once again there was the usual parade of scientists, and the inevitable squabbling between them as to their abilities, and the skill, or incompetence, with which they had carried out their analyses of the organs from the long-dead corpses. The defence continued to hammer the point that there was no direct evidence that Marie ever possessed a motive for poisoning anyone, or had been seen to do anything that suggested an attempt at poisoning. In 12 years of legal wrangling, Marie's lawyers stressed, the only likely explanation for arsenic in the bodies was that it came from the soil.

They were determined that this time the charges against Marie should be brought to a final conclusion—and the ultimate appeal to the jury was made by a beautiful, 38-year-old woman advocate who had joined the defence team, Maître Jacqueline Favreau-Colombier.

Say to yourselves," she pleaded, "that if today Marie Besnard is in the dock, tomorrow it might be you. Understand what it is to be the prey of public rumour . . . Don't be dupes. She came back to be judged, she trusts you, for she knows what she has not done." The ageing, accused widow gave vent to her long-pent-up emotions as the words were spoken, and sobbed uncontrollably.

Maître Favreau-Colombier had a word, too, to say about the letter-writing Madame Pintou. "I am convinced," she said, "that Madame Pintou always had a grudge against Marie Besnard because she had preserved the peace of her household and the love of her husband. She is a widow. She is said to be neurotic. What is neurosis? The psychiatrists say it is an earthquake of the mind. I had the curiosity to inquire into Mme Pintou's family. I found many odd deaths there, quite as many as in the Besnard affair, a mother, a husband, a son-in-law and so on. Why has not Mme Pintou been asked for explanations?"

On the afternoon of December 12, 1961, the jury retired to consider their verdict; 75 minutes later they returned. Marie, tired-eyed and pale, was brought in from an adjoining waiting-room where she had been nervously nibbling at cakes and sipping a glass of white wine. To the jury the court president read a list of 11 names, including Marie's husband, her father and mother, her father-in-law and other relatives and friends.

Prolonged cheering

As he read each name he asked whether "Marie Davaillaud, the widow Besnard, deliberately administered a poisonous substance likely to cause a more or less rapid death?" In each case the jury foreman answered with a firm "No".

At the end there was complete silence; then came a prolonged burst of cheering and applause. Above the din the court president bellowed, "Marie Besnard is acquitted!" The stolid countrywoman, who had waited so long to hear those words, rushed from her seat and threw herself into the outstretched arms of her defence lawyers. Oblivious of the dignity of the law, they wept with her—and in a moment the small emotional group was surrounded by men and women from the court's public benches, stretching out their hands to Marie in congratulation.

The brilliant white light of the photographers' flash bulbs stabbed the courtroom gloom and someone thrust a bouquet into Marie's arms. Outside the court, too, a huge crowd had gathered—laughing, cheering, turning the evening into a festival. Marie was whisked away by her lawyers to a quiet restaurant to eat her first meal as a completely free woman, and from there to embark upon the task of rebuilding her life as best she might at the age of 65.

CHARLES MILLES MANSON

UPI/Bettmann Newsphotos

On an August night, Sharon Tate and four others were murdered in Los Angeles. Twenty four hours later two more died, only a few miles away. The deaths were as bizarre as anything to have come out of Hollywood. The killers were even stranger – the commune disciples of Charles Manson.

ONE

THE MURDERS

Death In Los Angeles

Peace and love was the message for the young on the west coast of America in the 1960s. But there was a sinister undercurrent. A series of murders in wealthy Los Angeles was about to capture headlines throughout the world.

On 27 July 1969, Gary Hinman, a 34 year-old music teacher, became the first victim of the Manson Family. Three Family members, Bobby Beausoleil, Mary Brunner and Sadie Mae Glutz, had been sent round to his house to collect some money that was owed. They knew he had it – he ran a very profitable illegal drugs operation and the rumour was that he had just inherited $20,000 and had hidden it in his house on the Old Topanga Canyon Road, Los Angeles.

The three visitors argued with Hinman for two hours. Finally, Bobby Beausoleil lost patience, and pulled a gun – a 9mm Radom pistol. He handed it over to Sadie while he went to search the house. At that moment, Gary tried to escape and began struggling with Sadie. The gun went off, and the bullet ricocheted through the kitchen, embedding itself under the sink. Bobby ran back into the room, grabbed the gun and hit Gary around the head with it.

> **When I first saw them at the Tate house my first reaction was, 'Wow, they sure are beautiful people'**
>
> SUSAN ATKINS – FAMILY MEMBER

NEWS OF THE WO...

SUNDAY, AUGUST 10, 1969

No. 6,559 PRICE SEVENPENCE

Over 6,370,000 copies sold last week

FILM STAR DIES IN RITUAL MASSACRE

Sharon Tate found roped

VOICES FROM THE SPIRIT WORLD?

Read our evidence on PAGES 8 and 9

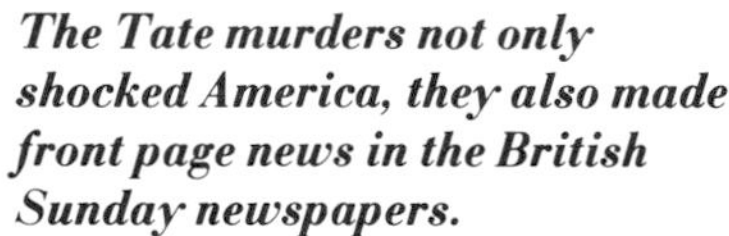

The Tate murders not only shocked America, they also made front page news in the British Sunday newspapers.

News of the World/John Frost Newspapers

First victim

They telephoned Charles Manson who came to the house himself, with Bruce Davis. Manson took a sword, which he used to cut Hinman's ear, leaving a 5in wound. He told Beausoleil to find out where the money was and then bring Hinman out to the ranch. He instructed the two girls to clean up his wounds.

Bobby, Mary and Sadie Mae tied Gary up and left him on the hearth rug while they ransacked the house. Mary Brunner then stitched up Hinman's cuts with dental floss, wrapped his wounds in bandages and gave him something to drink. All they got out of him were the pink slips signing his two cars over to them.

At dawn, Gary Hinman ran for the window and began to scream for help. Bobby Beausoleil panicked and, seizing a knife, stabbed Hinman twice through the chest, leaving him to bleed to death. The three wiped away all their fingerprints (except one) and bundled up incriminating blood-stained clothes and bandages. Somebody stuck a finger in Gary Hinman's blood and scrawled the words 'Political Piggy' on the wall above his head, another daubed a crude version of a cat's paw, the sign of the militant Black Panthers.

They had locked all the doors and were on their way out via the side window when they decided to climb back in and smother Hinman.

Hot-wiring Hinman's VW minibus, they all drove home to Spahn Ranch, stopping off on the way at the Topanga Kitchen for coffee and cherry cake.

Three weeks later, at around mid-

Wide World Photos

Popperfoto

Sharon Tate, actress and wife of Roman Polanski, was eight months pregnant when she and her guests were brutally murdered by the Manson Family.

KEY DATES

JULY-AUG 69

27.7.69	Murder of Gary Hinman, Malibu, LA
31.7.69	Discovery of Hinman's body
8.8.69	Murder of Sharon Tate and four others, Hollywood, LA
9.8.69	Murder of Leno and Rosemary LaBianca, Los Feliz, LA

The Tate home after the massacre (top). The sheet on the lawn (circled) covers Frykowski's body. Bloodstains on the porch (above) are grisly evidence of Frykowski's final attempt to escape. Inside the house, Tate and Sebring were found on the couch (right).

All photos AP/Wide World Photos

night, on 8 August, a white and yellow Ford moved slowly down Cielo Drive, Hollywood, stopping opposite number 10050, the home of actress Sharon Tate. Tex Watson had been there before. While Linda Kasabian, Katie (Patricia Krenwinkel) and Sadie Mae Glutz watched, Tex shinned up a

> **Society has wronged me. We'll kill whatever pigs are in the house. Go in and get them**
> CHARLES MANSON

telegraph pole and cut the wires linking 10050 with the outside world.

Tex, Linda, Katie (Patricia Krenwinkel) and Sadie Mae climbed over the security fence, clutching their bundles of spare clothes and their double-edged knives. Tex carried the Family gun, a .22 Buntline Special and 43ft of three-ply white nylon rope, snaked round his shoulder. The house lay wide open.

Car headlights

A white, two-seater Nash Ambassador came down the drive, on the way out. Brandishing the gun, Tex leapt into the headlight beams screaming for the driver to stop. He thrust the gun into the car window and shot 18 year-old Steven Parent four times in the chest and pushed the car into the bushes.

Tex sent Linda, Katie and Sadie Mae to scout around the house, but they found no way in, so he began cutting his way through the screens of an empty room at the front. Linda stayed outside keeping watch and never entered the house. The three walked in and saw Voytek Frykowski, lying stretched out on a large couch.

Devil's business

Frykowski woke to find the Buntline thrust in his face. Tex, Katie and Sadie Mae surrounded him. When he asked what they wanted, Tex replied, 'I'm the Devil. I'm here to do the Devil's business. Give me your money.'

Sadie Mae went and found a towel to tie up Frykowski's hands. Then she wandered round the house, finding

A policeman stands guard at the entrance to the LaBianca home at 3301 Waverly Drive, where Mr and Mrs LaBianca were murdered.

UPI/Bettmann Newsphotos

Abigail Folger lying reading on her bed. Sadie walked past, and stood in the doorway of another bedroom, watching Sharon Tate, eight months pregnant, talking to Jay Sebring. Sadie reported back to Tex, who sent her back to get them.

Jay Sebring, an ex-navy man, demanded that Sharon be allowed to sit down and then he made a lunge for the gun. Tex shot Sebring through the armpit. When Tex demanded money, his victims were eager to give it to him. While Frykowski lay tied up on the couch, Tex yoked Abigail Folger and Sharon Tate to the unconscious Jay Sebring, pulled the nooses tight and threw the rope end over the wooden beam that ran across the living room. Sadie Mae hung on to it.

Tex then told Sadie to kill Frykowski. He went down fighting. As she raised her double-edged knife, he finally wrenched his hands free, reached up, pulled her by the hair and banged her head. She lashed out with the knife, stabbing him in the legs four times, then in the back twice. Somehow, in the struggle, she lost the knife (it was stuck in one of the armchairs) so she clung on to her victim's back and yelled. Tex shot Frykowski twice, but he continued to fight back. Panic gripped Tex and he began beating Frykowski round the face with the gun butt so hard that the walnut handle grip shattered.

The sight of Frykowski's last stand galvanized the other victims, who began to struggle for their lives. Abigail Folger, as yet unharmed, broke free and ran for the door, Katie followed her. Tex moved in on the wounded and struggling Sebring, stabbing him four times. Then he joined Katie. Tex had now given way to an uncontrolled blood-lust. Thrusting Katie out of the way, he fell upon Abigail, cutting her neck and stabbing her several times.

> **I felt so elated; tired but at peace with the world. I knew this was just the beginning of helter skelter. Now the world would listen**
>
> SUSAN ATKINS – FAMILY MEMBER

Meanwhile, the seemingly indestructible Frykowski had staggered out of the front door, screaming for help. Outraged, Tex rushed after him, stabbing him again and again. Voytek Frykowski was found to have 51 stab wounds after his death.

THOSE THAT DIED

THE VICTIMS

Robert Hunt Library

Sharon Tate, 26 year-old actress, and star of films such as *Valley of the Dolls* and *Rosemary's Baby*. Wife of Roman Polanski.

UPI Bettmann Newsphotos

Jay Sebring, 35 year-old Hollywood hair stylist and supplier of drugs to his society friends. A friend of Tate and Polanski.

UPI Bettmann Newsphotos

Wojiciech 'Voytek' Frykowski, 32 year-old playboy boyfriend of Abigail Folger. Financier of one of Polanski's earliest films.

Abigail Anne Folger, 25 year-old heiress to the Folger coffee fortune, and former volunteer social worker.

Steven Earl Parent, 18 year-old graduate from Arroyo High School. A chance visitor.

Leno A. LaBianca, 44 year-old President of Gateway Markets.

Rosemary LaBianca, 38 year-old businesswoman whose Boutique Carriage business left an estate valued at $2,600,000.

BACKGROUND

HOLLYWOOD

In the 1960s, Hollywood, the hub of the film world, was a desirable residential star resort to the north of the great sprawl of LA. Bel Air, Beverly Hills, Benedict Canyon were the smart addresses where the rich and famous, such as film director Roman Polanski and his wife Sharon Tate (below, second and third left), chose to live. So it was a natural target for the Manson group to attack for maximum publicity in their struggle against the 'fat pigs' of society. It also represented the society that had excluded Manson when he had knocked hopefully on its doors.

When Susan Atkins was fantasizing about future exploits to her horrified cell mate Virginia Graham, she spoke of doing unspeakably hideous things to Richard Burton, Elizabeth Taylor, Steve McQueen, Frank Sinatra, Tom Jones and many others.

This alleged death list was published in the more colourful press. Some celebrities moved out. It was a touch of pure Hollywood that this threat should come from an old movie lot.

Terry O'Neil

Evening News

Night Special

Commercial Union at Bentalls of Kingston

'Death to pigs' scrawled on door in copycat horror killing as police hunt Sharon execution squad

COUPLE DIE IN NEW HOLLYWOOD 'HOODED' MURDER

MENTAL PATIENTS 'KICKED AND PUNCHED'

Evening News Reporter

Knocked to floor

CATHERINE, 23, AND TWO FRIENDS DIE IN CRASH

Lord Longford's

Moon men go home

In the

John Frost Newspapers

News of another ritual murder quickly crossed the Atlantic. The LaBianca murders made the death toll eight.

Abigail Folger somehow got to her feet and blundered towards the French doors to the pool. Katie chased after her, leaving a print of her little finger on the blood smeared door frame. Abigail got out, and staggered across the grass, falling just before she reached the fence.

Final gesture

Inside the house, Sharon Tate, unguarded, unharmed as yet, but tied to a dead man, tried to make her escape. Katie came back in and caught her. She pleaded for her life and for the life of her unborn baby. Sadie Mae's response was brutal. Sadie Mae and Katie held her down while Tex stabbed her to death. Then, they all stabbed her.

Tex ordered the girls out while he went on a final rampage, stabbing and kicking at the lifeless bodies, and linking up Jay Sebring and Sharon Tate with twin nooses. Then Sadie dipped the towel used to tie Frykowski in Sharon Tate's blood and inscribed the word 'pig' on the front hall wall. She left, leaving the front door wide open, and two bloody footprints on the porch.

Tex, Linda, Sadie and Katie returned to Spahn Ranch, hurling their blood-stained clothes and knives away at random on the way.

Later that night, Charles Manson and another Family member came to clean up and look for Sadie's knife. They wiped Steven Parent's car clean and then got rid of fingerprints with the towel that had tied up Frykowski. They left it over Jay Sebring's face.

By dawn, everyone was tucked up in somebody's sleeping bag back at the ranch. Tex, Linda, Sadie and Katie slept all day.

The next night, at an hour after midnight, the yellow and white Ford pulled up outside 3301 Waverly Drive in the Los Feliz district of Los Angeles. Inside were Charles Manson, Tex Watson, Linda Kasabian, Sadie Mae Glutz, Katie and two new faces – Leslie Van Houten and Clem Grogan.

Manson took his sword and gun and got out of the car, with Tex following. They walked up the drive to the long low white house and found a way in. In the living room they found Leno LaBianca, in his pyjamas.

> **"I've killed no one. I've ordered no one to be killed. These children who come to you with their knives, they're your children. I didn't teach them – you did"**
>
> CHARLES MANSON

'Be calm, sit down and be quiet,' ordered Manson. Tex stood over Leno LaBianca while Manson took the gun into Rosemary LaBianca's bedroom and brought her back, tying them up using the two leather thongs Manson wore round his neck. Manson wanted money and the couple gave him their wallets. Leno LaBianca, a supermarket millionaire, offered to take Manson to his store for more. The offer was turned down and Manson walked out of the front door.

The LaBiancas breathed again, but not for long. Clutching their bundles of spare clothes and bayonets, Katie and Leslie entered the house. They

Leno LaBianca (far left) and his wife Rosemary (left) were discovered almost 24 hours after their murder by Mrs LaBianca's son and daughter. Their blood had been used to daub graffiti on the walls of their house (above) – a clear link with the Tate and Hinman murders.

went straight to the kitchen, pulled down the kitchen blinds and took out a carving fork and a serrated wooden-handled knife. Then they forced Rosemary LaBianca to lay face down on her bed, covered her head in a pillowcase and loosely noosed her with the flex of her bedside lamp.

With equal efficiency, Tex pulled up Leno LaBianca's pyjama top and stabbed him four times in the throat with the kitchen knife, leaving it in the last wound. Then using his own knife, he stabbed him eight times in the stomach. Leno LaBianca bled to death, helped on his way by a pillow Tex put over his face.

Reluctant accomplice

Leslie held Rosemary LaBianca while Katie stabbed her. She tried to crawl away pulling the lamp with her. Hearing the noise, Tex rushed in. He helped Katie stab Rosemary LaBianca 41 times. Tex and Katie wanted Leslie to have a turn but she was reluctant. When she finally did begin, it was too late. Mrs LaBianca was already dead – but she still stabbed her 16 times in the buttocks.

With a knife, Tex carved the word WAR on Leno LaBianca's abdomen. Katie perforated the bodies with a carving fork, finally leaving it buried in Mr LaBianca's stomach. They tied lamp flex round his neck and put a pillowcase over his head. Using Mrs LaBianca's blood, somebody used their fingers to scrawl DEATH TO PIGS on the wall. With a rolled up sheet of paper dipped in the same blood, somebody printed RISE over a painting in the living room. And finally Katie wrote HEALTER SKELTER on the refrigerator.

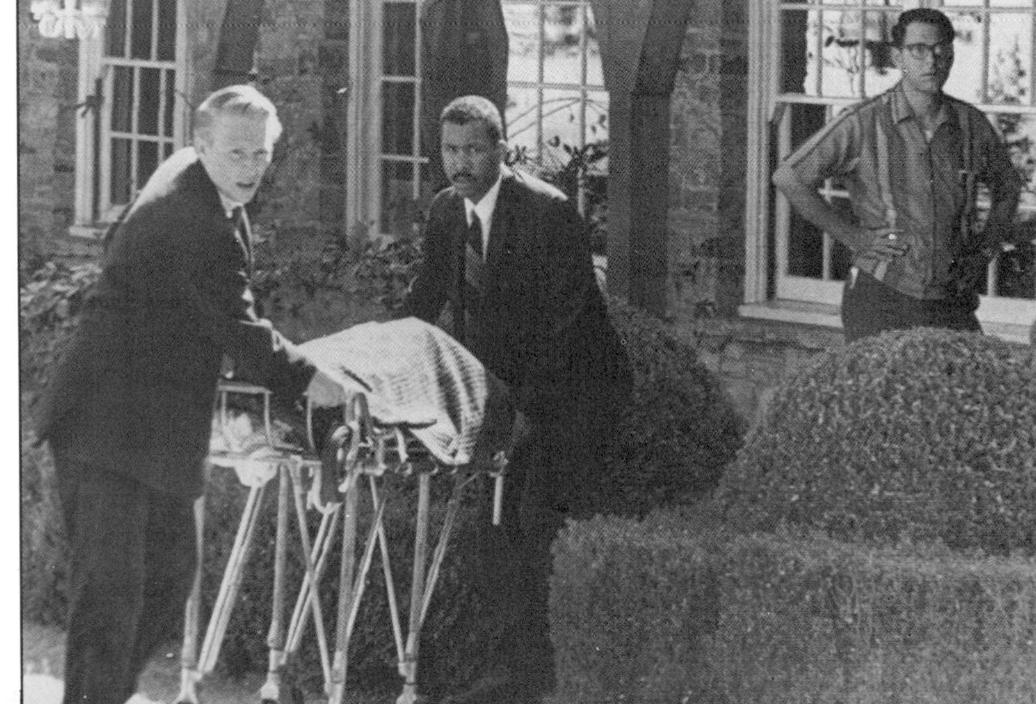

Men from the coroner's office wheel the body of Sharon Tate from the scene of the crime a couple of days after the murders.

SOCIETY OUTCAST

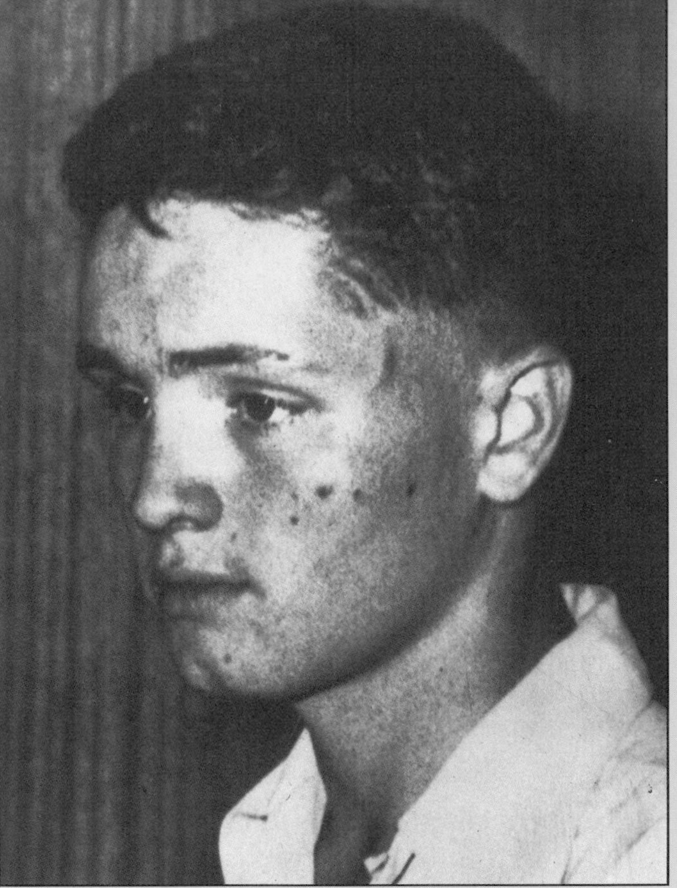

Shortly after his release from a juvenile home in 1948, Manson, aged 14, spent a brief spell working as a messenger boy.

UPI/Bettmann Newsphotos

Charles Manson never met his father and was deserted by his mother for years at a time. When she finally abandoned him at the age of 12, he trusted no one and was hardening into a tough and self-reliant petty criminal – more familiar with the inside of prisons and reform homes than the freedom of the streets.

Charles Milles Manson was born 'No Name Maddox' on 11 or 12 November 1934 – his mother could not remember which, so she chose the 11th. Kathleen Maddox was just 16, and had run away from her home in Ashland, Kentucky, because of the repressive Bible thumping behaviour of her mother. Manson's father was 'a drugstore cowboy' who called himself Colonel Scott. He did not stick around long enough to see the birth, however, and it was William Manson, to whom Kathleen was married for a brief time, who gave the boy his name.

Kathleen Maddox found it difficult to cope with motherhood so young, and Manson was regularly abandoned. When he was six, Manson was left with his grandparents while his mother and her brother, Luther, robbed a gas station. They were caught and jailed for five years. Manson went to live with his strict grandparents for a few weeks, and then his mother's sister, Joanne.

Nomadic Life

A year later, Kathleen Manson came back for Manson. The boy was ecstatic. They began a nomadic life together, but Manson could never be sure whether he would be with his mother or 'pawned off' on to someone else.

Manson and his mother moved around Ohio, Kentucky, West Virginia and Indiana. They lived a haphazard existence, that verged on the edge of crime, until Kathleen met a man who wanted her, but not Manson. She arranged for her son to be made a ward of court and Manson was sent to the Gibault Home for

Indiana Boys' School in Plainfield, Indiana, where Manson attended from the age of 13 to 16. He knew it as 'Painsville'.

Nuel Emmons

THE PRISON HABIT

Before his involvement with the murders, Manson was nothing more than a small time thief. He spent an inordinate amount of time behind bars for petty crimes: car theft, passing small value cheques, taking consenting girls across the state line, petty theft, violating parole. The sentences for all these crimes were made much heavier because they always involved crossing the state line.

Crimes that would merit only a few months in jail, a suspended sentence or a fine within a state, carry years when they become a federal matter. With Manson it seemed as if he was deliberately loading the dice against himself. When he could not cope in the outside world he would do something silly to ensure that he was safely locked up again. As he said himself, reformatories and prisons were his homes. He knew how the system worked and how to rig it – he had friends and a place in the hierarchy. In short, he belonged.

When he was released from Terminal Island in the spring of 1967, Manson said to the guards, 'You know what man, I don't want to leave! I don't have a home out there!

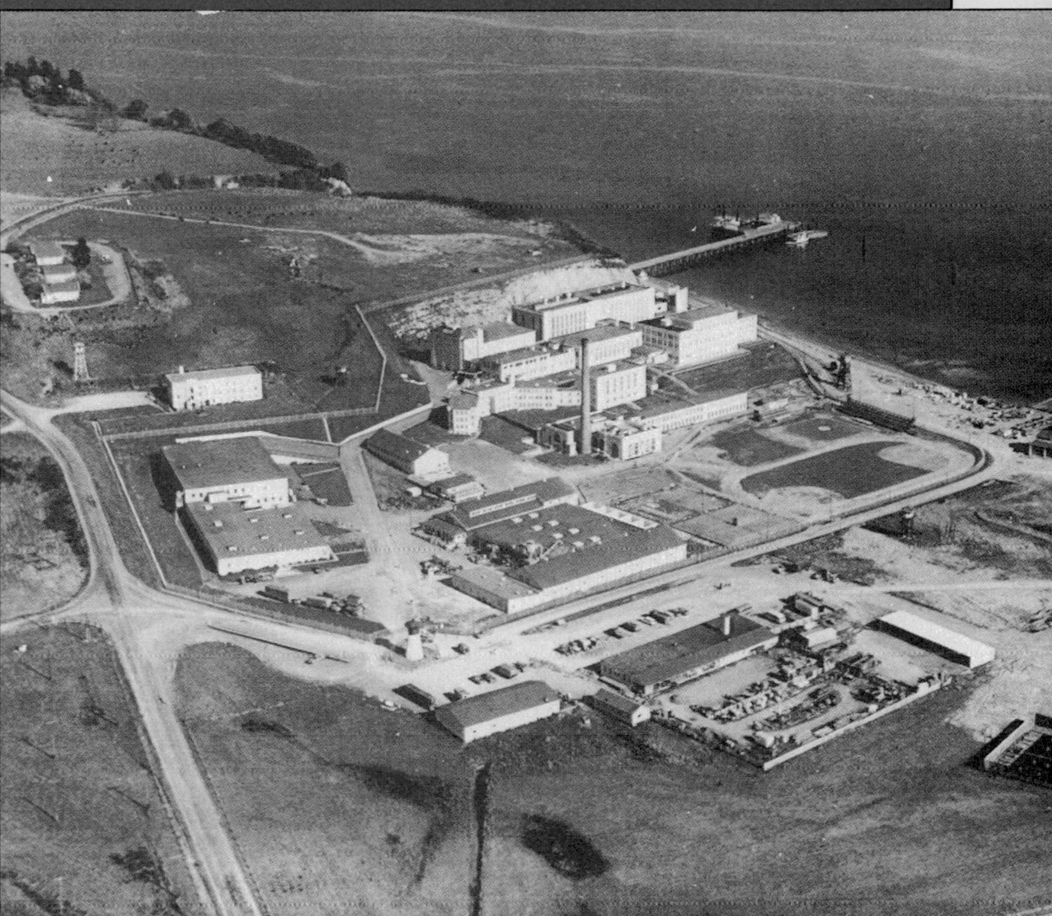

UPI/Bettmann Newsphotos

Boys in Terre Haute, Indiana. Although his mother visited him there and promised that 'pretty soon' he would be back with her, it never happened.

From then on, Manson's life is a sad tale of boys' homes and reformatories, running away, stealing cars and food, and trying to endure the sadism meted out in some of these establishments. He became increasingly hurt, bitter and angry. He also picked up some useful survival tricks on the way, to ensure that nobody messed with him.

Petty criminal

After the age of 16, he spent his time in reformatories, which were apparently an improvement on the Homes, and a great way to learn the ins and outs of petty crime.

In May 1954, Manson was paroled out on the recognizance of his aunt and uncle. He went to live with them in McMechen, where he met a miner's daughter, Rosalie Jean Willis, and married her in January 1955. Manson tried to go straight, but was soon seduced back into a life of crime by an older man who asked him to steal a car and drive it down to California. The deal backfired and for a while afterwards Manson wobbled along the thin line between crime and hustling.

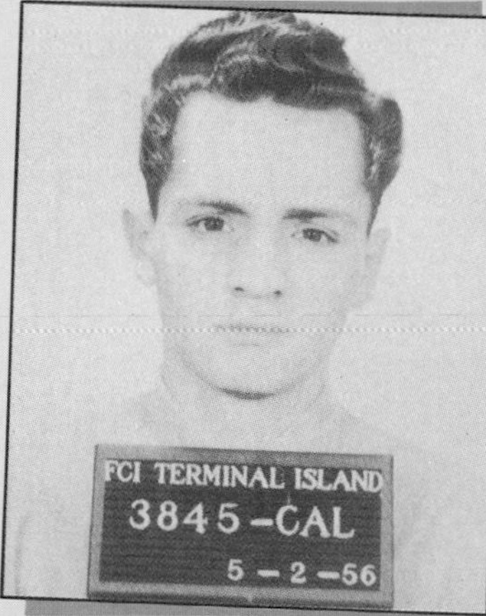

At the age of 21, Manson began a five year sentence at Terminal Island, California, for car theft.

But the car thefts caught up with him and he was jailed for five years. He was sent to Terminal Island, San Pedro. Soon afterwards his son was born, then Rosalie divorced him and went out of his life, taking little Charlie with her. Manson devoted himself to learning how to pimp, so that he would have a career when he got out. In 1958, he was released in Hollywood.

Soon he was arrested again for taking girls across the state line and trying to pass a stolen cheque worth $38. Manson ran to Mexico, but the police caught him and this time probation was turned into a ten year stretch at McNeil Island Penitentiary, and Terminal Island Penitentiary. He next saw the outside world in the spring of 1967.

It was shortly after his release in 1967, that the clean-cut Manson first established his 'Family'.

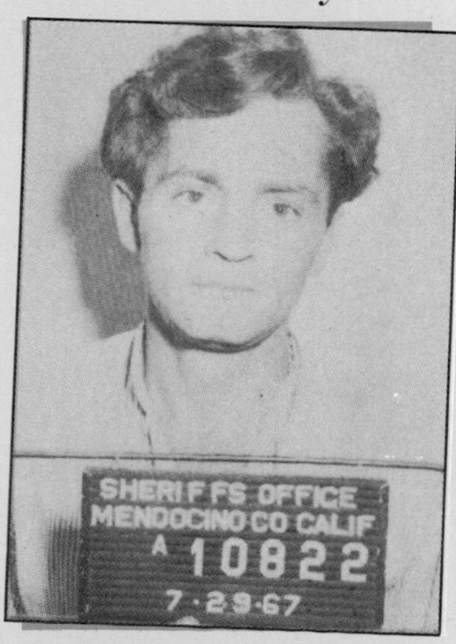

TWO

GENESIS

Forming Of The Family

Released from prison into a new world of liberation, Manson's appetite for female company was insatiable. Within two years he had surrounded himself with a loyal following of naive and willing disciples.

By July 1969 Charles Manson and his Family were living a primitive commune life on the edges of the desert. They were based at the old Spahn Movie Ranch near Chatsworth, often retreating to the more desolate and inaccessible Barker Ranch in Panamint Valley. They were a fluctuating population, but there was always around 30 or 35 followers, three quarters of them women and a few of them children. The murders were carried out by members of the hard core Family, people who had known Manson, or been under his influence for the last two years and were devoted to him.

When they were eventually picked up by the police, they were living like wild dogs, coyotes – a favourite Manson image of himself. But how had Manson turned a flower power commune into a training ground for mass murder, and why had white middle class Americans allowed their children to go to him?

When Charles Manson, small time hood and petty criminal, walked out of Terminal Island Penitentiary on 21 March 1967 he was 32 years old and everything had changed. The restrained, conservative world he had left behind when he started his prison sentence had been replaced by the new generation of love and peace and doing your own thing. Tuning in, turning on, dropping out were the new catch-phrases. Incoming inmates had told tales of what was going on outside the prison walls, but Manson had not believed them. Now he did.

> **Charlie is the only person I have met who tells the truth. It is hard to live with a person who tells the truth the whole time**
>
> CATHY SHARE – FAMILY MEMBER

Convict's dream

'Pretty little girls were running around every place with no panties or bras and asking for love. Grass and hallucinatory drugs were being handed to you on the streets. It was a different world than I had ever been in and one that I believed was too good to be true. It was a convict's dream and after being locked up for seven solid years, I didn't run from it. I joined it and the generation that lived in it,' Manson commented.

Manson came out from Terminal Island with $30.00 in his pocket and his guitar in his hand. All of young America was on the move, and they were all going where he was going – San Francisco. Everywhere, people were rebelling against authority, dropping out of college courses, refusing to toe the 'straight' line, mocking the establishment, trying to establish a counter culture. For the first time in his life, Charles Manson, the institutionalized reject, was in step with the rest of the world. His disaffected view of society was welcomed, approved, endorsed. Manson described that period, 'And we slept in the park and we loved on the streets and my hair got a little longer and I started playing music, and people liked my music and people smiled at me and people put their arms around me and hugged – I didn't know how to act. It just took me away.'

What the press called the Manson Family started out unspectacularly. Manson with his guitar and fashionably long hair quickly became a regular in the hippie scene on San Francisco's Haight Ashbury and on the campus at Berkeley (University of California). He would hang out, smoke marijuana, busk with his guitar. That was what he was doing when he met Mary Brunner, a librarian: a slim, flat-chested red-head, she was not pretty but definitely Manson's 'type' and he moved in with Mary.

A few weeks later he had acquired a VW minibus, and he and Mary took off, travelling up and down the West Coast (Manson's movements had to be

Wide World Photos Inset Michael Haering/L.A. Herald Examiner

As hippies across the United States dropped out to preach peace and love, Manson (foreground) and his followers abandoned society to prepare for an apocalyptic struggle of the races and the birth of a new world order.

KEY DATES

MAR 67-JULY 69

21.3.67	Manson released from Terminal Island
16.10.67	Family bus acquired
8.11.67	Susan Atkins joins Family
1.4.68	Mary Brunner gives birth to Manson's son
2.5.68	Manson arrested for marijuana possession – charges dropped
July 68	Family move to Spahn Ranch
Oct 68	Family move to Barker Ranch
23.3.69	Manson visits 10050 Cielo Drive

Michael Haering/L.A. Herald Examiner

approved by his parole officer) finding out for themselves about communal living and loving. Manson went to LA trying to set up his career as a rock superstar. On Venice Beach, he met Lynette Fromme, a slim red-haired girl who had just had a confrontation with her father. Manson brought her back to Mary, and the nucleus of the Family was formed. In September they were joined by disaffected legal clerk Patricia Krenwinkel.

Manson was establishing a harem: he and his busload of girls, all ten years or more younger than him, were invited to all the best parties.

His method of domination was acid (LSD) and sex. Half a lifetime ago, Charles Manson had been married and had fathered a son. While he was in prison his wife had divorced him and taken their son with her.

Calling the tune

In the 1950s, Manson had for a short period been an unsuccessful pimp, falling in love with his main girl, who had dumped him. With Mary and another girl called Darlene, whom he had picked up, he discovered something new. By sleeping with both girls on a rota basis, Manson called the tune, controlled the situation. He learned to wield the power of sex.

Later on, when there were more Family members Manson would be the one to choreograph their orgies, arranging the bodies artistically, directing who should do what to whom and how. Every woman who joined the Family was initiated by Manson, first with a 'tab' of LSD and then with a few hours of sex.

When university drop-out Bruce

IN CONTEXT

COMMUNE LIFE

In the 1960s young people all over America and Europe tried to find an alternative of living together, by sharing living space, responsibility, worldly goods and children. The shared lifestyle of the communes began to flourish. California and New Mexico were popular and Topanga Canyon, not far from the Spahn Ranch, in California was home to many communes, based on old houses and caves. Two famous commune experiments were the Hog Farm commune in California and the Diggers in San Francisco, where they took the philosophy of producing food to be distributed free to the poor.

Many young people on the move hitch-hiked from commune to commune. Until July 1969, Manson's Family had just been another commune, and many people passed through it, unaware of Manson's dark side.

UPI/Bettmann Newsphotos

Small caves dotted the land behind the Spahn Movie Ranch; ideal places, the Family believed, to hide out when their imagined enemies came to attack them. Lynette 'Squeaky' Fromme (below right), Manson's most consistent disciple, poses with room-mate Sandra Good for a 'Family' photo.

Popperfoto

Davis joined them, the VW needed to be replaced, so Manson traded it in for an old school bus. They painted it black and wrote Hollywood (spelling it Holywood) Film Productions on the side to avoid trouble with police. The black bus became famous in the vicinity. Manson and his group moved around in all the fashionable places in town, with Manson trying to establish himself on the fringes of the movie and music worlds.

More joined in: the delinquent Susan Atkins (Sadie Mae Glutz); Ruth Ann Moorehouse, the preacher's daughter who married a hapless bus driver in order to leave home and join the Family. Red-haired Dianne Lake, whose parents had dropped out to join the Hog Farm commune; Bobby Beausoleil, the pretty boy actor and musician who had starred in Kenneth Anger's underground film *Lucifer Rising*. Through Bobby, Manson was to meet Kitty Lutesinger, Cathy Share (Gypsy), Leslie Van Houten and Gary Hinman, among others. Charles (Tex) Watson, the All American ex-athlete, met the Family through Beach Boy (Californian band) Dennis Wilson. Wilson was so fascinated by their lifestyle that he allowed them to freeload on him unmercifully. He housed them, fed them and supplied them all with clothes from his own wardrobe.

> **Most of the people at the ranch were just people you did not want, people that were alongside the road**
>
> CHARLES MANSON

By mid 1968 Manson had most of his Family. There were three girls to every boy. The size of the Family had grown so rapidly that the bus could no longer cope and they had started living in and around Topanga Canyon in various shacks. It is probably impossible to document every person wandering the West Coast who blundered into the Manson circle and out again, but the people listed above formed the permanent Family. They were joined by Brooks Poston, TJ (the Terrible) Walleman, Steve Grogan (Clem), Juan Flynn, Nancy Pitman, Cathy Gillies, Sandra Good, Juan Flynn, Joan Wildebush (Juanita).

Mary Brunner had given birth on 1 April to Manson's son Valentine

Wide World Photos

CULTS AND GURUS

The 1960s was the decade of cults. Some, like the satanists, were merely sects of violence, but most arose in response to people's urge to break out of the conservatism of the '50s. They wanted to explore new ways of thinking and living. Some joined communes, others turned to the ancient civilization of the East, discovering a new word: guru, meaning master or teacher.

A guru was meant to help an individual in the search for truth. All a follower had to do was submit, surrendering his will to the guru. The Beatles and other celebrities (including Mia Farrow, the star of Polanski's *Rosemary's Baby*) looked for enlightenment in India, where they sat at the feet of the Maharishi Masheesh Yogi (above).

All over India, Ashrams (communes in which followers of a guru live and work collectively) were flooded by Europeans and Americans offering all their worldly goods and abasing their souls in the search for understanding. The Maharishi and other Indian teachers such as the Swami Satchidananda and Swami Bhakivedanta visited the West, turning up at key events such as Woodstock. In California it became as fashionable to have a guru as it had been to have an analyst.

IN CONTEXT

Elliot Landy/Redferns

THE DRUG CULTURE

From the crowds who flocked to the rock concerts at Woodstock (above), to the commune lifestyle of the new generation, drug culture dominated the 1960s – particularly on the west coast of America. Drugs were taken to expand consciousness. Unfortunately, most people gained no useful insight whatsoever, because the drugs were taken in an uncontrolled manner. Marijuana was considered comparatively harmless, and was grown and harvested on a commerical basis. Wild desert plants such as telache, magic mushrooms and jimson weed, were dangerously narcotic, and could be fatal when taken by people unused to them.

The mainstream drug of the decade, however, was LSD (lysergic acid diethylamide). LSD was a laboratory synthesized drug, used in the treatment of schizophrenia. But it produced schizophrenic-type symptoms in healthy people, hallucinations, feelings of invincibility, a fractured perception of the world and unhinged the mind from reality. In street talk, the hallucinatory drug LSD was known simply as 'acid'.

As LSD was a synthesized drug, any amount of it could be manufactured. In Los Angeles, the main supplier was a dropped-out chemist, Owsley, who produced the crystalline compound in his mobile lab in an old bus.

Manson took to LSD very quickly. His first encounter with it was in 1967 when, fresh out of prison, he went to a concert given by the Grateful Dead – the definitive acid rock band. The effect was electrifying. People remember Manson dancing like a man possessed and then falling into a trance curled up in the foetal position. From then on, Manson always had a 'tab' or two of LSD on him, which he would give to his girls before they had sex.

As a Family, Manson and the girls would go to parties, sit in a circle, and take LSD together for a group trip. Family member, Paul Watkins, noted that Manson was always the one to ration out the acid, and that he always made sure he took less than anyone else. He was always in control.

Michael (named after Robert Heinlein's hero in the cult science fiction book *Stranger in a Strange Land*). Susan Atkins was soon to produce her son Zezozoze C. Zadfrack. When twice-married young mother Linda Kasabian and Stephanie Schram joined the Family in 1969 the cast was complete.

Misfits and outcasts

The Family was not made up of obvious misfits and social outcasts, although they may have become so. Manson did not surround himself with

> **Charles Manson changes from second to second. He can be anybody he wants to be. He can put on any face he wants**
>
> SUSAN ATKINS

people like himself – paranoid petty crooks. The majority of the Family members were easily led and impressionable young people. Many were middle class white girls – librarians, clerks, students, university graduates, teachers. They provided easy guru-fodder for Manson. Only Susan Atkins had a criminal record. The material possessions various Family members brought with them – cars (Juanita),

AP/Wide World Photos

The Family's 'command vehicle', an armour-plated dune buggy. The furs covering the rear platform concealed a machine gun mounting.

access to property (Sandra Good, Cathy Gillies), substantial amounts of money (Linda Kasabian), daddy's credit cards (Patricia Krenwinkel) – allowed the Family to carry on.

Through an associate of San Diego socialite Sandra Good, the Family moved on to the Spahn Movie Ranch and began to live as counterculture outcasts, feeding themselves from the perfectly good food thrown away by supermarkets every night, helping out on the ranch, hustling dope, stealing or 'borrowing' credit cards and cars. Through Cathy Gillies they acquired the Barker Ranch, handing over one of Dennis Wilson's gold records to its bemused old owner as rent.

In the desert, Manson ruled supreme. Some Family members found the isolation, Manson's increasing paranoia and the menacing presence of the Straight Satans biker gang too much, and left – or rather escaped. However, Manson's earliest adherents proved his most devoted; they would do anything he wanted, or they thought he wanted. They were ready to kill without mercy or remorse.

SCIENTOLOGY

Popperfoto

Scientology – the modern science of mental health – was devised in 1950 in the fertile brain of the late Lafayette Ron Hubbard, the famous science fiction writer (right). It is a matter for debate whether Hubbard was sincerely attempting to find a new way to cure mental ills, or whether his was merely a cynical money-making experiment in people manipulation.

Hubbard's theory is full of a bewildering amount of jargon, which proved extremely appealing to the young or immature and ill-educated. Although there is great claim to scientific accuracy, no data, statistics or methodology are provided. Hubbard proposes that most mental problems are caused by physically or emotionally painful experiences 'recorded' by the body cells when a person is unconscious, ill, or in the womb.

These recordings are called engrams and are stored in the mind's 'engram bank'. They can be restimulated by outside events in the world, and block rational behaviour. To achieve optimum mental health, all that needs to be done is to relive these experiences a few times under a light hypnotic trance called a reverie. A person who has lifted all their engrams, such as Charles Manson, is called a 'clear'.

In the early years, scientology was a reasonably harmless crank theory as people 'cleared' each other. However, when Hubbard established the scientology organization (orgs), making 'clearing' something one had to pay for he also introduced the brainwashing and manipulative techniques at which Manson grew so adept.

Manson was introduced to scientology in prison. While there is no evidence that Manson actually believed in the theory, he certainly understood its uses. Working on young minds, or minds voluntarily softened by drugs, he used all the techniques – payment to enter the group, eye contact, impossible commands, threatened expulsion from the group, cultivated loathing for the outside world and death threats – to anyone who dared to leave or betray him.

The Family collected food thrown out of supermarkets, often making their pick-ups in a Rolls Royce. Lynette Fromme, Sandra Good, Mary Brunner and Ruth Ann Moorehouse await delivery in a garbage bin.

Michael Haering/L.A. Herald Examiner

THE RANCHES

The Manson Family settled in two communes outside Los Angeles during 1968. The first was the Spahn Ranch, an old movie lot where visitors came across Family members living in and around the buildings. It was from here that the Tate/LaBianca killers set out on 9-10 August. The second was the Barker Ranch, a rugged and inaccessible spot in the heart of Death Valley, where the Family were in hiding when they were arrested – waiting for the start of the revolution.

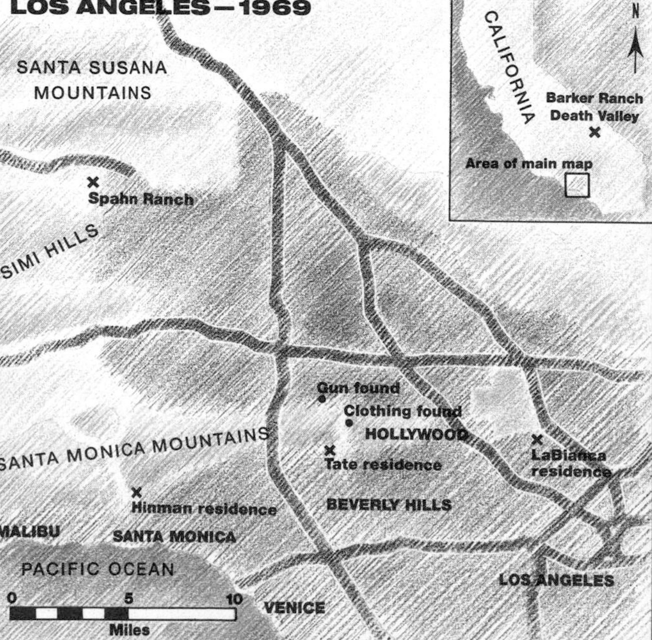

John Hutchinson

UPI/Bettmann Newsphotos

UPI/Bettmann Newsphotos

George Spahn (above) was the owner of the Spahn Ranch. Eighty years old and virtually blind, he had allowed the Family to settle there. In return the girls would clean, cook and, according to some, provide sexual favours for him. Twenty year-old Family member Lynette Fromme claimed, in an interview with prosecution attorney Vincent Bugliosi, that she was in love with Spahn and would marry him if he asked her to.

Nuel Emmons

Left and background: Michael Haering/L.A. Herald Examiner

AP/Wide World Photos

Spahn Ranch, August 1970 (above left). The remnants of the Family tried to carry on as normal while Manson and the others faced trial for the Tate/LaBianca murders. From left to right, Ginny Gentry, Catherine Share, Sue Bartlett, Danny DeCarlo, Sandra Good, Lynette Fromme, Chuck Lovett and Ruth Ann Moorehouse. The more remote Barker Ranch (above) became deserted after the police raid in October 1969. Manson was discovered by the police during the raid, hiding in a small cabinet under the kitchen sink.

Police raided the Spahn Ranch in August 1969 (above and right), after reports that stolen Volkswagens were being converted into dune buggies. An arsenal of weapons was found, but no connection between the commune and the murders in Los Angeles had yet been made. It was treated as no more than a local news story and all the suspects, including Manson himself, were released after it was discovered they had been arrested on a misdated arrest warrant.

THREE

AT LARGE

Clues In The Desert

A link was made between the Manson Family and the murders. How did Los Angeles detectives eventually arrive at this conclusion and what was the evidence? Was it sufficient to make arrests?

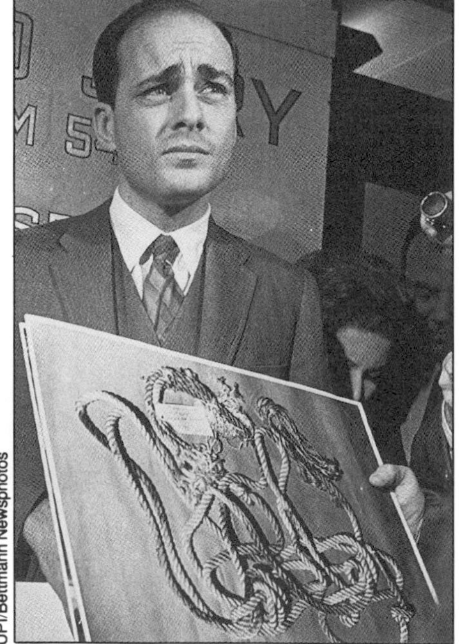
UPI/Bettmann Newsphotos

Aaron Stovitz, DA, with the nylon cord found around the necks of Sharon Tate and Jay Sebring.

Gary Hinman and the Tate-LaBianca victims were all killed within a fortnight of each other. Each murder appeared motiveless. All died in a particularly bloody manner and their blood was used to inscribe words on the wall. The words all had the same connecting theme. And yet at the beginning, the police made no connection between them.

Gary Hinman's body was found by friends on 31 July 1969, four days after he had been murdered. They called the Los Angeles Sherriff's Office (LASO), which deals with crimes outside the metropolitan area. Sergeant Paul Whiteley and Deputy Charles Guenther were assigned to the case, and it was to be their persistence which finally cracked the whole Family affair.

One of Hinman's killers, Bobby Beausoleil, was picked up very quickly, on 6 August. When Whiteley and Guenther read police reports on the Tate/LaBianca killings, they were

Both AP/Wide World Photos

The Barker Ranch (above and left) after being raided by the police. It was the final refuge of the Family when they were arrested in October 1969.

intrigued. They knew Bobby could not have been involved with them because he was in custody. But they wondered about the bloody scrawling of the words PIG and DEATH TO PIGS on Hinman's wall.

Family connection

They suspected Bobby had not been alone in the Hinman killing. He hung out with a weird bunch of hippies who lived at the Spahn Movie Ranch, led by Charles Manson. Perhaps whoever had been with Bobby had gone on to do the Tate/LaBianca murders? Whiteley passed on his ideas to Sergeant Jesse Buckles, an officer on the Tate investigation team in the Los Angeles Police Department (LAPD). Buckles dismissed the idea as a non-starter, and did not even bother to report it to his superior officer.

It took weeks for either team to get anywhere. The Tate investigation looked promising at first. The grisly scene had been discovered by the live-out housekeeper, Mrs Winifred Chapman. There was one person alive and unharmed on the Tate property residence – William Garretson, the young caretaker who lived in the guest house in the back garden and claimed he had not heard anything. He was dazed, confused, frightened. But above all, he had been on the grounds of the residence when the murders took place. They leant on him, but could prove nothing.

> **"We wanted to do a crime that the world would have to stand up and take notice"**
>
> SUSAN ATKINS

Drugs clue

The next day, when the LaBianca killings broke, all police could say definitely was that Garretson had not done it: he was in custody. In uptown LA, panic swept the poolsides. Gun sales shot up, security dog handlers had never had it so good and social life ceased. The pressure was on the police to be seen to act.

Hulton-Deutsch Collection

ROMAN POLANSKI

Sharon Tate's husband, the film director Roman Polanski, initially found himself suspect in the Tate murders. To some, it was possible that he could have set up the killings himself to satisfy some artistic desire.

Much of his work was dominated by violence and death. *Repulsion* was about a demented young girl who stabbed her lover to death in the bath: *Cul de Sac* was the harrowing tale of an isolated group who murdered each other.

When his pregnant wife, Sharon Tate was murdered, Polanski was in Europe, putting the finishing touches to his film *Rosemary's Baby*. But Polanski, who had nothing to do with the killings, offered a large reward to anyone who could help find the murderers.

KEY DATES

AUG-DEC 69

6.8.69	Arrest of Bobby Beausoleil
16.8.69	Police raid Spahn Ranch
12.10.69	Police raid Barker Ranch
15.10.69	Link made between Hinman and LaBianca murders
6.11.69	Susan Atkins' confession to cell-mate
30.11.69	Arrest of Tex Watson

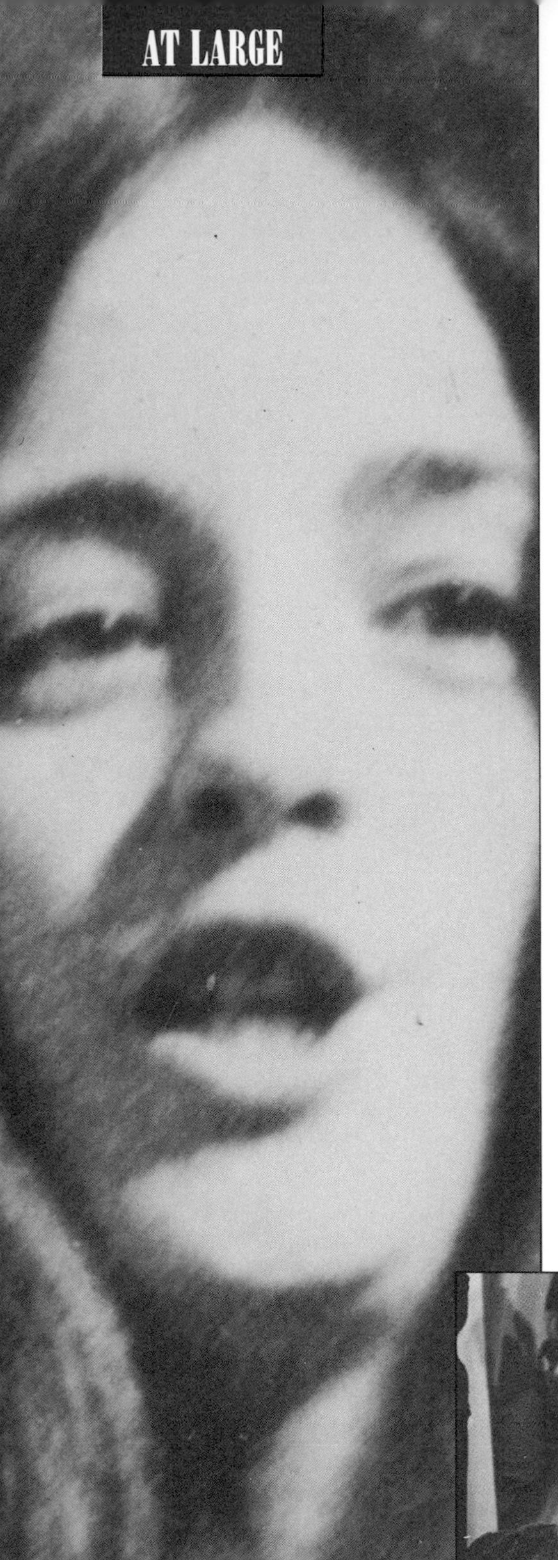

Susan Atkins (left) turned the whole course of the investigation when she made her startling confession to her prison cell-mate, Ronnie Howard.

In the Tate murder case, the most promising lead seemed to be drugs. A terrified Polish friend told the police that Voytek Frykowski was being set up as a drugs dealer. And the LAPD was well aware that Jay Sebring, hairdresser to the stars, was involved in the drug scene, discreetly supplying the rich and famous.

In contrast, the LaBiancas were eminently respectable, successful, rich and contented. Leno LaBianca was a supermarket supremo and Mrs LaBianca had her own retail business. Without much conviction, police explored the idea of some sort of mafia connection, or a gambling vendetta (Leno LaBianca had been a keen gambler and race horse owner), but there were no convincing leads.

It was not until 15 October that one of the LaBianca team thought about checking out similar murders on the LASO patch and found out about the Hinman case. Unlike the Tate detectives, they considered it an important lead. But as they were gearing up, news came in from Whiteley and Guenther about the activities of the desert hippies. All had not been quiet on the Spahn Ranch. On 16 August, it had been raided by LASO officers in pursuit of stolen cars and credit cards.

> **"If I'm looking for a motive, I'd look for something that doesn't fit your habitual standard"**
>
> ROMAN POLANSKI to the detectives

Two months later, on 12 October, Inyo County Police raided the remote Barker Ranch, in pursuit of car thieves, arsonists and illegal firearms. This time, they arrested 24 Family members, again including the scruffy guru himself. The remoteness of the ranch meant that the raid took three days. During this time, two frightened young women stumbled out of a dry gully and begged the police for protection. They were Kitty Lutesinger, five months pregnant with Bobby Beausoleil's child, and Stephanie Schram, Charles Manson's latest and last love. They had been trying to escape.

Inyo County Police informed LASO of the raid, and Whiteley and Guen-

Both AP/Wide World Photos

EVIDENCE?

THE BUNTLINE SPECIAL

On 1 September 1969, DA Aaron Stovitz showed the Press the gun used in the Tate/LaBianca killings. It was found on a hillside in Los Angeles by 10 year-old Stephen Weiss. It was a .22 Standard Longhorn revolver or Buntline Special, carrying nine cartridges in its cylinder. Only two live rounds were left and the gun was also missing its right hand grip. The police failed to recognize the gun's significance, tagging it, filing it away in a manila envelope and forgetting about it.

It resurfaced three and a half months later, only because of the perseverence of the Weiss father who recognized a description of the gun issued in the *Los Angeles Times*. By linking possession of the gun to Spahn Ranch and hence to Charles Manson it proved to be a crucial piece of evidence at the trial.

UPI/Bettmann Newsphotos

> **"When they catch me, it's going to be like feeding me to the lions. They're going to put me far away because I have no family, no one that will help me"**
> CHARLES MANSON

ther, who had been looking for Lutesinger for months in connection with the Hinman case, drove the 200-odd miles up to Independence to interview her. Kitty had devastating news. She had heard that Manson had told Bobby and Sadie Mae to go and collect money from Hinman. She had also heard Sadie Mae talk to other Family members at the ranch about stabbing a man in the legs and him pulling her hair. Sadie Mae, alias Susan Atkins, was also locked up at Independence. When interviewed, she told them she was at Hinman's house when Bobby murdered him. She was booked on suspicion of murder, and eventually detained in the Sybil Brand Institute in Los Angeles.

The LaBianca detectives, although not too impressed by the Hinman connection, nevertheless set their formidable intelligence gathering machine in motion, pursuing information on anyone who had anything to do with Manson and his followers.

Something Kitty had said about Sadie stuck in the minds of Whiteley and Guenther. Hinman had not been stabbed in the legs. Voytek Frykowski had. Could Sadie have been talking about the Tate murders? Whiteley thought the Tate detectives should know, and so he told them. But to their shame, they did nothing at all about it for 11 days. Kitty Lutesinger was not interviewed until 31 October.

A direct link between the Manson Family and all three murders was becoming visible. Sadie Mae, who loved to talk, had begun talking in jail to her cellmate, Ronnie Howard, and her workmate Virginia Graham. It took them some time to decide she was not making it up, and even longer to find someone to listen to them.

Linking evidence

The LaBianca conscientiousness paid off, netting Al Springer and then Danny de Carlo of the Straight Satans who had lots to say by way of hearsay and circumstantial evidence. People outside the Manson set such as record producer Terry Melcher and Greg Jakobsen gave evidence that Manson had been to the Tate residence (it used to be Terry Melcher's house) among other things. On 5 December, Susan Atkins took the stand to testify to the Grand Jury and describe what really happened on the night of 8 August at 10050 Cielo Drive.

A pair of spectacles (left) found on the floor at the Tate residence turned out to be a false lead left deliberately by Manson.

CLIMATE OF VIOLENCE

In 1968 waves of unrest followed Martin Luther King's assassination, while police turned on Vietnam protest students.

The 1960s was a decade of change, the overturning of established order, revolution and violence. The Manson murders were horrific, but they took place against a backcloth of institutionalized and politically motivated violence.

At the beginning of the 1960s, the world teetered on the edge of nuclear war, as the USA confronted Cuba under its communist leader Fidel Castro. In 1961, there was the Bay of Pigs incident, in which President John F Kennedy supported the unsuccessful counter-revolution. This was followed in 1962 by the Cuban Missile Crisis, when it was discovered that Cuba had deployed nuclear missiles, all pointing at the USA – a mere 150 miles away. President Kennedy ordered a blockade, which successfully forced the Cubans to dismantle their missiles.

But it was the Vietnam war that stained the decade. There were more than 100 US 'advisers' in Vietnam in the early 60s, monitoring the conflict between the communist North and South Vietnam – supporting the South to prevent communism over-running America. By the end of the decade, there were half a million American troops in Vietnam and the war was costing over $4 billion a month. More US soldiers had been killed than in the Korean war, and more bombs drop-

ped than the combined amount dropped by both sides in World War II.

As the war intensified, the world was taught some distasteful new vocabulary: escalation, deforestation, agent orange and napalm. The war was hugely unpopular in the US, as people wondered why so many of their boys were being killed. A draft system was introduced and resisted by many who burnt their draft cards and fled the country. Anti-war demonstrations – reaching their peak in 1968 – occurred all over the USA and Europe.

A dreadful emblem of the whole experience was the shameful My Lai massacre in 1969. Lieutenant Paul Calley 'captured' the village of My Lai (the soldiers called it Pinkville) and ordered his men to kill the inhabitants: 109 old men, women, children and babies. The war gradually wound down, ending in ignominy and shame for America in 1973. The war had cost a fortune, thousands had been killed or maimed and nothing was achieved.

Americans demonstrated in Central Park, New York, against the continuation of the Vietnam War.

In the US, violence also took political shape. On 22 November 1963, President John F Kennedy was assassinated in Dallas, Texas. His alleged murderer, Lee Harvey Oswald, was in his turn murdered by Jack Ruby, who subsequently died of a heart attack. The Warren Commission, set up by President Lyndon B Johnson to investigate Oswald's murder has never reached a satisfactory conclusion.

Early in 1968, Civil Rights leader, the Reverend Martin Luther King was assassinated, presumably in an attempt to halt the burgeoning and successful civil rights movement. Then in June that same year, Senator Robert Kennedy – brother of John F Kennedy was assassinated,by Sirhan Sirhan.

Race Riots

The Civil Rights movement, led by Martin Luther King, had been growing strongly, and since the start of the 60s, American blacks had fought for and gradually – on the whole peacefully – gained their rights as American citizens.

Shops and schools were de-segregated and in 1965, James Meredith, an air force veteran, became the first black to register at the University of Mississippi (after President Kennedy had sent in the army).

After Martin Luther King was assassinated, the campaign became more violent, and there were riots in many states including Watts, Cleveland, Chicago and Detroit. More than 100 people were killed.

BLACK PANTHERS

The Black Panthers proclaimed strict adherence to the African Muslim religion. They wanted to establish a separate Negro society within America. They had an intense dislike for all figures of authority, in particular the police, whom they labelled 'pigs', the most abhorrent of all creatures to devout Muslims. Their criminal activities were well-known but evidence against individuals was hard to obtain. Five members of the gang walked free from Omaha Central police station (left), after questioning. They were thought to be involved in the violence which erupted in the area of Omaha.

Background picture: Protestors marched to the United Nations Building in New York, appalled by US involvement in Vietnam. One year later, Robert Kennedy (above), whose brother had sent troops to Vietnam, was assassinated.

Below: AP/Wide World Photos All others Popperfoto

FOUR

THE TRIALS

Guilty But Unbowed

Manson and three others faced Judge Older for the Tate/LaBianca killings and other trials followed. The star prosecution witness was kept in solitary confinement to protect her life.

The Manson trial began on 15 June 1970. Lasting for nine and a half months, it was the longest ever American murder trial, with a transcript running to over eight million words. The jury of seven men and five women were sequestered – that is kept in a hotel supervised by bailiffs, for the entire trial – 225 days longer than any other jury before.

There were vast amounts of evidence and information to collect, and a mass of witnesses to find. It also took an age to build a defence team, as Manson wanted to represent himself (his request was refused) and rejected many of the attorneys appointed for him. He was enough of a prison lawyer to know all the ways to win time by delaying tactics. Manson was also desperate to control the defence – he did not want the girls' attorneys doing their proper job representing their clients interests individually. The whole team was there to defend Manson, and the girls could take the rap.

> **"My faith in me is stronger than all your armies, governments, gas chambers or anything you may want to do to me"**
> CHARLES MANSON

Manson was eventually defended by Irving Kanarek. Although Manson did not choose him, he was the ideal attorney for the man who wanted to win time. He was notorious for his obstructionist behaviour and had once stretched a simple theft case into two years' worth of court time. Manson challenged the right for the first judge, William Keene, to preside over the trial (this is allowed by law), and he was replaced by Judge Charles Older. For the people, the prosecution team was led by the indefatigable Vincent Bugliosi supported by Aaron Stovitz.

From the start, the trial was characterized by bizarre scenes and unprecedented behaviour both in and outside the courtroom. On day one, 24 July, Manson appeared with a cross on his forehead, which he had inflicted on himself with a hacksaw blade. He said nothing, but issued a typewritten statement: 'I have Xd myself from your society.' A few days later, his co-defendents were sporting the same mark and by the end of the week, devoted Family girls, encamped on a corner near the courthouse, had done the same. When Manson shaved his head, so did all the girls. When he was obstructive in court, turning his back on the judge, they did likewise. At one point, Manson leapt from the dock towards the judge, screaming that he should have his head cut off.

In August, newly elected President Richard Nixon (who should have known better as he was himself an

Manson heads for court in June 1970. It had taken a total of 8,750 hours of police work to get him and his followers there.

attorney) endangered the legality of the trial by declaring *sub-judice* that Manson was guilty, and allowing this to appear in the press.

Death threats

Bugliosi had to present the prosecution case in an eerie atmosphere of death threats and anonymous phone calls from the zealous Family members who wanted their friends freed. Judge and attorneys had to be protected by bodyguards and were issued with walkie-talkies for communication, in case their phones were cut off.

Bugliosi's star prosecution witness was Linda Kasabian, who had actually been present at the Tate killings and had heard about the LaBiancas'. Susan Atkins had promised to testify, but retracted. Linda, who had said to Manson, 'I'm not like you Charlie: I can't kill anyone,' seemed to have no fear of telling all she knew. She had to be kept in solitary confinement during her time at court for fear of her life.

Probably the most damaging witness was Tex Watson, finally extracted from the Texas jailhouse where he had first been arrested. Manson had been trying desperately to establish him as the evil mastermind of the killings, but when the jury saw All-American Tex, they could not believe it. What he said was more damaging: 'Charlie called me over behind a car. He said for me to take the gun and knife and go up to where Terry Melcher used to live. He said to kill everyone in the house as gruesome as I could.'

The Family trial shocked the world. But it gave Manson what he wanted – fame.

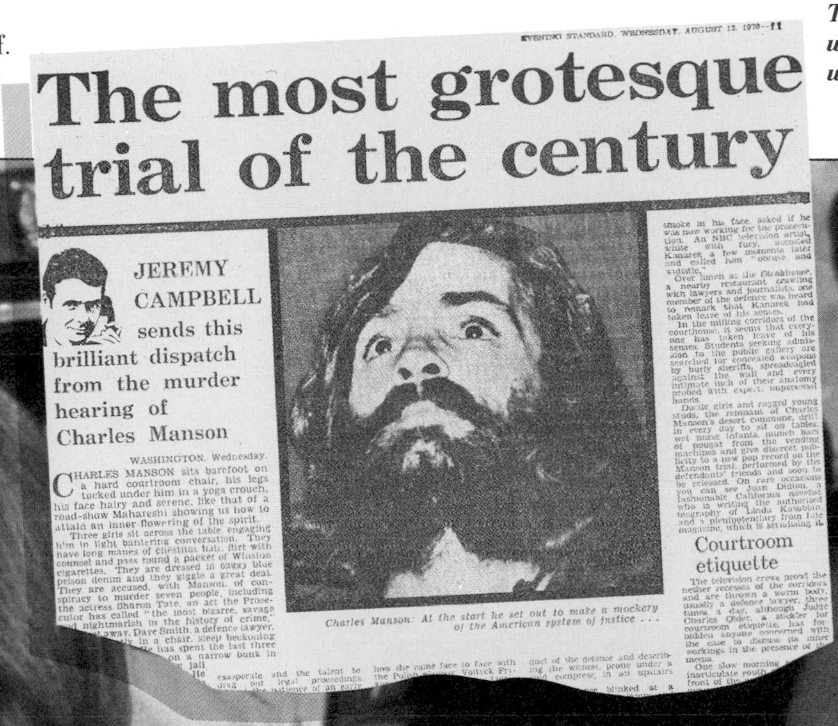

Inset Evening Standard/John Frost Newspapers
Wide World Photos

EVENING STANDARD, WEDNESDAY, AUGUST 12, 1970—11

The most grotesque trial of the century

JEREMY CAMPBELL sends this brilliant dispatch from the murder hearing of Charles Manson

WASHINGTON, Wednesday.

CHARLES MANSON sits barefoot on a hard courtroom chair, his legs tucked under him in a yoga crouch, his face hairy and serene, like that of a road-show Mahareshi showing us how to attain an inner flowering of the spirit.

Courtroom etiquette

Charles Manson: At the start he set out to make a mockery of the American system of justice ...

JUNE 70-FEB 72

KEY DATES

15.6.70	Tate/LaBianca trial begins
3.8.70	President Nixon declares Manson 'guilty'
Nov 70	Robert Hughes murdered
25.1.71	Jury finds verdict of guilty on all counts
29.3.71	Death sentence passed on Manson, Krenwinkel, Atkins and Van Houten
21.10.71	Death sentence passed on Watson
16.2.72	Californian death penalty abolished

> **I may have implied that I may have been Jesus Christ, but I haven't decided yet what I am**
> CHARLES MANSON

At last, on 15 January 1971, the jury went out, seven months to the day since the beginning of the trial. They took ten days to come to a decision, announcing a verdict of guilty on all counts on 25 January 1971. Californian law demands two trials – one for guilt to be established and the second for the sentence to be decided. In the second trial, fraught with further courtroom antics, Vincent Bugliosi asked for the death sentence. Manson, Atkins, Krenwinkel and Van Houten had the death sentence passed on them on 19 April 1971. They were not to die, however, because on 16 February 1972, California revoked the death sentence. The four of them were saved by the very society they planned to destroy.

Further trials

After the Manson trial, there were others. Tex Watson was finally brought to justice for the Tate/LaBianca murders. Steve Grogan, Bruce Davis, Manson and Susan Atkins were brought into court for the murder of Gary Hinman and Shorty Shea.

The death of Shorty Shea, ranch hand and out of work actor on the Spahn Ranch, has never properly been explained. He and Manson did not get on with each other and after the police raid at the Spahn ranch for stolen cars and credit cards in August 1969, Manson decided that it was Shea who had informed to the police. Shortly after the raid, Shea disappeared and was never seen alive again. On the evidence given by the others, it was accepted he was the

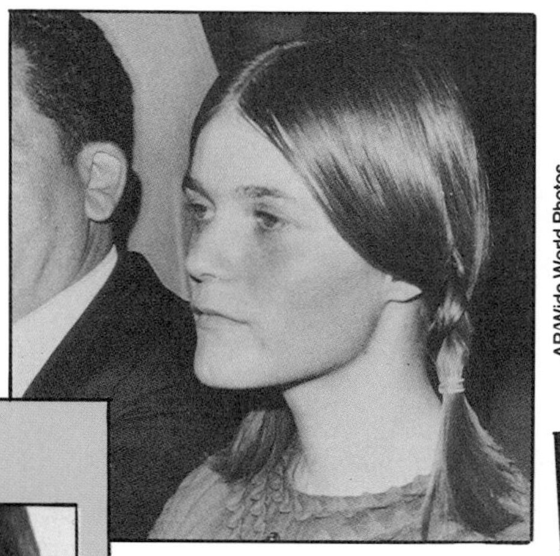

AP/Wide World Photos

Linda Kasabian (above) was the prosecution's principal witness. Manson's defence, led by Irving Kanarek (right), claimed she had taken LSD at least 300 times and was incapable of testifying. Prosecution attorney Vincent Bugliosi (below) was complimented by Manson after the trial for doing a 'fantastic, remarkable job' in managing to secure his conviction.

ACCUSED

A FAMILY GATHERING

Topham

CHARLES MANSON
Age 32. Although charged with one murder and conspiracy for seven others, Manson claimed responsibility for up to 35.

AP/Wide World Photos

CHARLES 'TEX' WATSON
Age 23. Former record-holding schoolboy athlete. Dropped out of college to run a wig shop before meeting Manson in 1968.

Topham

SUSAN ATKINS
Age 21. Quit school at 15 to hang out with armed robbers in San Francisco. Later became a topless dancer. Met Manson in 1967.

Topham

LESLIE VAN HOUTEN
Age 20. Exemplary childhood wrecked by divorce of parents. Maintained she did what she did for Beausoleil, not Manson.

PATRICIA KRENWINKEL
Age 21. Ex-school teacher and insurance clerk who found meaning in life after being subjected to Manson's 'sexual healing'.

AP/Wide World Photos

ROBERT 'BOBBY' BEAUSOLEIL Age 22. Cult film actor and competent musician songwriter. Resented by Manson for his success with women.

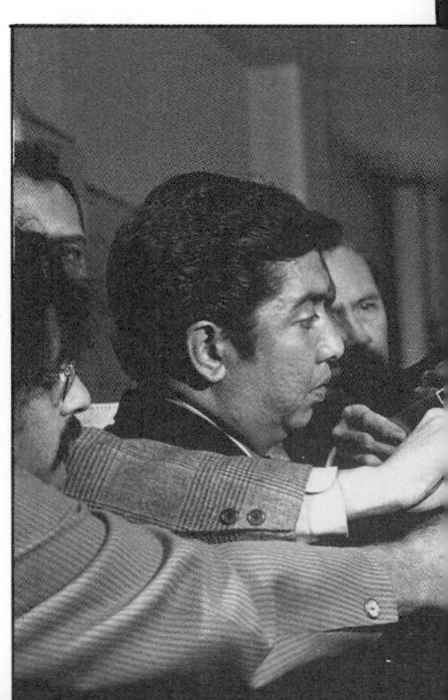

ninth victim of the Manson Family.

Vincent Bugliosi, barely rested from the Manson trial, prosecuted Tex Watson. The jury were sequestered, but this time it was all over within three months. The jury found him guilty on 12 October and he was sentenced to death on 21 October, after only a few hours deliberation.

Susan Atkins was sentenced to death for her part in the Hinman murder. Bobby Beausoleil was already on death row. Manson, Bruce Davis and Steve Grogan were tried separately. Manson and Davis got life; Steve Grogan was given the death sentence, but Judge James Kolts commuted it to life on 23 December 1971, finding Grogan incapable of deciding anything on his own.

It is by no means certain that the Family death toll rests at nine. Various other deaths occurred throughout the period from 1969 to 1972, most of which have never been solved.

In a beach house on 5 November 1969, Family member John Philip Haught alias Zero, apparently shot himself. At the time he was with other Family members – Cathy Share, Linda Baldwin, Sue Bartell and Bruce Davis. They claimed he was playing Russian roulette. But the gun was fully loaded and it had been wiped clean of fingerprints – even Zero's own.

On 16 November 1969, the body of a young girl dumped in Laurel Canyon was identified as a Family member. She had been stabbed 157 times. No one has ever found out her name. On 21 November, the bodies of two young scientologists, James Sharp and Doreen Gaul, were found in an alley in Los Angeles. Doreen Gaul had been a girlfriend of Bruce Davis, himself an ex-scientologist. Although the police suspected Family involvement, nothing was ever proved.

London death

On 1 December 1969, the body of Joel Pugh was found in the Talgarth Hotel in West London. His throat had been cut and there were razor slash marks on both wrists. Police put it down to suicide. It was not until later that it was discovered that Joel Dean Pugh, ex-Family member, was the former husband of Sandra Cood.

In November 1970, Leslie Van Houten's attorney, Robert Hughes, went away camping for the weekend and did not return. The trial had to be adjourned. His body was found in Sespe Creek, Ventura County, four months later.

Both below UPI/Bettmann Newsphotos

IN CONTEXT

THE TRIAL SYSTEM

The US trial procedure works in much the same way as in England and Wales. However, there are variations. In the case of the Manson trial, Judge Charles H. Older (below) summed up only as to the law before the lawyers made their final speeches, and did not comment on the evidence. In California, during a death penalty trial, the defence and prosecution can each make over 20 peremptory challenges as well as a limitless number for cause.

In a death penalty case the jury deliberates not only on the guilt or innocence of the defendant but at a later stage on whether the death penalty should be imposed. Before they try the main issue, jurors are always asked whether, if there is a guilty verdict, they would have any objections to bringing in a verdict for the death penalty.

Wide World Photos

Manson's response to Nixon: 'Here's a man who is accused of murdering hundreds of thousands in Vietnam . . .'

TUESDAY PREVIEW EDITION

COMPLETE STOCKS

Los Angeles Times

LATE SPORTS

VOL. LXXXIX FIVE PARTS—PART ONE

TUESDAY MORNING, AUGUST 4, 1970

74 PAGES

DAILY 10c

MANSON GUILTY, NIXON DECLARES

Rams Game Saturday
SEE SPORTS SECTION

AP/Wide World Photos

MESSIAH OR MADMAN?

Charles Manson was capable of articulation and understanding. Yet, his attitudes revealed stark contradictions – he respected nature but thought nothing of human life.

UPI/Bettmann Newsphotos

Charles Manson is unique among mass murderers. There have been many such killers in the United States, but none like Manson – for Manson murdered by proxy. The power of his personality made others want to do his killing for him. But how could this happen?

Interviews with Manson himself and with people who knew or followed him, bring out very different pictures. To some, he is a racist, misogynist, ill-educated bigot, to others he is the most dangerous man alive; or even God or the Devil. To himself, he is a small-time pimp and thief. And yet, something in his personality allowed Manson to dominate and manipulate a large group of people.

Any study of Manson and his personality yields two overriding images. One is of the chameleon, the other is the dog. Manson frequently characterized himself as a mirror to humanity, a reflection of the sickness inherent in the society of his time. Family members attest that he was a changeling, he could be whatever the other people wanted him to be, he could reflect their views.

For example, in conversation with Vincent Bugliosi, the prosecuting attorney, he could be rational and quick witted – bringing out his prison lawyer skills. Yet Bugliosi could see the mesmerizing effect Manson had on Lynette Fromme and Sandra Good.

Many people, including himself, describe Manson as the man with a thousand masks, ready to be whatever ingratiated him with companions. For a physically small man (Manson is 5ft 2in) who spent half his life in prison, the ability to agree with all men is obviously a powerful survival strategy. When it is coupled with the mind control techniques of scientology, and fuelled by a paranoid anger at the world, the result is a powerful persona indeed.

The image of Manson as a dog, and all that that entails, is his favourite

MANSON'S HANDWRITING

Manson's handwriting reveals a man who has a deep-seated fear of authority. There is a significant difference between his normal writing and his signature. The first indicates a man who is introverted and unassuming. In his signature, however, he seeks to give the impression of being busy and under pressure.

A 'B' open at base = talkative

B 'E' with two arcs = quick mind

C 'R' with inflated top = ability to appear kind and friendly

D End stroke of 'M' = dislike of compromise

E Higher first stroke of 'M' = egoistic

F 'H' tall and narrow = reserved and inhibited

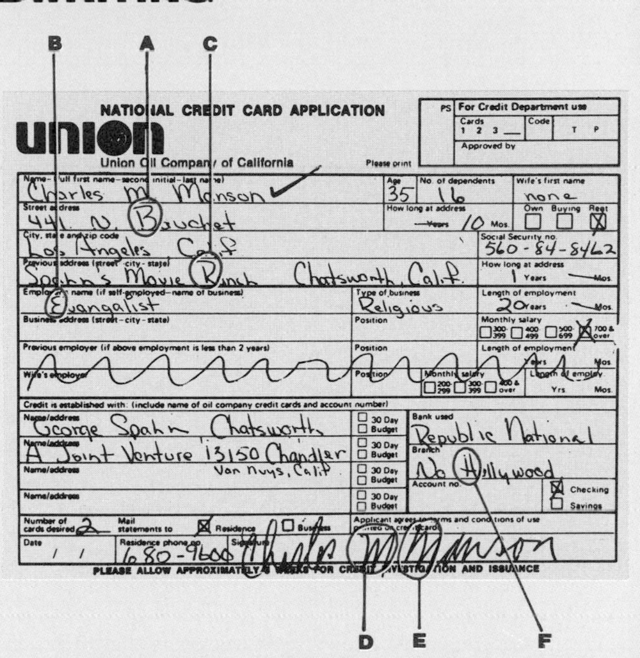

B A C

NATIONAL CREDIT CARD APPLICATION

UNION

Union Oil Company of California

Please print

PS For Credit Department use

Cards 1 2 3 ___ Code T P

Approved by

Name – (full first name – second initial – last name): Charles M Manson ✓

Age: 35

No. of dependents: 16

Wife's first name: none

Street address: 441 N. Bucket

How long at address: Years 10 Mos.

Own / Buying / Rent: [X] Rent

City, state and zip code: Los Angeles, Calif

Social Security no.: 560-84-8462

Previous address (street – city – state): Spahn's Movie Ranch Chatsworth, Calif.

How long at address: 1 Years Mos.

Employer's name (if self-employed – name of business): Evangalist

Type of business: Religious

Length of employment: 20 Years Mos.

Business address (street – city – state)

Position

Monthly salary: 300-399 / 400-499 / 500-699 / [X] 700 & over

Previous employer (if above employment is less than 2 years)

Position

Length of employment: Years Mos.

Wife's employer

Position

Monthly salary: 200-299 / 300-399 / 400 & over

Length of employ Yrs Mos.

Credit is established with: (include name of oil company credit cards and account number)

Name/address: George Spahn Chatsworth

Name/address: A Joint Venture 13150 Chandler Van Nuys, Calif

Name/address

Name/address

30 Day / Budget

Bank used: Republic National

Branch: No Hollywood

Account no.

[X] Checking / Savings

Number of cards desired: 2

Mail statements to: [X] Residence / Business

Applicant agrees to terms and conditions of use printed on credit card.

Date: / /

Residence phone no.: 680-9600

Signature: Charles M Manson

PLEASE ALLOW APPROXIMATELY 6 WEEKS FOR CREDIT INVESTIGATION AND ISSUANCE

D E F

James Woodward, PO Box 310, London SE20 7RA.

AP/Wide World Photos

Members of Manson's Family who kept a vigil outside the LA courtroom in 1971, followed his example and shaved their heads.

AP/Wide World Photos

metaphor for himself. Loyal friend, rejected puppy, coyote pariah are all repeated Manson images.

At the same time, when he came across other dominant males – the biker gangs' Juan Flynn who had survived Vietnam – Manson felt it necessary to establish his position by boasting of the killing he had done. Like an unsocialized dog, Manson fed on other's fear. People who showed fear were punished, assigned to a lowly position in the pack hierarchy. People who could outstare or out threaten, or showed that they were not frightened were left alone, or fawned upon.

Even his strategies were dog-like. In contrast to the communal values he talked about, there was no doubt that Manson had to be leader of the pack, and everyone did what he said.

Manson emerged in the 1960s when authority was being questioned on all levels, and young people were looking for an alternative way to live. He offered a way, and certainly inspired, great love and loyalty in many of his followers. Even when Linda Kasabian was testifying against him, she still claimed that she loved him. Manson did not force people to kill for him. He made it possible for those with a mind to murder to allow themselves to do it.

Has the myth outgrown the man? Prison psychologists diagnosed him as a paranoid schizophrenic. There is still no satisfactory explanation as to how he turned into 'the most dangerous man in the world'.

Five different images of Manson (above), which emphasized his ability to adopt a personality for each occasion. From 'scruffy little guru' as the Beach Boys saw him, to 'Jesus Christ', who preached to disciples in the desert wilderness and prepared them for the forthcoming revolution, as his followers believed. Strangers who met Manson found him submissive and ready to agree with their own philosophies and opinions.

FIVE

MOTIVES

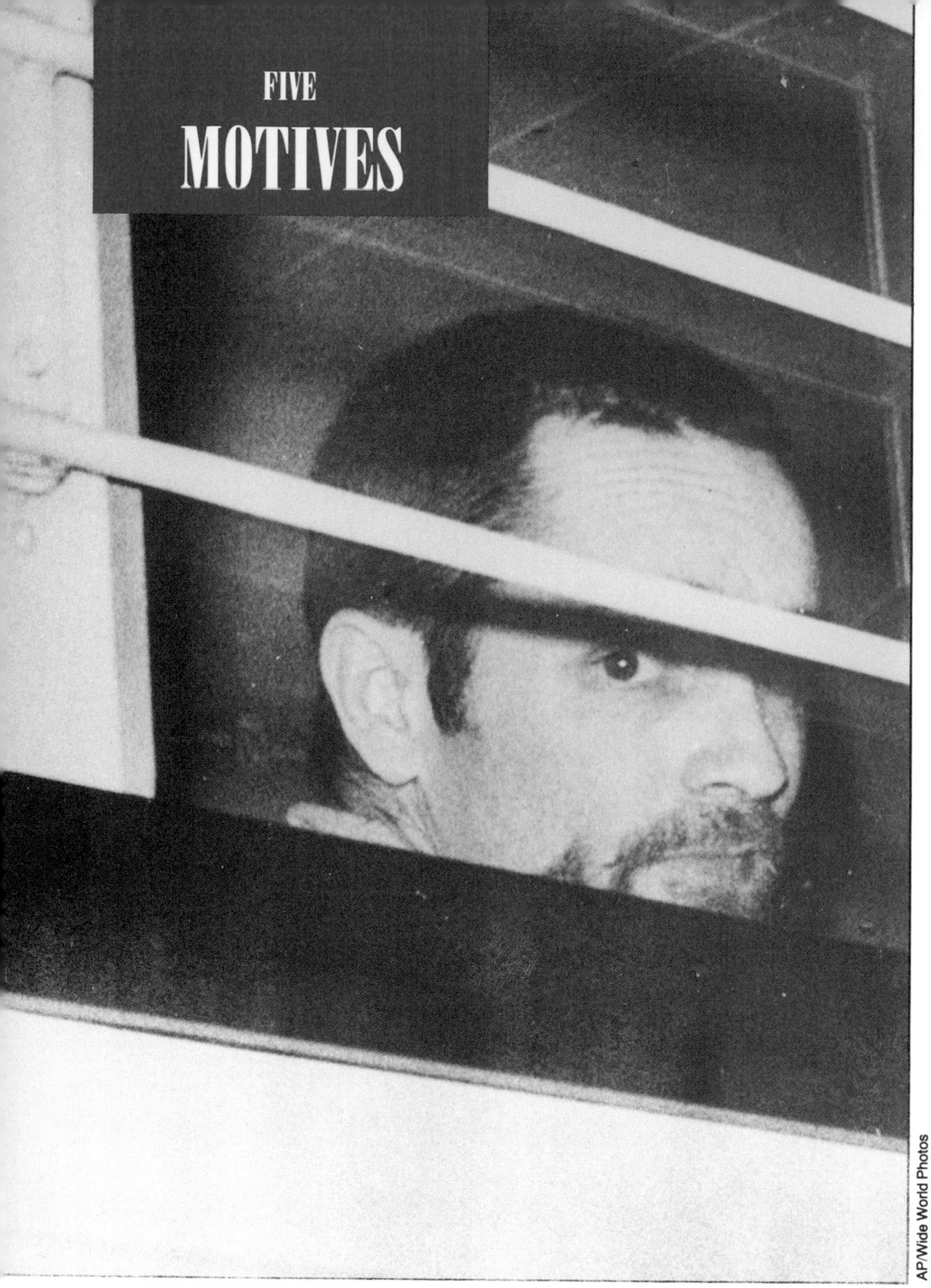

There is no obligation to prove motive in a murder trial. Confession and evidence proved beyond doubt that the accused in the Manson trial were guilty. Why they did it is another story.

To find one possible reason, it is necessary to go back to July 1969. Tex Watson was involved with a black drug dealer called Bernard Crowe. Tex bought $2,400 worth of drugs from him, but refused to pay. Crowe and two minders burst into Watson's girlfriend's flat. Tex had disappeared and Crowe became threatening. Manson and another Family member, TJ Wallemann, went to the flat, and Manson shot Crowe.

Fortifications

Manson believed he had killed him and the very next day news came out that a Black Panther had been found shot dead. In fact Crowe had not died and the Black Panther was someone completely different, but Manson was paranoid that the wrath of the Black Panthers was about to descend on him and the Family. He began to fortify the Spahn Ranch, buying guns and preparing additional hiding places out in the desert.

While Manson awaited the revenge

AP/Wide World Photos

Manson (left) was returned to San Quentin's Death Row after being convicted of the murders of Gary Hinman and Shorty Shea. In 1968, Beach Boy Dennis Wilson (centre, below) introduced Manson to record producer Terry Melcher, then living at 10050 Cielo Drive.

Bizarre Vision

With the killers behind bars, the Manson story still endures – some believe that his influence went way beyond the West Coast. What were the true motives behind the events of 1969?

of the Panthers, Gary Hinman, drugs supplier, was accused by a biker gang of supplying a bad batch. They began to apply pressure on Bobby Beausoleil. It was Hinman's inability to provide the money that led to his death. As an afterthought, Bobby Beausoleil and Sadie Mae Glutz tried to involve the Panthers, perhaps get the police after them, by daubing the Panther sign and also a Panther word for white authority – PIG.

When Beausoleil was picked up and accused of Hinman's murder, Sadie and the girls decided to try to free him. According to Manson, they thought some copycat murders would be the answer. If Bobby was in jail and similar murders were committed, he would be free from suspicion.

Manson always denied that he was the instigator, but he instructed Tex to go to the Tate residence. He also chose the houses they were to go to, though he did not know the victims. He had gone to 10050 Cielo Drive with Dennis Wilson. He had also been to the house next door to 3301 Waverley Drive, the home of a drug dealer called Harold True.

At the trial, prosecutor Vincent Bugliosi put forward a much more bizarre motive, which he called Helter Skelter. Bugliosi claimed that Manson had evolved an apocalyptic world vision from a set of unlikely sources: the Bible, particularly Revelation 9; the lyrics of the Beatles; scientology and Robert Heinlein's science fiction classic, *Stranger in a Strange Land.*

According to Bugliosi, Manson believed that there was about to be a bloody revolution when the black man rose up and that he was meant to find a great pit in the desert to hide his followers underground while racial war raged above. When the fighting was over, with the blacks victorious, he and his followers would emerge, and the stupid and inexperienced blacks would beg him to be their leader. This gothic theory was called Helter Skelter, after a Beatles' song. The murders were done, to stir up black and white antipathy, in effect to start the revolution.

> **What do you think would have happened if the Family hadn't done what they did? You seen the Vietnam war stopped didn't you?**
>
> CHARLES MANSON

Split identity

Manson himself in *Without Conscience* plays down the whole idea. But what Manson says he thinks and what other people think of Manson are two different things. Probably the motive was a mixture of various things: Manson wanted to frighten off the Panthers, and to get his own back on the 'fat cats' who had rejected him and refused to listen to his music.

EVIDENCE?

REVELATION

'Neither repented they of their murders, nor of their sorceries, not of their fornication, nor of their theft.' Revelation Chapter 9 Verse 21.

Although he was illiterate until his early 20s, Charles Manson was brought up with a thorough knowledge of the Bible. Chapter Nine of the Book of Revelation became a source of particular fascination for him and he developed an extraordinary interpretation of its meaning, which tied in with his lifestyle on the communes and the murders in Los Angeles. He saw himself as Appollyon, the Exterminating Angel mentioned in the Chapter, and believed that by carrying out the Tate/LaBianca murders he would initiate the killing of a third of mankind, emerging afterwards as a new leader of society. His interpretation was linked in closely with the messages that he believed were left exclusively for him in the Beatles White Album.

In any event, his followers were persuaded to kill. He brainwashed them through a mixture of scientology techniques and the warping of language. A favourite word for kill was 'discorporate', which is what Heinlein's hero, Valentine Smith, did to his enemies.

In the end the Manson murders were a result of the lethal cocktail of Manson's philosophy finding a place in the hollowed out souls of Bobby and Mary, Tex and Katie, Leslie and Sadie Mae.

London Features International

BEATLE MANIA

Manson saw the Beatles' White Album as a message, which only he was fully able to interpret properly. The raucous rock song *Helter Skelter* was seen as describing the collapse of society; *Piggies* sneered at the establishment. *Sexy Sadie* was regarded as a hymn to Susan Atkins; *Blackbird* was a song urging black people to revolt. And *Revolution 9* was aural chaos. Revolution 9, Revelation 9. For Manson and his Family, Helter Skelter was certainly coming down.

BACKGROUND

David Redfern

AFTERMATH

The story of Charles Manson and his accomplices since their conviction has revolved chiefly around how soon they will be granted parole. Only one of them, Steven Grogan, has been released, after serving 13 years of his sentence. He was probably helped by leading the authorities to the previously undiscovered body of Shorty Shea. On his release he began working as a house painter in the San Fernando Valley.

■ The murderers first became eligible for parole in 1978, six years after the abolition of the Californian death penalty. Since then a running battle has been fought to ensure that none of them, particularly Manson, come out any sooner than they have to.

■ Stephen Kay, a Los Angeles County district attorney, who worked as an assistant to Vincent Bugliosi during the original trials, has kept up a close scrutiny of each of the murderers.

■ The chances of Manson ever being released are unlikely. At a 1981 parole hearing he warned that Kay would be killed in the car park afterwards. A year later he was put into a maximum security cell at Vacaville prison in California after reports that he was planning an escape by balloon. A catalogue for hot air balloons, a hacksaw and other items including rope and a container of flammable liquid were discovered in the jail.

■ It is different for Manson's accomplices, however, particularly the three girls, Susan Atkins, Patricia Krenwinkel and Leslie Van Houten. Using

In August 1978, Manson (above) began to live his fantasy as a rock star. He still practises in the prison chapel.

UPI/Bettmann Newsphotos

Charles 'Tex' Watson was interviewed in his office behind the chapel at California Men's Colony in 1978 (above). As an inmate, he served as assistant pastor, but then went on to become a prison car mechanic.

Both photos Syndication International

Manson (below) is serving nine life terms in Vacaville jail, in Southern California. He works as a gardener in the chapel garden. He remains unrepentant about his past. Even in prison, public fascination with him continues.

skilled lawyers they have worked hard to find loopholes that will help towards their release.

■ The most likely candidate is Leslie Van Houten. She has become a model prisoner at the California Institution for Women at Frontera, where she gained a degree in psychology and literature. This is combined with the fact that her involvement in the LaBianca murders may have been only secondary, since she stabbed Rosemary LaBianca after she was already dead.

■ But while Vincent Bugliosi believes it certain that the three girls will be released eventually, the future of Charles 'Tex' Watson, whose direct involvement in the murders was the most appalling, remains less certain. His period as assistant Protestant pastor in prison at San Luis Obispo – with fellow Family murderer Bruce Davis as his assistant – came to an end when DA Kay complained that he was trying to build himself a personal power base within the prison.

EXTRA

CLOSING N.Y. STOCKS

Los Angeles Times

FRIDAY LATE FINAL

MANSON GIRL TRIES TO SHOOT PRESIDENT

Pulls Gun in Crowd at Sacramento

John Frost Newspapers

In Sacramento, in 1975, Lynette Fromme pointed a gun at US President Gerald Ford. Fortunately, she failed to pull the trigger, but the Manson connection caught the headlines yet again (above).

AP/Wide World Photos

A bullet-ridden van was the result of a shoot out with police after a failed raid on a gun store in 1971. The Family had planned to use guns from the raid to hijack an airliner and demand the release of Manson and the others.

In the summer of 1987 Manson spoke to author Nuel Emmons in San Quentin jail, California. Emmons twice served sentences with Manson before writing Without Conscience – Charles Manson in his Own Words.

From 1976 to 1982, Manson was kept under constant supervision in segregated quarters at Vacaville Medical Facility, where he regularly sought parole.

Topham Picture Library

Syndication International

PUBLISH OR BE DAMNED

When Sir Travers Twiss (below) married his charming and beautiful young wife, Marie, he accepted without question that she was of "respectable" social origins. He reckoned without the insidious menaces of a blackmailer . . .

"Do you feel a creeping, shrinking sensation, Watson, when you stand before the serpents in the Zoo, and see the slithery, gliding, venomous creatures, with their deadly eyes and wicked, flattened faces? Well, that's how Milverton impresses me. I've had to do with fifty murderers, but the worst of them never gave me the repulsion which I have for this fellow."

The speaker is, of course, Sherlock Holmes, and the man he is referring to is the blackmailer, Charles Augustus Milverton, "the worst man in London". The story of Milverton was first published in *Collier's Magazine* in 1904. The date is interesting because the slithery Milverton was probably the first blackmailer ever to make his appearance in fiction.

In fact, the crime itself was relatively new; a law against "threatening to publish with intent to extort money" was not passed until 1893, though the word "blackmail" dates back to the time of Queen Elizabeth I, when certain free-booting Scottish chieftains used to extort money from farmers along the Scottish border. This "protection money" was called black-mail, or black-rent, to distinguish it from the rent the farmer paid to his proper landlord.

This was not actually a crime – the law taking the view that if a farmer chose to pay black-rent, that was his own business. It was not until 1873 that the British parliament decided that "demanding money with menaces" was just as unlawful as pointing a gun at somebody's head and taking his wallet.

Medium dominance

It may seem curious that English law – and this also applies to America – took so long to take account of blackmail, but the reason can be seen in *Charles Augustus Milverton*. Milverton makes a living by buying up "compromising letters" written by ladies and gentlemen in high society, and threatening to send them to the husband or wife of the imprudent writer. Holmes is engaged to try to recover certain indiscreet letters written by a young lady to a penniless country squire; now she is about to marry an Earl, and the blackmailer threatens to send the letters to the future husband.

And, in fact, real-life Milvertons *were* making money in exactly this way. A century earlier, it would have been absurd; people in high society took mistresses – or lovers – all the time, and nobody gave a damn. Then Queen Victoria came to the throne, married a serious and religious German prince named Albert, and all that changed; in England, high society took its tone from the royal family. The Age of Respectability had arrived, and there were suddenly dozens of things that were just Not Done.

The "breath of scandal" could ruin a man – and totally destroy a woman; Queen Victoria turned violently and passionately against her own son when she heard he was having an affair with an actress, whereas her predecessors on the throne of England would have thought there was something seriously wrong with a son who *didn't* fornicate with actresses,

IRONICALLY, blackmail only blossomed as a crime when Queen Victoria turned licentiousness into a social offence . . .

Radio Times Hulton

chambermaids and ladies-in-waiting. But the First Lady of England, being a woman of only "medium dominance", was a romantic, one-man woman, who thought sex was rather dirty, and high society had to live up to her standards – or else.

The case that made the Victorians aware of the curious legal problems involved in blackmail took place in 1872. The lady in the case was called Lady Twiss; the blackmailer was a London solicitor named Alexander Chaffers. Lady Twiss was the wife of Sir Travers Twiss, a well-known Victorian advocate, and professor of International Law at King's College, London. She was regarded as thoroughly respectable – she had even been presented at Court to Queen Victoria. And now, to the horrified incredulity of British high society, she was accused by Mr. Chaffers of being a common prostitute.

Sir Travers Twiss had been a highly successful man of fifty when he had met a pretty Polish girl at his mother's house in 1859. Her name was Marie Van Lynseele, and she was the daughter of a Polish Major-General. Three years later, Sir Travers was in Dresden, and again met the pretty Pole. They fell in love, and married at the British Legation. On their return to England, Lady Twiss was presented first to the Prince of Wales, then to Queen Victoria.

ONE DAY in Kew Gardens (below) the cosy world of Lady Twiss and her eminent husband began to crumble – with a seemingly innocuous encounter . . .

One day, when she and her husband were walking in Kew Gardens, a man suddenly raised his hat and said hello. Lady Twiss introduced him to her husband as a solicitor, Alexander Chaffers. Chaffers congratulated her on her marriage, and not long after, Lady Twiss received a bill for £46 from Mr. Chaffers "for services rendered". She ignored it. He sent another letter, this time asking for £150. Lady Twiss showed it to her husband, and explained that she really owed Chaffers some money for legal work he had once done for a maid in her employment. Whereupon Sir Travers Twiss arranged a meeting with Chaffers, and paid him £50, asking for a receipt. This was marked "in full discharge".

HARDLY ELEMENTARY this time . . . Holmes and his friend Watson (above) were unused to tackling blackmailers.

But Chaffers was apparently not satisfied. He continued to ask Lady Twiss for money. He wrote a letter to the Lord Chamberlain – the Court official responsible for vetting the list of people who would be received by the Queen – telling him that Lady Twiss had been, to put it crudely, a French whore who had managed to worm her way into high society.

The Lord Chamberlain was baffled. Short of hiring a private detective, he couldn't think of any way of investigating the story, so he decided to treat it as a hoax and forget it. But he told Lord and Lady Twiss about the accusations. They were horrified, and confirmed his opinion that Chaffers was a madman. Chaffers certainly had the persistence of a madman. He had a writ for libel served on Sir Travers, claiming that Lady Twiss had been spreading all kinds of slanders about him, and then went to the Chief Magistrate at Bow Street to make a sworn statement of "the truth about Lady Twiss".

Mansell Collection

Made public

This statement declared that she was actually a prostitute named Marie Gelas, and that she had been intimate with Chaffers on several occasions in certain houses of ill-fame in Belgium. Now, as much as he disliked the idea, Sir Travers Twiss had to take action. In May, 1871, Mr. Chaffers appeared at Southwark Police Court, charged with having "published" various slanders against Sir Travers and Lady Twiss – in legal terminology, "published" means simply "made public". Mr. Chaffers' defence was that the "libels" were true.

Marie Van Lynseele claimed to be the daughter of a deceased Major-General, and that she had been brought up in Poland and Belgium as the adopted daughter of a Monsieur Jastrenski. Marie admitted that she *knew* someone called Marie Gelas; according to her, Marie Gelas had been her chaperone when she first came to England in 1859—the occasion when she had first met Sir Travers.

During that visit, Marie Van Lynseele had fallen seriously ill, and Marie Gelas had decided that her employer ought to make a will; she therefore sent for Mr. Chaffers, whom she already knew, and got him to draw up a suitable document. This, said Lady Twiss, was the full extent of her acquaintance with Mr. Chaffers, and he had been paid his £50 professional fee after the meeting in Kew Gardens.

Mr. Chaffers replied that there never *had* been a "chaperone" called Marie Gelas. Lady Twiss *was* Marie Gelas, and he had slept with her several times before she "struck it rich". Nowadays, this would be an open and shut case. Mr. Chaffers was admitting that he had tried to blackmail Lady Twiss by telling her husband about her past, and then, when that didn't work, trying to blackmail them both. But in 1872 there was no law against blackmail: only against libel.

Lady Twiss's problem was to prove that she was Marie Van Lynseele, daughter of a Major-General, not Marie Gelas. She called various witnesses to testify about her past, including a maid who swore on oath that Chaffers had tried to bribe her to support slanders against her mistress. Obviously Chaffers was a very nasty piece of work, and the judge made no attempt to hide his distaste.

Unsolved mystery

And then, quite unexpectedly, Lady Twiss surrendered. On the eighth day of the trial she decided she had had enough. Her counsel appeared in court to tell the judge that his client had left London, and decided not to continue the case. The judge had no alternative but to discharge Alexander Chaffers. He told him that for the rest of his life he would be "an object of contempt to all honest and well-thinking men"; but the fact remained that Chaffers had won.

A week later, Sir Travers Twiss resigned from all his various distinguished posts. His wife had vanished to the Continent, and, as far as we know, he never saw her again. The *London Gazette* published a paragraph saying that Lady Twiss's presentation to the Queen—which had taken place three years earlier—had been "cancelled"—which was the Victorian way of saying that it hadn't really happened at all, and the case remains an apparently unsolved mystery.

But it is easy enough to read between the lines. If Lady Twiss *had* been Marie Van Lynseele, she would presumably have fought to the last ditch. The court was already inclined heavily in her favour. Her foster-father, M. Jastrenski, had testified that she *was* Marie Van Lynseele, and many other witnesses had declared on oath that they knew Marie Gelas, and that she was *not* Marie Van Lynseele. It was a foregone conclusion that Chaffers would be found guilty and sent for trial.

What probably happened is that Marie Van Lynseele—or Gelas—had bribed various people to appear in her favour, but that she realized a trial would be a more serious matter; perhaps her witnesses refused to testify at a criminal trial, because they were afraid of the penalty for perjury. She decided the game was up, and vanished. If she was innocent, why did she tell her husband that she owed Chaffers the £50 for legal fees contracted on behalf of a maid, when she later testified in court that it was *her* will that Chaffers drew up?

Homosexual brothel

On the other hand, there remains the other possibility: that, persecuted by Chaffers, realizing that she had ruined her husband, no matter what the outcome of the case, Lady Twiss's nerve snapped and she fled. The case made upper-class Victorians aware how vulnerable they were to blackmail. A man like Chaffers didn't need any *evidence* that Lady Twiss was a prostitute. He only had to say so in court, and even if he was found guilty of libel, her reputation would never recover from the scandal.

It also made the Victorians aware that they needed a law to prevent people like Chaffers extorting money by threats: hence the statute of 1873 against "de-

Radio Times/Quartet

"EDDIE", the Duke of Clarence (right), was one of the clients at a homosexual brothel raided by police in 1889. Oscar Wilde (inset) was a famous fellow client.

Radio Times Hulton
Mary Evans
Radio Times Hulton/Quartet

RAVISHING . . . Lady Warwick (right) was certainly one of the great beauties of the age. Husband (top left) and lover Beresford (centre) no doubt thought so too! Below: Her home, Warwick Castle.

manding money with menaces". It cost Sir Travers Twiss his career, but his case had changed the law.

Unfortunately, a change in the law was not quite the answer. When a crime suddenly attracts public attention, criminals everywhere wonder whether this is not a new source of income. The Victorian poor had always been the prey of rich debauchees; there were few working-class girls who could refuse the offer of five shillings for the use of their bodies. Now the poor began to retaliate by exerting blackmail on the seducers.

Oscar Wilde was blackmailed by some of the working-class youths he slept with; when a homosexual brothel in Cleveland Street was raided by the police in 1889, the whole affair was quickly hushed up when they realized that one of the chief clients was the Duke of Clarence, the grandson of Queen Victoria. "Eddie"—as the Duke was known—was packed off on a world cruise, and endless possibilities of blackmail were averted.

But it was not only the lower classes who indulged in blackmail. Aristocrats could play the game just as ruthlessly. One of the most famous—and notorious—of Victorian aristocrats was Lady Warwick, known universally as Daisy—the song "Daisy, Daisy" was written with her in mind. The ravishingly beautiful Daisy married the future Earl of Warwick in 1881 and became mistress of Warwick Castle and a huge fortune. She soon found her husband's passion for hunting and fishing a bore, and began to take lovers.

Sexual promiscuity

For several years she conducted a passionate affair with the dashing Lord Charles Beresford—in the Victorian age there was nothing to stop you having love affairs provided you were discreet about it, and avoided "scandal". When Lord Charles finally broke it off she went to his closest friend, the Prince of Wales, to beg him to help her get back a certain compromising letter.

Edward, Prince of Wales, was the son who had alienated Queen Victoria through his affair with an actress, and ever since that time he had devoted his life to sexual promiscuity with the energy of a Casanova. He took one look at Daisy, and dragged her towards the nearest bed. Daisy was willing enough; for although the Prince was no longer young or handsome—he was fat and inclined to wheeze—she saw he was a valuable ally. As to Prince Edward, he was genuinely in love with the delicious Daisy.

In 1893 her father-in-law died, and Daisy became mistress of a fortune. She immediately had Warwick Castle re-landscaped, filled it with expensive carpets and furniture, and gave huge weekend parties that were famous for their extravagance. The socialist press attacked her for wasting so much money when the poor were starving; as a result she went to see the famous left-wing editor, W. T. Stead, and immediately became converted to socialism. She had the double pleasure of being immensely rich and being known as the defender of the poor.

As the years went by, Daisy's beauty

faded and her fortune dwindled. In 1912 she realized that she was close to bankruptcy. And then she had her inspiration. She would write her memoirs, make sure they were scandalously frank, and sell them to a publisher for some huge sum—£100,000 was her first estimate. In 1914, she contacted a journalist and writer named Frank Harris—now known chiefly as the author of the semi-pornographic *My Life and Loves*.

Harris was not only an editor, a novelist and a Don Juan; he was a completely unscrupulous blackmailer, and he instantly saw the enormous possibilities of her scheme. All she had to do was to make sure she included the love letters of the Prince of Wales—later King Edward VII, who had died in 1910—and then ask the Palace how much it was worth to suppress the book.

Two years earlier a Tory Member of Parliament, Charles du Cros, had lent Daisy £16,000, and he now wanted his interest on the sum. Daisy also happened to know that he wanted a knighthood, and that he had an attitude verging on adoration for King George V, Edward's son. She sent for du Cros, told him about the memoirs, and mentioned that she had letters from the late King in which, among more intimate and scandalous matters, he had given his frank opinion of such people as the Kaiser and the Tsar of Russia.

Du Cros rushed to see George V's A.D.C. and his solicitor. The solicitor suggested that he had better ask Daisy how much she would take to suppress the book. Daisy said £85,000—but told du Cros that he would have to see her

INVOLVED in the proposed scandal of Daisy's memoirs—though on opposite sides—were Charles du Cros (below) and the notorious hack Frank Harris (inset).

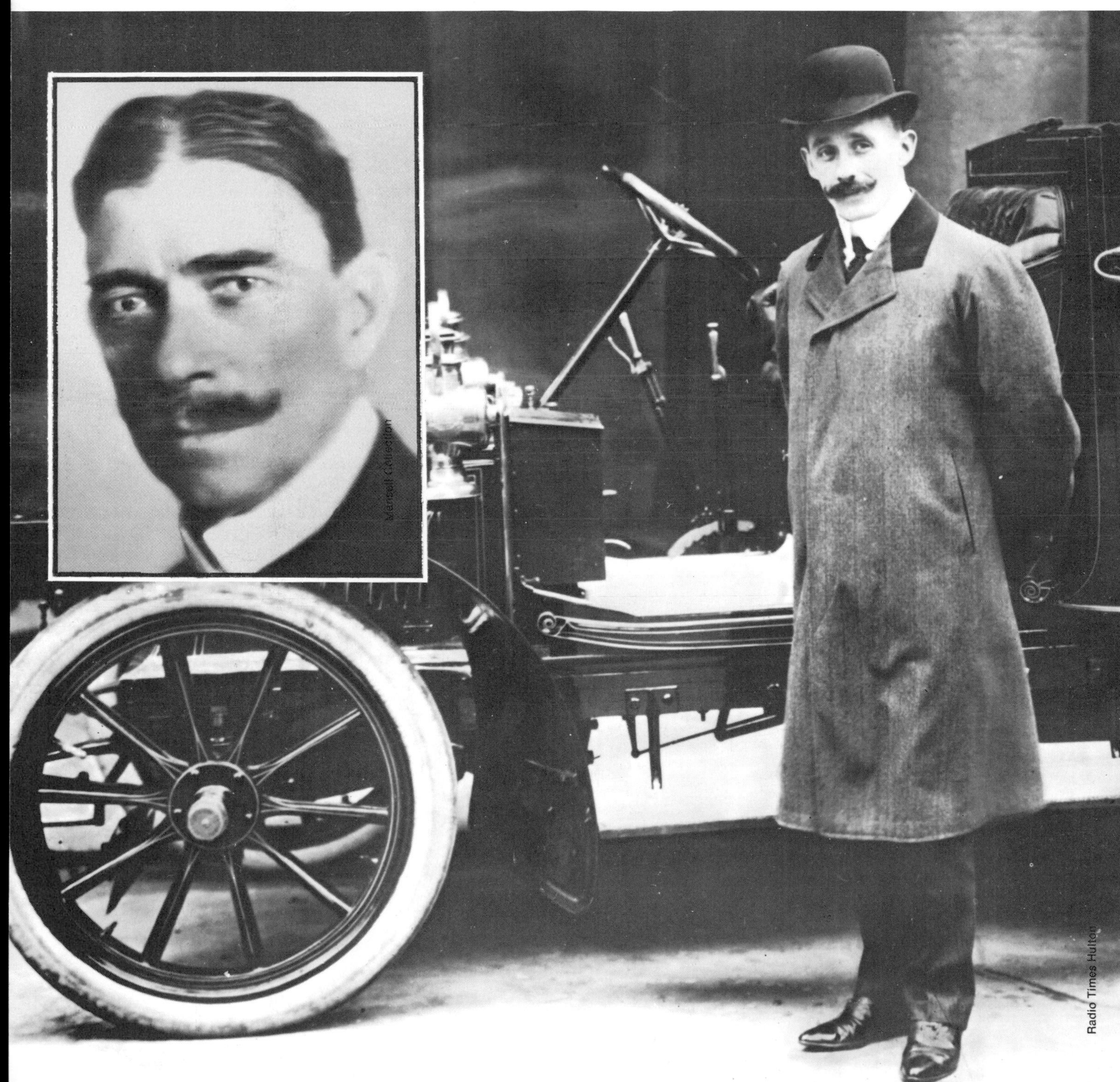

Mansell Collection

Radio Times Hulton

Radio Times Hulton

"partner", Frank Harris. Harris had fled to Paris, escaping his creditors; du Cros saw him at the Ritz Hotel, and was told that they would settle for a mere £125,000.

But the Establishment had its own way of dealing with blackmail. Instead of paying up, George V's solicitor asked for a court injunction to prevent Daisy publishing the late King's letters. Daisy at first found it incredible – to drag the affair into open court; but there she was mistaken. The Establishment co-operated admirably. The case was heard in chambers – a closed court. Edward VII's name was not mentioned; it was simply a matter of preventing the publication of "certain letters". The letters had to be handed over to the court. The injunction was granted, and the court also ordered that the letters were to be destroyed.

Two-way mirrors

This was not quite the end of the story. Before the letters were handed over, Frank Harris went to stay with Daisy Warwick at her house, Easton Lodge – she had been forced by debts to move out of Warwick Castle. He asked to see the letters – and when Harris left for America, the letters went with him. In order to get them back, Daisy had to pay Harris for them. She was the loser all round . . . Her only consolation was that du Cros, feeling sorry for her, took over £50,000-worth of her debts.

CONFIRMED SOCIALIST William Stead (left) converted Daisy to the defence of the poor – for a time. Edward VII (right) saw only her more obvious charms.

Since Daisy's time the art of blackmail has been turned into an exact science – particularly by the espionage and counter-espionage services of all the major countries. The West learnt a great deal about the techniques of the Soviet K.G.B. – for example, how they blackmailed the American sergeant James Harris, who appeared in the Rudolph Abel case, or of the pressure they brought to bear on the homosexual British naval clerk, Vassall. But there can be no doubt that the C.I.A. and Britain's M.I.5 were, and probably still are, skilled in its uses.

A favourite technique with both sides was to lure a diplomat – or member of the government – into a sexually compromising position. The Russians are credited with the discovery of the use of two-way mirrors for this purpose – the English and American method was cruder, using a picture or photograph with tiny holes in it, usually in the pupils of the eyes, with the camera concealed behind it.

The invention of transistors enabled the C.I.A. to perfect a whole new range of "bugging devices". One of these was a tiny pill that emitted a radio signal. The girl who has been chosen as the decoy swallows a pill that makes a "bleep" noise. Another pill – which emits a "bloop" – is concealed in the food of the victim, so he swallows it. Agents are then able to follow the couple with radio receivers, and when their receivers pick up simultaneous bloops and bleeps, they can assume that the bellies of both parties are in sufficiently close contact to warrant a sudden intrusion.

Blackmail is the least documented of all crimes for an obvious reason: if a blackmailer is caught by the police, it is in everybody's interests to make sure that the case receives no publicity. And in most civilized countries, it is generally agreed that when victims report blackmail to the police, they will not lay themselves open to criminal charges, even if they are being blackmailed for a crime they had committed. Although this is a convention, not a law, it is seldom broken – the only exception being in cases involving treason. Slowly, very slowly, society is learning to combat the blackmailer. The day may yet come when blackmail, like piracy, is no more than a relic of the past.

MURDER WEAPON...?

Behind the courtroom jargon can lurk every imaginable weapon of death. The murder kit in the notorious Ruth Snyder case, for example, included chloroform, picture-wire . . . and a sash-weight bludgeon.

WOUNDS caused by the ubiquitous "blunt instruments" of fiction are usually found on parts of the body where bone is lying just beneath the skin; common sites are the scalp, eyebrows, cheeks, nose, elbows and knees. Blunt weapons such as iron bars, axes, shovels, hammers and pieces of wood cause split wounds or lacerations.

Lacerations are made when a blow crushes and stretches the skin and causes it to split open; a ragged wound is made with grazed and bruised edges. Such injuries often bleed less profusely than might be expected, and this is because the blood vessels which are torn and crushed when the wound is inflicted retract and allow clots to form more easily.

Close inspection of lacerated wounds shows fatty tissue bulging out at the edges of the split. Strands of tissue, nerves and blood vessels may be seen stretched across the base of the wound; local bruising is a distinctive feature as the tissues are crushed rather than cut as in knife wounds.

Assault with a poker

Because of the "splitting" nature of the wound it does not hold the shape of the weapon and identification is thus more difficult. Examination of the wound may reveal useful clues in the form of fragments or foreign particles. For example, bone fragments in the depths of a scalp wound would suggest that a heavy weapon such as an axe had been used. Foreign matter such as dust, paint or fibres might indicate the type and origin of the weapon—coal ash, for instance, suggesting an assault with a poker.

It is not usually difficult to distinguish between lacerated and incised wounds. But a wound over underlying bone might superficially appear to have been caused by a sharp weapon. Careful examination of the margins of the injury with a hand lens will determine the nature of the weapon which caused it. In wounds caused by blunt instruments the hair follicles lying under the skin are torn out whole and may be picked out of the edges of the split, but not in the case of incised wounds.

In multiple wounding, injuries may have been caused by more than one kind of weapon. The forensic expert will examine each wound and note:

Position
Shape
Dimensions
Depth
Appearance of edges
Appearance of base
Presence of foreign matter

The scene of death will also bear important clues enabling a reconstruction of the wounding to be made. Wounds caused by blunt instruments are usually associated with a murderous assault. But accident and suicide cannot be ruled out—self-inflicted scalp wounds with an axe are not unknown.

The position of the body, evidence of a struggle and nature of any blood splashes are especially significant; accidental wounding is a possibility where the body is found with injuries which might be consistent with a fall against a fireplace or piece of heavy furniture. Where suicide is suspected the weapon will obviously be close to hand, there will be no signs of a struggle and the wound—there will probably be only one—must be on an accessible part of the body.

Deciding factors in a homicide will be evidence of a struggle—an assault with a blunt weapon, often wielded with both hands, frequently entails a violent struggle. Protective wounds on the victim's forearms where he attempted to fend off his assailant's blows would be expected.

The position and direction of blood splashes on walls and furniture is significant in placing the relative positions of attacker and victim. Blood splashes which drop obliquely onto a flat surface show the direction from which they travelled and suggest their likely point of origin.

In the Sheppard murder case in Cleveland, Ohio, in 1954, the absence of blood splashes on the ceiling of the murder room was noted as a curious feature. A woman had been battered to death on the bed and all four walls of the room were blood spattered. It was contended that the weapon used was wielded in a sideways fashion which prevented blood being

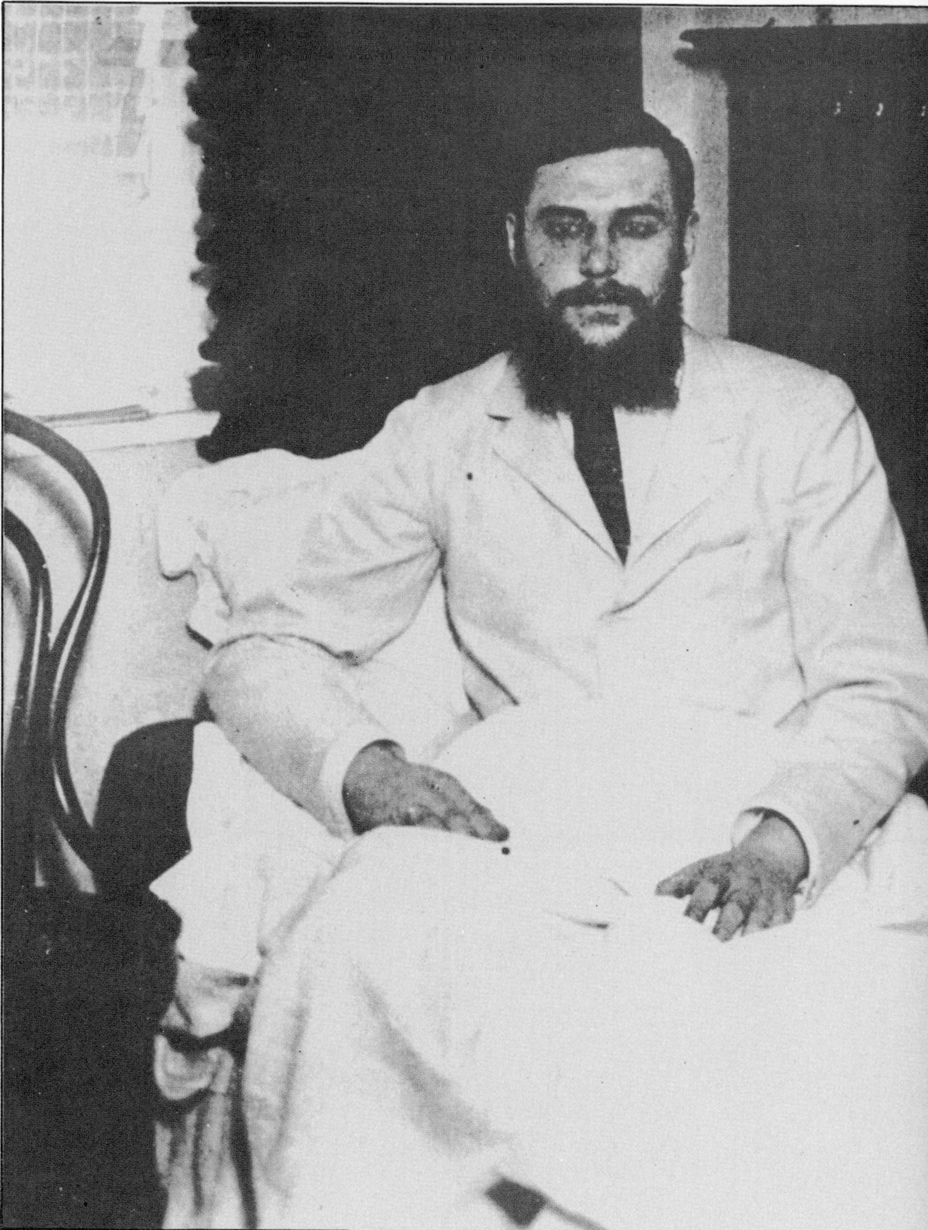

SHE HELPED SEVER her husband's leg for the insurance money. When that failed, Martha Marek turned poisoner, murdering four people with a compound of thallium before, ironically, the executioner's axe ended her career.

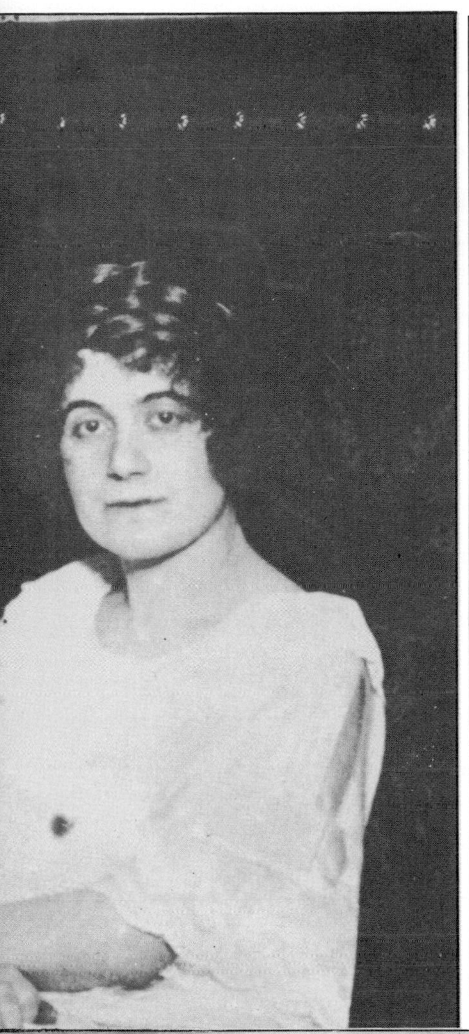

thrown up onto the ceiling.

An axe murder in which the weapon was matched to the wound was one which featured Sir Bernard Spilsbury and two improbable characters called "Moosh" and "Tiggy". On June 2, 1931, a labourer passing a smouldering rubbish tip by some railway sidings near Elstree, not far from London, noticed a human hand sticking out of the refuse. Police were called and the burned body of a man was dragged out. The remains were those of a middle-aged man. The body had been badly charred by the slow combustion of the rubbish tip.

A rectangular fracture

Spilsbury was called in to make a pathological examination of the body. From the state of decomposition of the unburned parts of the corpse, he judged that death had occurred three or four days previously. The cause of death he identified as a blow to the left side of the head with a heavy object. There was a rectangular-shaped fracture of the skull, and the victim's left hand was bruised.

From the clothing remains the dead man was thought to have been a labourer. Fortunately part of the left forearm was intact and this bore a tattoo which enabled the police to identify the man as Herbert Ayres, or "Pigsticker", as he was known in the locality. He was forty-five years of age. "Pigsticker" was one of a group of men who did casual labouring and lived in shacks near the railway. The men lived rough and had habits to match; they frightened the local inhabitants and were thought to be dishonest. For the most part they were known only by their nicknames.

Police enquiries were aided by information volunteered by a man called Armstrong. He said that he shared a hut at the railway sidings on the night of May 30 with two men called "Moosh" and "Tiggy". On that night Armstrong was inside the hut trying to sleep when he heard sounds of a quarrel going on outside. He looked out and saw "Moosh" and "Tiggy" beating up another man.

"Moosh" and "Tiggy", whose real names were Oliver Newman and William Shelley, were arrested. Under the floor of their hut was found a blood-stained axe. Spilsbury fitted the squared back of the axe head into the fracture in the dead man's skull. He was sure the murder weapon had been found. The bruises on the victim's hand he thought were caused by efforts to protect his head from the raining blows.

Newman and Shelley admitted beating up "Pigsticker" because they thought he had stolen food from their hut. When they realized they had killed him they buried his body in the rubbish tip. The two men were tried at the Old Bailey and sentenced to death; they were hanged on August 5, 1931.

A bludgeon formed part of the unique murder kit assembled for the slaying of Albert Snyder. Albert and Ruth Snyder lived in Long Island, New York. They had been married twelve years and had one daughter. Albert was art editor on a boating magazine. The Snyders led an uneventful life and Ruth was bored. In a New York restaurant, Ruth met Judd Gray, a handsome, lively man who was a commercial traveller selling corsets. Ruth began to confide in her new companion, who was himself happily married; she spoke of her own dull marriage and her longings for freedom. She also said that she had tried several times to do away with her husband. Gray advised her to take up Christian Science.

A pair of new corsets

Ruth, however, had taken out $50,000 life insurance on her husband. She thought now that it was worth expediting his death. Gray, her lover for two years, was persuaded to help her, and she sent him shopping. From different towns he bought a heavy sash-weight, a length of picture wire and a bottle of chloroform. These he gave to Ruth in a parcel which also contained a pair of new corsets.

Murder was planned for the night of March 19, 1927. The Snyders spent the evening with neighbours, where Albert became drunk and aggressive. They returned home after midnight and went to

Both Popperfoto

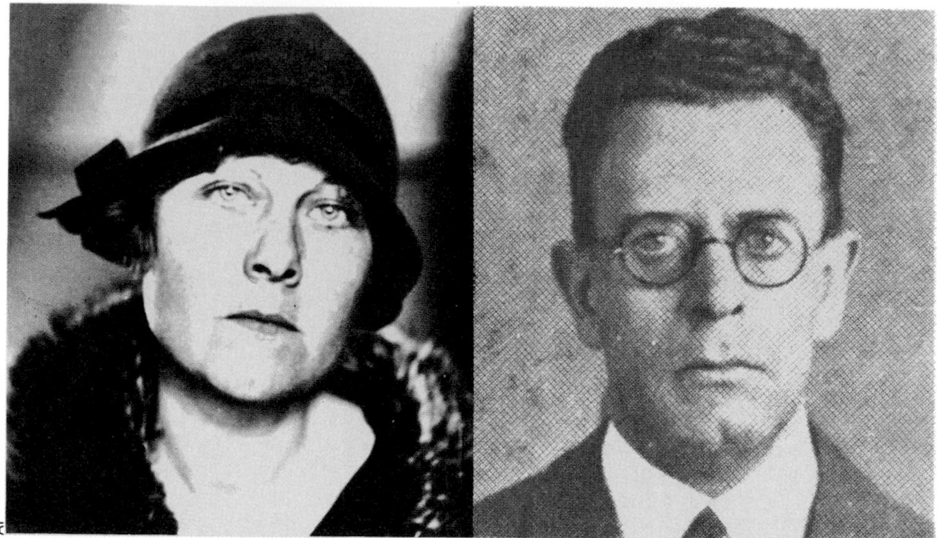

THE GRANITE WOMAN, as the press called Ruth Snyder, was bored—so she and lover Judd Gray brutally murdered her husband. Both were electrocuted.

bed. The following morning Albert was found dead in bed by his distraught wife; his head had been battered in, a wire was fastened around his neck and his nostrils were plugged with chloroform-impregnated cotton wool. The house was in great disorder. Drawers had been opened and their contents scattered on the floor. Some furs and jewellery were said by Ruth to be missing, and a police search of the premises revealed a blood-stained sash weight, in a tool chest in the cellar.

Ruth Snyder broke down under police questioning and declared that her husband's killer was her lover Judd Gray. Gray had an alibi for the evening of the murder but the police were disbelieving. He then changed his story implicating himself in the murder but accusing Ruth Snyder of chloroforming and then strangling her husband with picture wire.

They were not impressed

Snyder and Gray were charged with murder—each accused the other. They were put on trial on April 25. Prejudice against Ruth Snyder had built up in the press. She was referred to as the "granite woman". The prosecution showed that she had carefully arranged her husband's life insurance without his knowledge; he did not even know what the premiums were. Snyder explained her attempts to mislead the police by saying that Gray had threatened her life, but witnesses came forward to testify to Gray's good character, and a picture was painted by his lawyer of a man led astray by the "granite woman". Neither judge nor jury was impressed and both Snyder and Gray were convicted and sentenced to death. They were both electrocuted on January 12, 1928.

The axe has featured in some remarkable crimes, such as those of Lizzie Borden and the mysterious axeman of New Orleans. But there is no axe crime more incredible than the mutilation of Emile Marek's leg. Marek, an engineer, was married to Martha Loewenstein, a young Viennese woman with a reputation for extravagant tastes.

In 1925 Marek insured himself against serious accident for $30,000. The insurance company was impressed with the Austrian government's interest in an electrification scheme which Marek had devised; the young engineer seemed to have a bright future and the proposal to insure him against the possibility of accident seemed reasonable.

A week after taking out this insurance Marek was rushed to hospital with one leg hanging only by a sinew. He had injured himself while cutting down a tree in the garden of his villa. His cries for help brought his wife Martha running to the scene. He was lying in a pool of blood. Martha applied several tourniquets to stem the bleeding. This was the story recounted to the doctors at the hospital.

Marek, shocked and suffering from loss of blood, had the leg amputated. The vice-president of the company insuring him against accident visited the hospital—he had been quickly notified of his client's injury. He inspected the severed limb and spoke to the surgeon who had amputated it—he was not satisfied that the injury had been an accident. The police were called and they conferred with the hospital authorities.

The surgeon was asked about the angle of the cut in the leg when Marek was admitted. He said that the cut was straight, which was puzzling, but accidental injuries were often freakish. The police appreciated that any suggestion that Marek had hacked off his own leg in order to collect the insurance money would be met with open-mouthed incredulity. Nevertheless, they pursued their enquiries.

A detective sent to Marek's home found a half-felled tree in the garden and beside it a large patch of blood and an axe with a very sharp blade. The axe had been wiped clean of any trace of blood and it carried no fingerprints. That was suspicious enough but further examination of the injured leg was even more revealing. A doctor at the Vienna Medical Institute told the police that there had been not one but three cuts in the leg. Three separate strokes of the axe, each deepening the wound, had nearly severed the limb. It was thought that Martha Marek must have helped in the deliberate mutilation of her husband's leg. The angle of the wound was such as to have made it impossible for the injury to be self-inflicted.

Confronted with this allegation Martha said that the insurance company representative and a surgeon at the hospital had been seen extending the wound on the amputated leg. Presumably the contention was that the insurance company was trying to get out of paying compensation. Martha gave this story to the press and created a minor sensation. She would not name her informant saying only that he was employed at the hospital.

Small compensation

The police had little difficulty in tracing her source. A hospital orderly, Karl Mraz, at first bore out her story but later admitted having been bribed by Martha. The Mareks were charged with attempted fraud and attempting to obscure the course of justice. The first charge was dismissed for lack of evidence, but the pair were found guilty on the second and given four months' imprisonment. The Mareks still pressed their insurance claim but were persuaded to settle for $2000. After their legal expenses had been paid it left very little to compensate Emile for his suffering and the loss of a limb.

A run of ill-fortune and death followed. Emile died, apparently of tuberculosis in July 1932 and their baby daughter died a month later. Martha went to live with an aged relative, Frau Loewenstein; the old lady died soon afterwards and Martha inherited her money and the house. Next, she set up as a lodging-house keeper, but when one of her lodgers died mysteriously relatives became suspicious and enquiries were started.

Exhumations were ordered and it was found that the lodger, Frau Loewenstein and Martha's husband and child had all been poisoned with a compound of thallium. Martha Marek was tried for murder. The death penalty had been restored in Austria in 1938—Martha suffered the ultimate penalty. Ironically, in her case, her head was severed from her body by the executioner's axe.

SHOT DOWN BY SOVIET AIRFORCE

Flight 007 – the Korean Airlines passenger jet that strayed too far, and paid the price.

A KOREAN AIRLINES 747 Jumbo Jet (below) and Soviet MiG-23 interceptor (right).

AT 18:26 HOURS plus 22 seconds, on the evening of August 31, 1983, pilot 805 of one of Russia's Sukhoi Su-15 interceptors was able to report: "805. The target is destroyed". He was already pulling up and away from the scything debris spewing from the collossal fireball that had burst in the sky ahead. And was well on his way home before the flaming fragments of Korean Air Lines Flight 007 hit the Sea of Japan almost seven miles below.

This act of aggression by an outwardly friendly power brought the leaders of both the US and USSR back from summer vacation, and possibly changed their personal destinies. It led to icy recriminations that continued until the Gorbachev era.

Above all, for 269 human souls, it was a totally unexpected way to die.

As we join Flight 007 at Anchorage, Alaska on the last leg of a routine run to Seoul the clock reads 3:30am local time. The passengers straggling back to the airliner after this stopover from New York are already weary. But their mood is good: the majority are Koreans on their way home. Others, like Muriel Kole, New York physiotherapist, are en route to academic conferences. Neil and Carol Ann Grenfell are among those Americans returning to work (he is a Kodak executive). Their main concern tonight is with daughters Stacey Mary and Noelle Ann, aged three and five respectively.

The new captain of Flight 007 on its final run is Chun Byung In. Aged 45, he is one of the airline's best. A lean, impressive figure as he treads across the space between the airport and the gleaming white Boeing 747-200B, he has the satisfaction of 10,600 flying hours under his belt. He is also qualified to wear a black belt in *Tae Kwon Do,* Korea's national martial art.

With him, approaching the tall tail fin of the massive airliner (brightly illuminated by KAL's distinctively proud red symbol of a flying bird) are Captain Chun's co-pilot Sohn Dong Hui and flight engineer Kim Eui Dong.

The idea that these three men are planning to drive an airliner into Soviet Airspace is laughable. So is the idea that they did not know where they were when Pilot 805 destroyed them.

Motorway in the sky

Route R20, as it is called, runs between Anchorage and Seoul. For pilots it is as visible as an urban motorway. It threads a gap, over the cold seas of the North Pacific, between two continents – two landmasses that are surprisingly close if you take your eyes off the flat schoolroom map and look at the globe.

East is east and West is west, but the run from Alaska to Korea is a brief one on the real map. The map that Captain Chun has in his cockpit tonight clearly states the penalties for deviating from route R20.

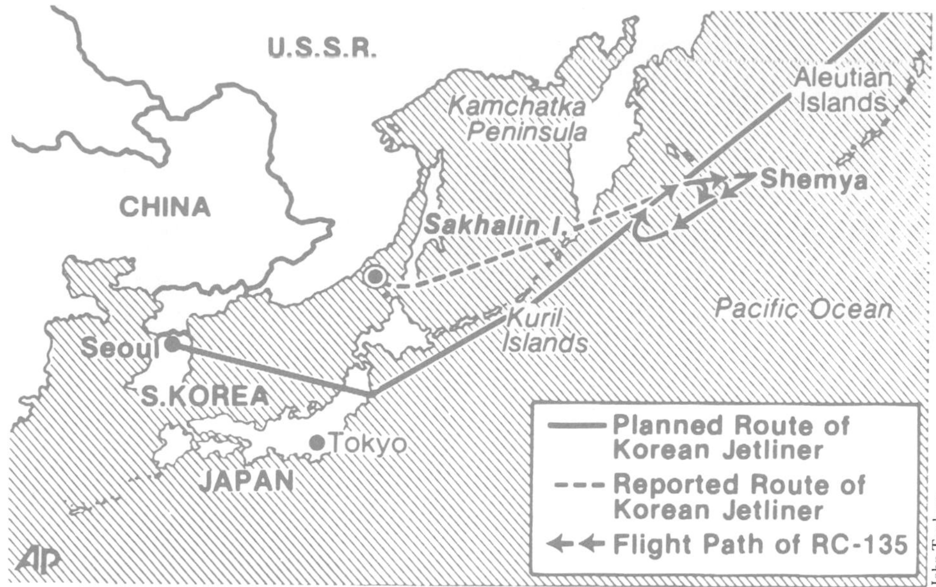

MAP SHOWING the flight paths of the US reconnaissance RC-135 and the off-course jet.

"Warning", the map reads, "Aircraft infringing upon Non-Free Flying Territory may be fired on without warning".

That bleak but explicit notice on Flight 007's charts serves as a reminder of the perils awaiting anyone straying north of R20. To do so is to venture into some of the most dangerous airspace in the world. Wander north of R20 and you fly into Russia's most sensitive front line: Kamchatka, the Sea of Okhotsk and mysterious Sakhalin Island.

Bristling with Soviet defence technology, this frontier is in the charge of a special arm of the Russian military machine: the Voiska Protivovozdushnoi Oborony (PVO) or Air Defense Forces.

On Russia's frontiers worldwide, this task force has some 10,000 SAM missiles and 2,250 interceptors at its disposal. Dangerously, in today's terms, these frontiersmen have something of the old freedom of those who guarded the borders of America's Wild West. They may not be entirely a law unto themselves – but they are certainly not part of the Soviet Air Force either.

Anyone who flies into their airspace – either to spy or bomb the nuclear bases in the North Pacific – does so at extreme peril.

As Flight 007 lifts off from Anchorage, 37,750 gallons of fuel freshly aboard, the Korean stewardesses in traditional long dress serve a Japanese *soba* soup to those among the women and children, already snuggling down for the night, who want it.

For the flight crew, as the 747's four engines power the airliner towards its correct cruising height, most of the hard work trip has already been completed. No less than three Inertial Navigation Systems have been programmed to take the plane safely down R20, along a chain of 'waymarks'. An amber light will show as the longitude of each waymark is passed.

Widely spaced at first, as route R20 traverses uncontentious international waters, the points become more frequent as R20 passes over Japan and homes in on Seoul. At preselected waymarks it is compulsory for the flight crew to report their position to base. The first such is *Nippi*. The aircraft should be more than half way to Tokyo by now, as Captain Chun duly beams the news to flight control at Japan's Narita Airport. In fact, as he does so, he is hundreds of miles to the north over Russia's Kamchatka peninsula.

And according to the Russians he has been doggedly off course almost as soon as he left Anchorage: north of waymarks *Nabie, Nukks, Neeva* and *Ninno* and heading staight for Sakhalin island.

Russian fighters scramble

As Russian interceptors are raised from the ground to meet the intruder on their radar screens it becomes urgent to discover just what is going wrong in the cabin of Flight 007 – if only to prevent such a disaster ever happening again.

Is the crew, for example, being forced to fly at gunpoint against their will? That theory is quickly discounted. Every airliner carries an alarm, discreetly hidden amidst the myriad controls, that will beam an instant message back to base if a hi-jacker is on board. It is inconceivable that a hi-jacker would be familiar enough with the controls to prevent its use.

Was the crew fast asleep? Alarming as the thought is to the fare-paying passenger, it is not unknown for everyone on board a long night flight to be soundly snoozing. Nor is it dangerous. The horizon is level; the revolving pulse of the strobe light is mesmerizing; the crew dozes off. It is no matter, for 'George' is in control. George, the automatic pilot, is checking the information fed from the Inertial Navigation Systems and nudging the plane back on course if wind and weather are pushing the plane elsewhere.

Perhaps George and the three INS systems aboard are suffering some electronic brainstorm? That is mechanically impossible. This plane is not careering about the sky; it is following a course that has been painstakingly punched into its memory back at Anchorage.

And that course is the wrong one. Indeed, it is *so* wrong that it defies belief that Captain Chun's team could have accidentally mis-programed the computer. Just as it defies belief that the crew could be ignoring the evidence of their own on-board radar screens. As Flight 007 cruised serenely at 33,000 feet, the coastline of Russia must have been clearly visible.

In the Russian camp by this stage, it is now known, concern is moving swiftly towards wrath. Six MiG-23 pilots have failed to catch the mystery plane over Kamchatka and have returned to base. The intruder is now proceeding steadily towards Sakhalin Island.

Russia's 'spy' claim

Such was the disbelief in the West (initially, at least) when Russia first justified herself as legitimately gunning down a plane on a spy mission, that the claim deserves inspection. Surely, baffled and enraged commentators in the West retorted, in these days of spy satellites that can read a newspaper from outer space, who could seriously imagine that Flight 007 would discover anything of interest by overflying the fringe of Russia by night?

The truth is less simple. In fact, US officials admit, spy planes *regularly* probe Russian airspace. With batteries of monitoring equipment aboard, they play out a war of nerves that is, understandably, kept well out of the headlines.

Several years ago, for example, an RC-135V spy plane was seen at a US airbase in Suffolk, England with five small red silhouettes of the Soviet Sukhoi interceptor on its nose. Normally, such markings denote a 'kill'. But the RC-135 was unarmed and presumably just celebrating successful penetrations. The game is not always so lighthearted: some 900 attempts to shoot down the high flying 'Blackbird' spy planes have been admitted. So have the deaths of over 140 US servicemen engaged on reconnaissance missions since 1950.

The aim of the game was to probe the Soviet 'electronic order of battle'. As the intruder provocatively advances on Russian air space the network of Soviet radar stations and anti-aircraft missile bases goes on alert. Dotted across the northern coast of Hokkaido Island, Japan, is a whole chain of US listening stations.

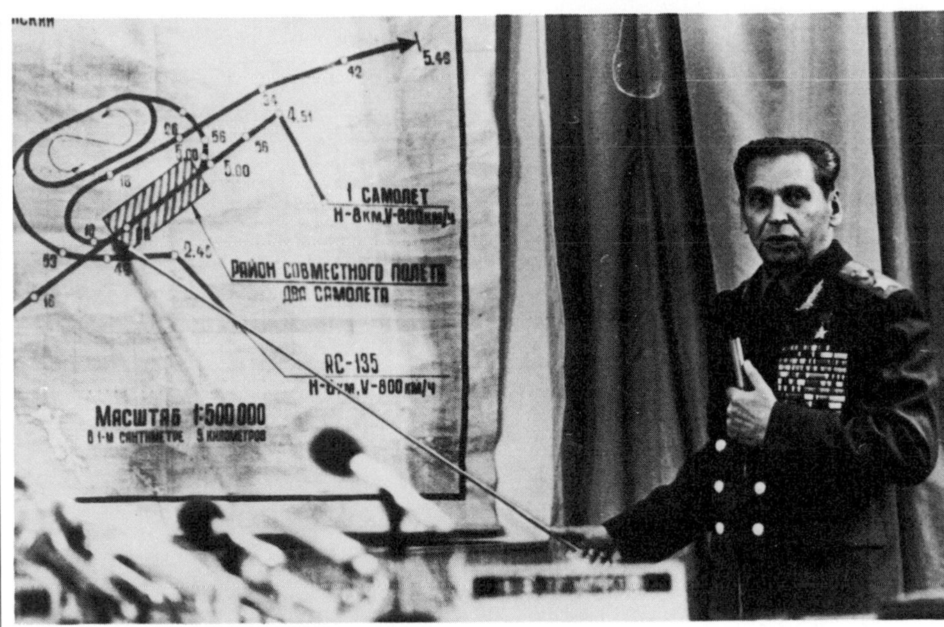

CHIEF OF STAFF Nikolai Ogarkov explains Soviet version of events to the Press.

At Misawa Air Base alone there were at the time over 1600 intelligence operators and analysts, routinely monitoring all radio signals between Soviet pilots and their ground controllers. The mission is to gain knowledge of Soviet defence strengths and weaknesses, so that, in the event of war, US bombers may be able to find chinks in the armour.

If the professionals on both sides know exactly what the other is up to (indeed, on one occasion, Soviet radio operators cordially wished a US monitoring station a Merry Christmas) the general public in the West was – until the 007 disaster – unaware. Disbelief turned to thoughtfulness when, in the aftermath, transcripts of the messages from the destroyer of Flight 007 were made available in detail. And thoughtfulness turned to alarm when – almost casually – it was the US that admitted an RC-135V spy plane *had* been in the area that night. For Russia, that admission would serve as a heaven-sent opportunity to cloud the issue for ever after.

In plain truth, as the pilot of the Su-15 detailed to deal with Flight 007 shot skywards, neither he nor anyone in the control chain running back to Moscow could have mistaken the jumbo jet on their radar screens for an RC-135. The RC-135 (a modified version of a 707) is 125 knots slower and a great deal smaller. Tracking both kinds of plane across the north Pacific was bread and butter work for Soviet defenders.

Intruder had to be stopped

What counted, to the Russian general who served as air commander of the Biya region (and to the duty officer at the National Command Post of the Air Defense Forces in Kalinin, near Moscow), was that an intruder was heading straight for Soviet territory.

It is 18:03 Zulu (Greenwich Mean Time) as the Su-15 pilot's two Lyulka engines power him almost vertically to an altitude of six miles in less than a minute. Behind him, communications with Moscow are humming. *Whatever* is out there in the pre-dawn sky cannot be allowed to ride on unchallenged. Years of combat-readiness have now prepared the Russian frontiersmen for just such an event. If the unknown intruder is not an RC-135 up to its usual games, it might well be a nuclear bomber.

On Flight 007 the stewardesses are preparing to draw back the window curtains and serve a distinctive Korean Airlines breakfast. They have not yet done so, and the plane is still in darkness. But the passengers are stirring. Among them is US Congressman Larry McDonald, chairman of the extreme right-wing John Birch Society. A vehement anti-communist, he is a man to whom no one in the Soviet leadership would wish a long life. Later, the Society will advance the theory that Soviet agents monitored the two million airline bookings made by US citizens each day so effectively that they knew he was on board and acted accordingly.

At 18:05:56 the 40 year old Su-15 pilot number 805 shouts back to base: "805. I see it!" Flight 007 has just 20 minutes left to live. What happened in those 20 minutes, though pilot 805's tapes have been played a thousand times since, remains mysterious.

Never does he identify the target as a civilian airliner, or report the distinctive KAL flying bird on the 747's tail.

At 18:22:17 he reports "805. I am going

Soviet fighter pilot (right) goes on TV to justify his attack on the airliner. Over 100,000 gather for a memorial service (below) at Seoul Stadium to mourn those killed a few days previously on the fatal KAL flight from Anchorage to Seoul. A year later, flowers and makeshift cardboard headstones (below right) were symbolically placed opposite the White House in protest.

John Topham

John Topham

around it. I'm already moving in front of target''. But Flight 007 doesn't seem to notice. Nor, in the intervening minutes has Captain Chun responded to 805's IFF transmission – a standard request for ''Identification: Friend or Foe''. However, only military aircraft are geared to receive such messages.

Cannons fired

More amazingly, Captain Chun has also made no visible response to the fact that at 18:20:49 pilot 805 fired 120 rounds in four bursts from the all-weather fighter's cannon. Whether these were invisible or tracer shells remains unknown. Certainly Flight 007 was changing altitude at precisely this moment because he has just asked Japanese air traffic control for permission to do so. He wants to climb 2,000 feet to 35,000 feet and now does so. To pilot 805 that looked like an evasive manoeuvre.

The grim certainties of slaughter now take over from the many mysteries of Flight 007's journey so far. At 18:25:46 hours the Soviet interceptor pilot's message is a brief ''805. ZG''. That means his twin ANAB missiles are locked onto target and firing.

In just two seconds they rip into Flight 007 and blow it apart in a holocaust that combines the massive explosive powers of the missiles; the inrushing decompression of the airliner's shell; the fireball of thousands of gallons of fuel.

Maybe, in those appalling moments, the front end of the aircraft is thrown clear and wierdly intact. Certainly the last message from 007 is 38 seconds later than pilot 805's claim of a kill. To the professional listeners on the ground, East and West, the garbled words that emerged from the cockpit will haunt them for ever. ''Radio . . . Korean Air007 . . . All engines . . . Rapid decompression . . . 101 . . . two . . . Delta''.

Russians blame Americans

In the stunned aftermath of 007's plunge, some images stand out. There is Marshal Kinolai V Ogarkov, wearing his Hero of the Soviet Union medal and nine rows of campaign ribbons – and authoritatively stabbing a map at a world press conference to explain the iniquity of the US for sending a spy mission.

There is the President of the United States, taking a firm line about an event that has rightly shocked the world. A year later, he was re-elected with a massive majority.

And there is the image of distraught mourners at the Korean quaysides: for Buddhists, as the majority of these victims were, to be buried without an accompanying shred of clothing is no passport to a good reincarnation. Few shreds of cloth, let alone a revealing 'black box' of aviation secrets surfaced from the Sea of Japan.

What really happened? One answer, favoured by many, is to take a closer look at the map.

It happens that the *shortest* route between Anchorage and Seoul runs the way that Captain Chun was trying to take it. On a straight line, there is money and time to be saved by going direct.

Not much money and not much time: but no one can deny that in August 1983 the finances of Korean Airlines were in a critical state. The history of KAL is one of dramatic expansion. In the early 1980s its revenues were some 180 times higher than its base in 1969. It could offer more than 130 international flights a week on a 41 strong fleet of modern airliners. And the debt burden of those aircraft stood, at the end of business 1982, at $1.1 billion. It was a figure that neatly cancelled out the year's operating profit.

In 1982, a new management philosophy, under chairman Harry Cho, turned a sombre $47.8 million loss into a $6 million profit. The key was cost cutting.

In such programs, every little helps. It might be that if Captain Chun shaved twenty minutes off his flying time on a Seoul trip the net saving would be little more than $2000 dollars. But if *each* pilot did that on *every* flight – why, you quickly get to cancelling out the deficit.

Pilots are, as a breed, loyal and dedicated. Some are more aggressive than others. And Captain Chun had a reputation for an aggressive, competitive spirit.

Certainly the ELINT (Electronic Intelligence Specialists) of both East and West learnt a great deal about their respective opponents on that night.

The postscript to this tragedy came during President Gorbachev's first state visit to South Korea in 1992, when he ceremoniously handed over the cockpit voice and data records of KAL 007, ''as a show of friendship and apology'', after the signing of a friendship treaty.

John Topham

TOXICOLOGY

For the modern forensic scientist, toxicology can be divided into two main areas: narcotics and poisons. While the former are usually self-administered and the crime lies in the illegality of possession itself, poisons are usually associated with deliberate acts of harm or murder to a third party.

Although the work of a forensic laboratory is increasingly devoted to the battle against drug-abuse, there is ample evidence that the Victorian pastime of poisoning still finds adherents amongst the wilfully criminal.

Above: *Drugs and the associated paraphernalia of their abuse play an increasingly dominant role in the work of today's forensic toxicologist.*

'Poisoner!' hissed the crowd outside Stafford gaol when Dr William Palmer was publicly hanged there in 1856 for murdering 14 people with antimony. The same cry followed Florence Bravo and her companion Jane Cox in 1876, when they were released due to insufficient evidence, though a coroner had found that Florence's husband Charles had been 'wilfully murdered' at their sedate Balham home.

Three years earlier, nurse Mary Ann Cotton had been strangled slowly to death when the hangman bungled his job at Durham Prison. This time the crowd outside approved, for Mary Ann had killed between 15 and 20 people – husbands, lovers, and children – with arsenic, becoming Britain's greatest ever mass murderer. Across the Atlantic, an aristocratic American, Florence Maybrick, gained grudging sympathy when she was sentenced to life for using arsenic to kill her unfaithful husband in 1889. To end the century, another American, Dr Thomas Neill Cream, the 'Lambeth Poisoner', killed at least five prostitutes with strychnine before going to the gallows in 1892, equalling the Ripper's record and, in fact, falsely claiming to be him on the scaffold.

The art of the Victorian poisoner did not, however, end with the death of the old Queen. In 1907 Richard Brinkley went to the gallows for killing his elderly, well to do woman friend by pouring prussic acid into her bottle of stout – a classic Victorian touch – while in 1916 Frederick Henry Seddon, who had murdered his lodger with arsenic in a particularly squalid fashion for her money, appealed to the judge from the dock of the Old Bailey as a 'fellow Freemason'. The judge wept, but sentenced him to death. Only two years before, Dr Hawley Harvey Crippen, perhaps the best known poisoner of modern times, had died on the scaffold for the murder of his promiscuous wife with the vegetable drug hyoscine – then used in small doses for the treatment of sexually unbalanced mental patients.

A personal affair

All these people had something in common besides poison: they killed for love and money – or greed and lust – which are very personal motives. The

Above: *The notorious doctor Crippen being escorted off the* Montrose *by Inspector Drew. After poisoning his wife, he tried to escape by sea with his mistress, who was disguised as a boy. This ship was alerted by radio — the first time it was ever used in crime detection.*

poisoner has to have close contact with his victim, and it is this which usually causes his downfall. As crime writer Colin Wilson puts it: 'In real life – as in fiction – it is always easier to identify and bring a poisoner to trial than it is to get the bandit before the jury for the dollars stolen from a bank. Poisoning is usually a personal affair, with a motive like a shining beacon. This is why the clear up rate for poisoners . . . is far higher than any type of crime.'

The determined poisoner has a vast range of materials to hand, but in fact few poisons are as obviously toxic as arsenic, strychnine, or cyanide. Any bright schoolboy with a slight knowledge of organic chemistry could pick a dozen or more lethal substances from the average hedgerow on a nature walk, and in fact any chemical is poisonous if taken in quantity or by the wrong person. Conversely, some substances which appear to be deadly may not kill at all.

In the spring of 1978 a German laboratory technician was convicted of attempting to murder his wife by administering cancer cells to her. He had smuggled a cancer culture from the research laboratory in which he worked and mixed it into her food. Although she became ill, she did not die for the culture was not in itself dangerous in that form. Similarly the scare which followed the news, in the late 1970s, that a large consignment of Israeli oranges had been injected with mercury was without foundation, although the fruit was withdrawn from the market in the face of public alarm. Throughout the 1980s, there was a spate of deliberate supermarket poisonings – usually involving randomly contaminated foodstuffs which were then used as the basis for a ransom demand.

The Rasputin case

Frequently, the body may manufacture its own antidote, as Professor Keith Simpson, the eminent British pathologist, has pointed out could well have been the case with Rasputin, the monk who dominated the Russian Imperial family immediately before the Revolution. In December, 1916,

Rasputin was lured to the house of Prince Felix Yussopov with the promise of an orgy. Yussopov and three friends had, in fact, determined to kill the powerful peasant, and had prepared wine and chocolate cake laced with what Yussopov described as 'enough potassium cyanide to kill a monastery of monks'.

Rasputin ate and drank vast quantities without any apparent effect, and in the end Yussopov shot him in the back at point blank range. Two hours later the monk revived and vigorously attacked the Prince. He was then beaten about the head with a heavy instrument, and thrown into the River Neva. Two days later his body was washed up; there were signs that he had regained consciousness again.

Rasputin, a man of giant stature and constitution, might well have survived the bullet and the battering and even the icy water failed to drown him immediately. But what about the cyanide? Professor Simpson pointed out that cyanide is more or less harmless until it comes into contact with the gastric juices, so that its action on the body may be delayed by 'dyspepsia'. 'Should the victim suffer from chronic gastritis as Rasputin probably did,' he wrote, 'he may swallow many times the fatal dose and escape the fate an ordinary subject would quickly meet.'

The toxicologist's role in crime

Forensic toxicologists are called upon to prove or disprove conjectures such as the one quoted above practically every day of their working lives: not as dramatic, perhaps, but usually much more important to the cause of justice. In the United States they usually operate as part of the Coroner's Department alongside the Medical Examiner; in Britain and Europe they either work full time in the government forensic laboratories or from the clinical chemistry departments of the great teaching hospitals.

Toxicology means the study of substances such as chemicals and bacteria which are harmful to human beings, although in practice bacteriologists usually handle cases in their own field. The average

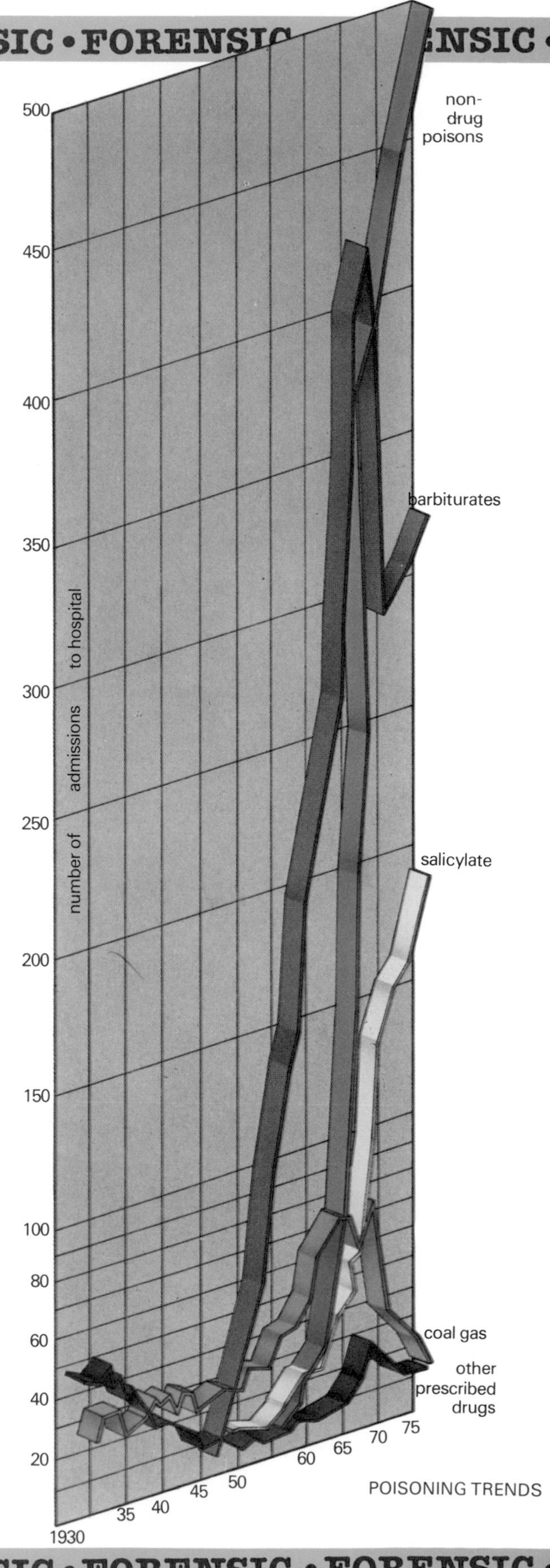

Right: *The graph illustrates the changing trends in poison abuse over a 45 year period.*

forensic toxicologist is a doctor of science who has specialist qualifications in analytical or clinical chemistry, or in clinical pharmacology. In cooperation with the forensic pathologist who performs post-mortem work he will examine and identify suspected poisons and illicit drugs in body tissues and fluids, and perform examinations and conduct tests in serious drink and driving cases – although the more routine cases are handled by assistants. In recent years, the toxicologist has been frequently called upon to carry out similar tests and examinations on athletes suspected of using stimulants such as anabolic steroids, beta-blockers and peptide hormones (notably 100-metre runner Ben Johnson, stripped of his gold medal and banned during the 1988 Seoul Games).

The use of drugs to enhance performance in sport is nothing new: two thousand years ago hallucinogenic mushrooms were in use during the original Olympic games. Tom Hicks allegedly won the 1904 Marathon on brandy and strychnine, and it is over 30 years since the drug induced death of the Danish cyclist at the Rome Olympics. Nowadays there is substantial profit to be made from the sale of controlled agents such as anabolic steroids.

Cries for help

Much of the work toxicologists do is concerned with 'routine' poisoning cases. Every year in Britain alone, 100,000 people are admitted to hospital with suspected poisoning, and a further 4,000 die from poisoning of all kinds. Most of the latter are never admitted to hospital, being 'successful' suicides.

Careful distinction must be made between 'genuine' attempted suicides and those which are merely 'cries for help' which go too far. As very few deaths occur in the group that reaches hospital, it would appear that many of these cases are not 'genuine'. Sometimes they are kept in hospital merely so that they can be seen and helped by a psychiatrist. They represent a very much younger age group than those found dead at home.

One group certainly not intending to kill themselves, though their life style may represent a form of death wish, are the drug addicts; one rarely finds the death of a so-called addict much above the age of 30. There are examples of this group who have injected themselves with narcotics or taken a large quantity of barbiturates, just to cure themselves of a hangover.

Above: *The self-administering of toxins, principally narcotics, is an increasing part of the modern forensic toxicologist's investigations.*

Another group who do not intend to kill themselves are the ones who take what can be described as a moderate dose of paracetamol, a common analgesic which can be bought without prescription. A massive dose of this is usually fatal and is fairly obviously genuine. But many of the 'moderate' overdose group, who take maybe five or six tablets to knock themselves out and attract attention, begin to recover only to succumb to the incredibly toxic effect of compounds – metabolites – which destroy the liver several days later.

Murder by poison

Although suicide and 'accidental' suicides of the type quoted make up the bulk of the toxicological work carried on in the West, murder by poison did not by any means die out with the Palmers, Maybricks and Crippens. As an officer of London's Metropolitan Police Forensic Science Laboratory points out, of the annual number of people who die or are admitted to hospital suffering from poisoning, perhaps 99% are suicidal or accidental. That still leaves 40 deaths and 1,000 non-fatal poisonings which may be criminal. Without suspicion there is no investigation, and therefore no analysis.

Normally if a person dies under suspicious or dubious circumstances, the pathologist passes on samples of the major organs for further analysis in the laboratory. But 'suspicion' becomes the key word in hunting down deliberate poisoners. As Professor Alexandre Lacassagne, founder of the Department of Forensic Science at Lyons University impressed on the nineteenth century toxicologists under his guidance: 'One must know how to doubt.'

The scene of the crime

Often, the first suspicion must be voiced by the police officer called to a scene of sudden death, and detectives are given careful schooling in what to watch for. Poison should always be considered, they are told, if death or illness occurs rapidly, without warning in young children, alcoholics, the insane, the senile, and the chronically sick. All these people can be described as 'classic' potential victims. For one thing they are more vulnerable than healthy adults, and for another they can be a nuisance: they tend to be in someone's way.

It is far more difficult to dope the healthy adult in reality than it is in fiction. The single sleeping tablet in the security guard's cup of tea will not cause him to suddenly fall asleep. Most of the sedative or narcotic pharmaceuticals do not dissolve completely in drinks and they usually taste very bitter. Anybody taking the old fashioned 'Micky Finn' would be possessed of neither taste nor smell!

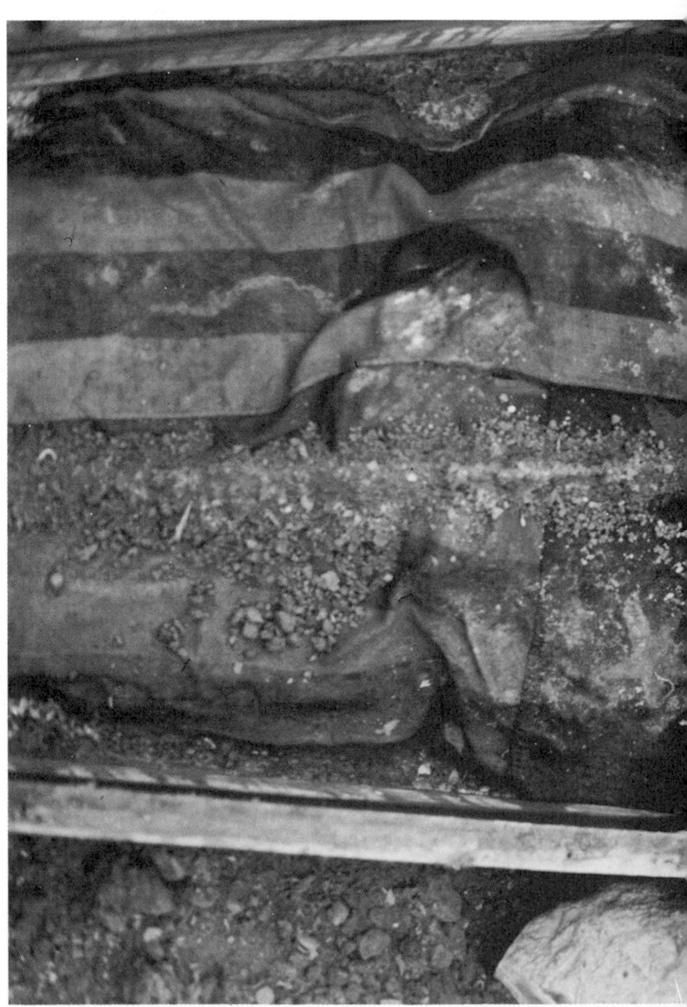

Right: *An American explorer, Charles Francis Hall, who died in suspicious circumstances at the North Pole in 1871. As he was buried there, his body was well preserved. Nearly a century later, scientists found a lethal dose of arsenic in his body tissues.*

When in doubt, therefore, the officer specially trained to work at the scene of a crime is very careful indeed. Tablets, capsules and medicines found near the victim are sent off with their containers carefully labelled and with a note of the position in which they were found. Similarly, cups, glasses and bottles are taken for examination, their contents drained into test tubes, along with any other odd tubes, packets, or bottles which lie in the house unlabelled.

Anything which has a warning label on it is noted, though not submitted unless it seems to have been used recently, or unless it is in an unusual place.

Obviously, the police are interested if they find anti-freeze in the lounge, ant powder in the bathroom, or even cleaner in the bedroom. They also examine sugar basins, tea caddies, coffee jars – 'do they appear to be contaminated?'

Above: *Graham Young, the mass poisoner. His trial shocked the British public in the 1970s, when it was revealed that at 14 he had already tried to poison several people. He was then sent to a special prison for mentally disturbed criminals, and had been released as "cured".*

The police officer with little or no knowledge of chemistry is asked to smell cautiously at strange substances, but, of course, never to taste. Any unusual odours are important, and officers are required to make a note of them, trying to relate them to something they are familiar with – for instance fruit, fish, bad eggs, sour milk, nail varnish.

In a full scale investigation, perhaps in the hunt for a multiple poisoner, a much more thorough search will be instigated. Dustbins will be emptied and rummaged through, sink traps and lavatory pans will be drained, and stains of vomit or urine will be gathered, as well as quantities of the liquid – up to eight pints – used to wash out the stomach of any survivors in hospital.

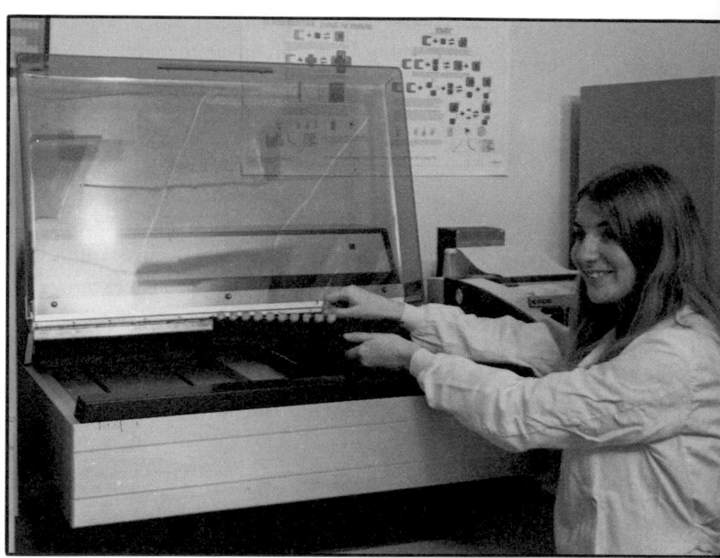

Above: *Examining a liquid chromatograph chart.*
Below: *Rapid screening tests for drugs can be made automatically on this EMIT (enzyme multiplied immuno-assay technique) device. EMIT is used to detect a wide range of drugs, including opiates, cocaine, barbiturates and amphetamines, and is of immeasurable help to the toxicologist.*

Above right: *Radioimmunoassay. Samples of test solution are incubated with a series of radioactively labelled antibodies. If a drug is present, it will combine with its specific antibody. Amounts are estimated by measuring the radioactivity.*
Below: *Thin layer chromatogram. This technique can analyse about 90% of common poisons.*

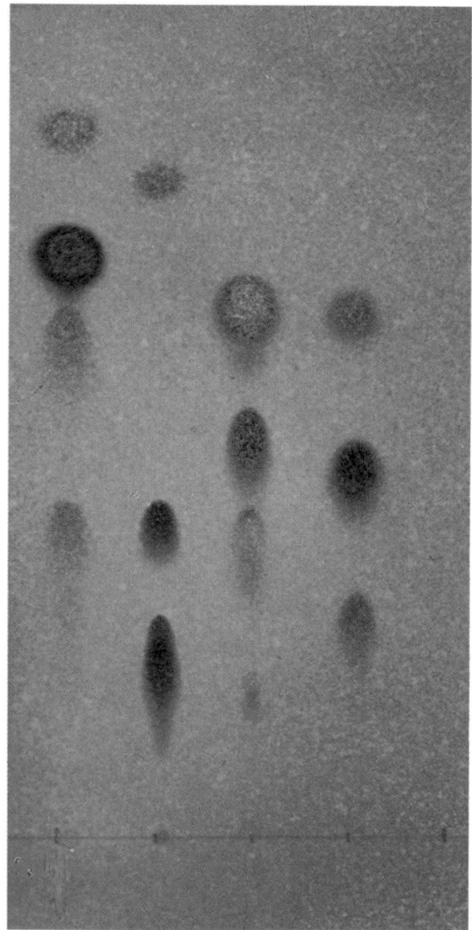

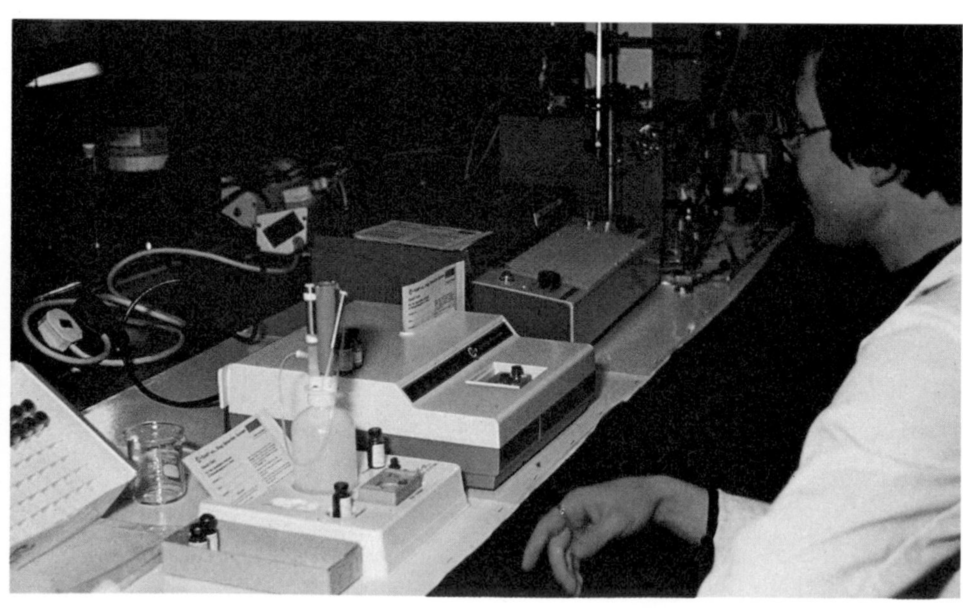

Taking samples

If a toxicologist is unable to perform or attend at the post mortem, the scene of crime officer will watch it and take notes from the pathologist. Eventually he will leave with a container of sealed jars destined for the laboratory. In every case of poisoning these will contain the stomach and its contents, at least one third of the liver, a minimum of 25 milligrams of blood from both chambers of the heart and various other sites in the body, and urine from the bladder. If a volatile toxic is suspected – one that evaporates quickly – the brain and lungs will be taken, while if death is due to cyanide the spleen will be removed. Signs of vomiting and diarrhoea might mean that a closer examination of a kidney is called for, while portions of hair, nails, and a segment of bone, preferably from the femur, will tell the toxicologist if arsenical poisoning caused death. Even when the body is putrid or badly crushed, vitreous humour from the eyeball may have been invaded by the poison, and will reveal its nature under analysis.

Although there are very few homicides in relation to the number of suspected suicides examined, the amount of extra work that is entailed in a full scale murder investigation is often out of all proportion to its scientific requirement, though not, of course, to the requirements of the courts. Every angle has to be scrutinized.

Changes in toxicology

It was Mathieu Joseph Bonaventure Orfila, born in Minorca in 1787, who is generally recognized as the father of modern toxicology. In the early nineteenth century at the University of Paris, he began the monumental task of cataloguing poisons and their effects. He received fortuitous assistance from a contemporary and colleague, Marie Guillaume Alphonse Devergie, the man who first brought the microscope to bear on practical forensic pathology and published the results in 1835 in his classic *Médecine légale, théorique et pratique.*

In the 150 years since then, the practical application of the principles laid down by both men has come on apace. In a modern laboratory, the two pioneers would recognize items such as test tubes, conical flasks, and jars, and Devergie might just discern the vague outline of his early instrument in the shape of its modern successor, but little else except the poisons and the human tissue itself would be familiar.

Lab technology

Today's toxicologist is largely dependent on a battery of analytical techniques using various forms of chromatography – a method of separating, measuring and analysing chemical mixtures. The machines used are complex, but in basic terms chemicals are fed into an electronic machine which the toxicologist adjusts to his requirements; the amounts of each substance present emerge in the form of either a graph or, in modern instruments, a computer print out.

There are several methods for different jobs: mass spectrometry, gas chromatography, paper and thin layer chromatography, and most recently high pressure liquid chromatography. This can detect tiny traces of such formerly 'difficult' substances as LSD in the urine, and monitor the strength present by a process known as radio-immunoassay. Thus in a sample of blood, urine or other liquid the measurement of drugs or poison present using these methods need be no more than .000000001 gram. No toxicology laboratory can now do an up-to-date and thorough job without at least two of these appliances.

Drug-abuse

Drugs are a major part of the modern toxicologist's work, and identification of the huge range of narcotics in existence requires continuous updating and modification, in line with the rapidly increasing distribution of new drugs available to the abuser.

Amphetamine-based drugs such as Ecstacy, or opiates like 'Crack' cocaine are being joined by new 'superdrugs' such as the 'designer' cannabis, skunk. Skunkweed, grown in Holland, is the latest in 'hybrid' drugs, having a high THC (active ingredient) content achieved by cross-breeding ever stronger breeds of cannabis. Each time a new form or variety of known substance like this is discovered, lab technicians have to evaluate its contents and type so that it can be quickly and accurately identified in future.

Carbon monoxide

A common by-product of the modern age, carbon monoxide is most often associated with automobile exhaust emissions. It is highly toxic, and easily obtained – a colourless, odourless gas used in many suicides as well as the cause of many industrial and domestic accidents, though only rarely has it been used as a means of murder.

On a warm summer day in the mid-1980s a CID officer attached to the coroner's office in Yorkshire in the north of England, following routine practice, called to see a man in hospital whose wife had died from an apparent gas leak accident the previous night. The couple had slept in a caravan, which was parked in the driveway of their home (the victim's parents, who were staying the night, were using their bedroom). The man, a university science lecturer who appeared himself to be suffering the after effects of carbon monoxide poisoning, described tearfully how a faulty gas fire or lamp they had been using in the caravan must have been the cause. It seemed a perfectly plausible, indeed, tragic tale – but for one small thing. The night of the accident had been the hottest of an already record-breaking summer . . . why would anyone have a fire on in such high temperatures? The officer decided to ask forensic colleagues to take a closer look at the caravan – and the appliances.

At first, Forensic Toxicologist Dr Les King accepted the possibility of an accident – indeed a remarkably similar event had occurred in the region and been widely publicised not long before. On inspecting the caravan, however, the seeds of doubt began to grow. Not only were both fire and lamp working normally, with no more than trace emissions even after many hours of continuous running, but he found all the ventilation sources taped up – except for the base of the door, where the man had been found by his son the morning after the accident.

The caravan was then taken in for detailed forensic examination since its owner had developed a sudden urge to sell it. Suspecting his equipment might be at fault, Dr King decided to check his analyser probes against a known source. Placing the probe by the exhaust of a car with its

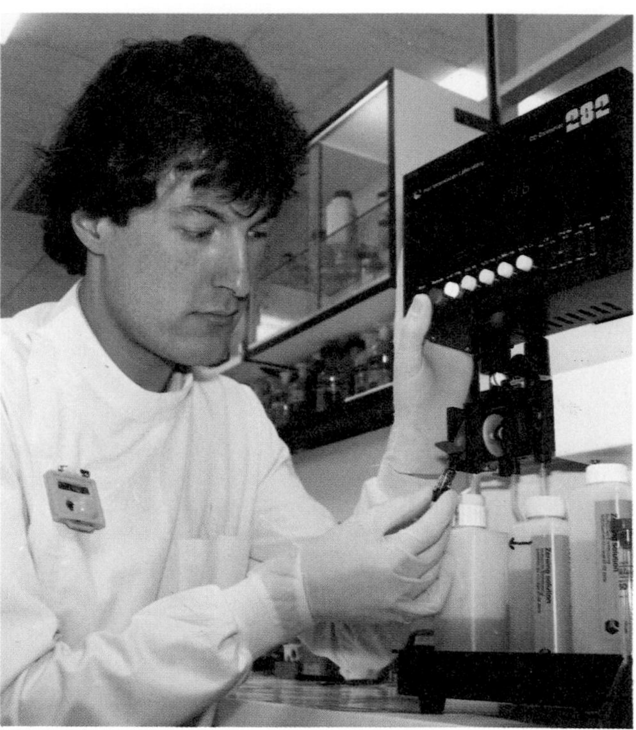

Above: *A microprocessor-driven analyser was used to measure differing carbon monoxide levels in blood samples taken from the lecturer and the body of his dead wife. The difference was so marked that Dr Les King, the Forensic Toxicologist, after checking his equipment against a known source for accuracy, immediately reported the death as suspicious.*

engine running, he was immediately able to prove that the readings were accurate. Furthermore, a sample of the scientist's blood had shown a carbon monoxide level of just 14% – not enough to cause any measurable ill-effects, whereas a similar sample taken from the victim's body showed lethal levels of 85%. How could two people in the same confined space have received such hugely differing doses – from a demonstrably harmless appliance? The accident was beginning to look somewhat contrived, and the toxicologist decided to advise the CID.

Confronted with the forensic evidence, the lecturer stuck to his original story, claiming that his wife was particularly sensitive to the cold (to explain the fire) and that she had a phobia about insects (to explain the masking tape). Pressed by the detective to account for his wife's death from an appliance that the forensic scientist had shown to be safe and the different toxicity levels, he could only suggest lamely that "somebody was making a mistake". This was not very convincing, especially coming from a scientist, and he eventually changed the story – saying that his wife had been depressed over her husband's career failure, and that he had found her asphyxiated from exhaust fumes in the garage. Wishing to spare the family from the pain and humiliation of her suicide, he claimed, he had decided to fake the accident.

Sceptical of this version of events, the police carried out further tests: not only were there no traces of the soot normally associated with car exhaust fumes in the victim's lungs, but the investigating officer was also sure that it would have been impossible for the man to have carried his wife's 13-stone body from the garage to the caravan without leaving visible evidence. Recalled for questioning after being left to 'sweat it out' at home, the suspect eventually confessed.

Taunted by a domineering wife as being 'pathetic' following dismissal from his job at the university, the 50-year-old academic had decided first to commit suicide, then to take his wife with him using two carbon monoxide gas cylinders he had easily obtained from his university department. Surprised by how rapidly she had succumbed to the gas, he had panicked, baulked at taking his own life and resolved to make the whole thing look like an accident. Taking his state of mind into consideration, the court accepted a plea of guilty to manslaughter.

Below: *Forensic analysis of a suspected drug using the mass spectrometer, one of several technical aids available to the examiner.*

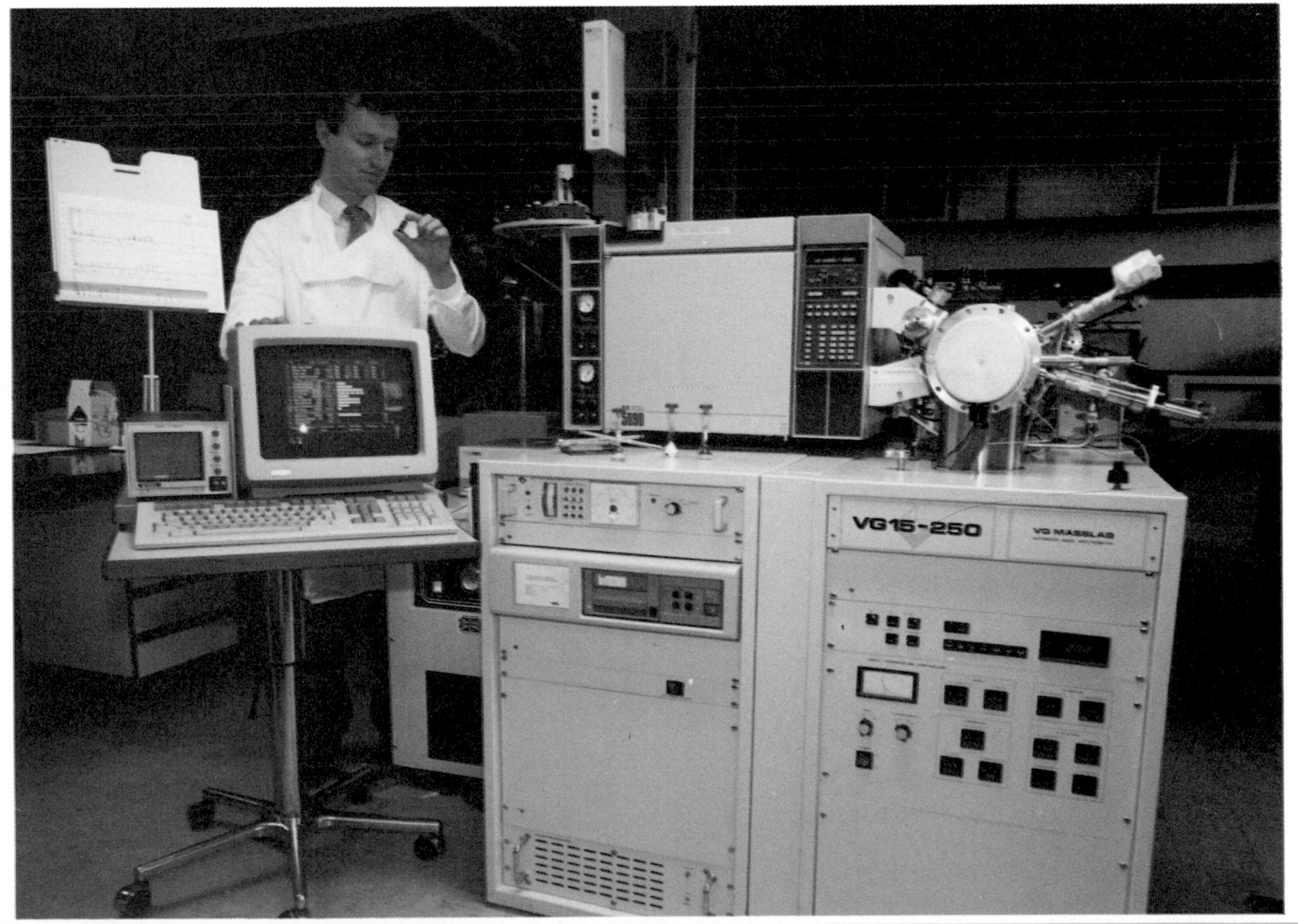

FROM RUSSIA WITH LOVE? The Markov murder

The slaying of Georgi Markov will remain one of the most chilling demonstrations of science and technology harnessed to murderous ends.

By September 1978 Markov, a healthy six-foot-tall Bulgarian of 49 years, working in London for the BBC World Service, was a thorn in the side of the regime that ran his native country. There was every reason for Bulgaria's communist government to wish his courageous, provocative broadcasts could suddenly cease.

On September 7, Markov was waiting for his evening bus home on Waterloo Bridge when a jab in his right thigh caused him to turn in surprise. The man behind him dropped the offending furled umbrella, muttered an apology, and hastened to hail a taxi. His problem in explaining his destination suggested, later, that he was probably a foreigner. Bemused but little concerned, Markov went home to his wife.

That night he slept in his study. He was due on early shift next day and did not wish to disturb the family. But they were disturbed. In the small hours Markov began running a temperature of 104° and vomiting.

"I have a horrible suspicion" he confided to his wife, "that it might be connected with something that happened today." They examined the mysterious puncture. It looked as if someone had jabbed him with a ball point pen. There were a few drops of blood on his jeans.

Next morning, Markov seemed well enough to be left, but his wife arranged for the family doctor to call, before departing for work. The doctor was alarmed enough to have Georgi hospitalized immediately. His decline thereafter was swift. A circular area of inflammation now surrounded the original puncture. His temperature and blood pressure fell rapidly. Septicemia was diagnosed. Over the weekend the patient became violent and confused. He died on Monday morning. To their astonishment, the hospital found that Markov's white blood count had risen to 33,000 per cubic millimetre – a normal count is between five and ten thousand.

The death was sufficiently mysterious to provoke a high level investigation that reached from London's Metropolitan Police Laboratory to the governmental microbiological research institute at Porton Down. Here pathologist Rufus Crompton examined the section of flesh excised from the dead Bulgarian's thigh. One inch from the puncture, and just below the skin, he felt a small hard object that he first guessed was a pinhead. On removal it turned out to be a minute metal ball. Crompton, bemused, put it in a paper bag, and turned it over to Dr Ray Williams at the Metropolitan Police Laboratory.

Electron microscopy revealed an impressive piece of precision engineering. The pellet, a mere 1.52mm in diameter, had two holes bored through it, crossing at the centre. In composition, the pellet proved to be an alloy, 90% platinum and 10% iridium. To drill holes .35mm wide in such a notably hard substance plainly involved someone with access to highly specialized equipment.

The position of the pellet in the body suggested that the mysterious assailant's umbrella had been equally specialized. Everything indicated a firing device in the ferrule, silently powered by a gas cylinder. The whereabouts of the umbrella remained a mystery. So, for the moment, did the identity of a poison sufficiently lethal to be effective in the minute quantity the pellet was able to hold.

Tests ruled out a radioactive source. The only other known candidates in the toxicologist's book were derivatives from two widespread – and at first acquaintance innocent-seeming – plants. One, the so called Rosary Bean, was already familiar as the world's commonest lethal source of vegetable poison. The beans, widely used to make simple rosaries, yield a toxin called abrin. Chemically, this is close to the residue of another bean, fruit of the castor oil plant: and castor oil plants are commonly cultivated in the countries where Markov's enemies could reasonably be expected to lurk.

Ricin, or ricinine, is not present in castor oil itself (despite the testimony of generations of children that castor oil is pure poison). It remains in the bean once the oil is extracted – anyone unwise enough to chew a bean thoroughly has a one in 20 chance of dying. Efficiently extracted however, ricin is twice as deadly as cobra venom. An albumen, it causes red blood cells to agglutinate; then it goes on to attack other body cells with devastating effect. High temperature, vomiting, disorientation and diarrhea are among the immediate host of effects. Significantly, the toxin is most effective at an astonishing dilution of one part in a million. For some years, cancer specialists had been experimenting with both ricin and abrin as a weapon against rogue cells.

At Porton Down, the pathologists experimentally injected a pig with the amount of ricin the Markov pellet could have contained. It died within

Above: *The ill-fated Georgi Markov.*
Below: *A microscope picture of the tiny pellet in Markov's body, photographed alongside a pinhead.*

24 hours. The evidence was hardening but still circumstantial – for no trace of ricin itself had been found in Markov's corpse.

Yet that fact was only another indicator that ricin was the likely agent. One property of the toxin that makes it elegantly suitable as a murder agent is that the body's natural protein-making cells break ricin down so that, having done its damage, it disappears from the body.

The clinching conclusion to the investigation lay not in the laboratory but walking in the streets of Paris. In an incident outside a metro station the previous year another Bulgarian emigré had been mysteriously jabbed, fallen sick, but recovered. After some persuasion, he was now visited by a surgeon, who extracted a small metallic object from his flesh. It was brought by police escort to the lab in London, eagerly awaited by Dr Ray Williams and his assistant. There, an electron microscope revealed a pellet identical to the one that killed Markov.

Although investigations failed to reveal the perpetrator, the implications seemed clear.

Following the collapse of the Warsaw Pact and the end of communism in Eastern Europe, the new authorities in Bulgaria confirmed that agents from the previous regime had, as suspected, carried out both attacks.

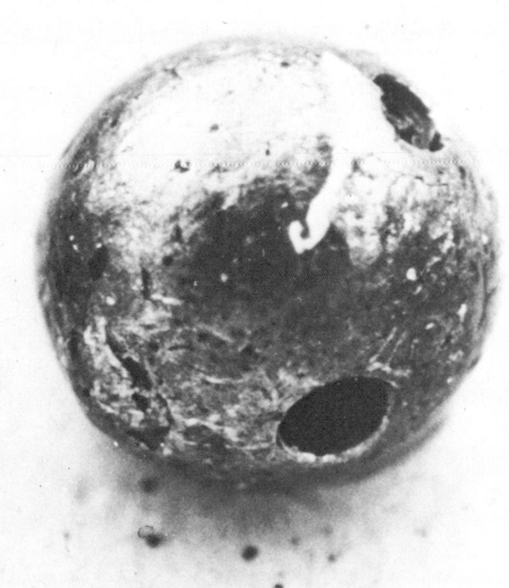

The cyanide case

One of the oddest cases concerning the build up of a 'tolerance' – in this instance to a large dose of cyanide – concerned a heavy drinker who had smoked 60 cigarettes a day for over 25 years. While he was a patient in hospital, a routine blood sample was taken and found to contain a considerable quantity of cyanide. In fact, had it been taken in acute form – all at once, it could have been fatal. The picric acid test is one of the sensitive standard methods used by toxicologists for measuring cyanide levels in the blood. A blood-acid mixture is heated at the bottom of a flask and as the cyanide gas is eliminated from this mixture it is trapped by a dye forming process in a cup suspended from the flask's stopper. The quantity of cyanide in the blood is directly related to the strength of the purple colour that develops in the cup.

A deep purple would indicate death by cyanide ingestion or from breathing cyanide fumes from burning polyurethane plastics. Alternatively, it could be the result of the burning of a great deal of protein. Cyanide vapour is produced when protein is burned, and cigarettes contain protein. Calculations showed that over the years he had inhaled minute quantities of cyanide vapour with each cigarette; normally the liver dissipates the substance in a short time, but the patient's liver was not in very good condition after his drinking and the poison had stayed. However, the process had taken so long that his body had built up a truly amazing resistance to one of the most agonizing and deadly poisons known.

Below: *Samples of cyanide taken from the stomach (40), liver (41), brain (42) and stomach in a picric acid test (43) of a New York man in 1931. The man's car was in flames, and his body slumped over the front mudguard. At first it was thought that he had burned to death accidentally. However these lab samples helped prove that he had taken a fatal dose of cyanide.*

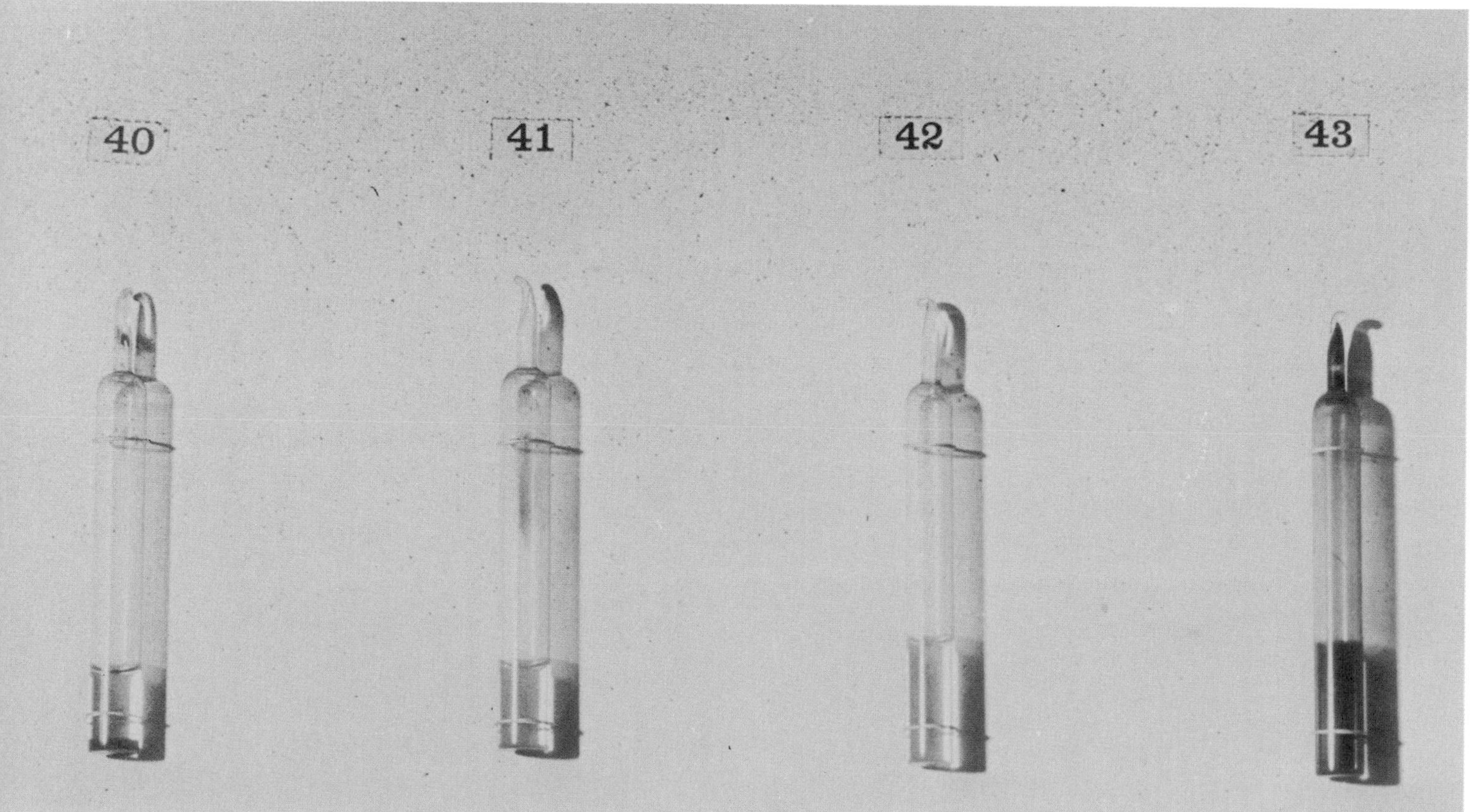

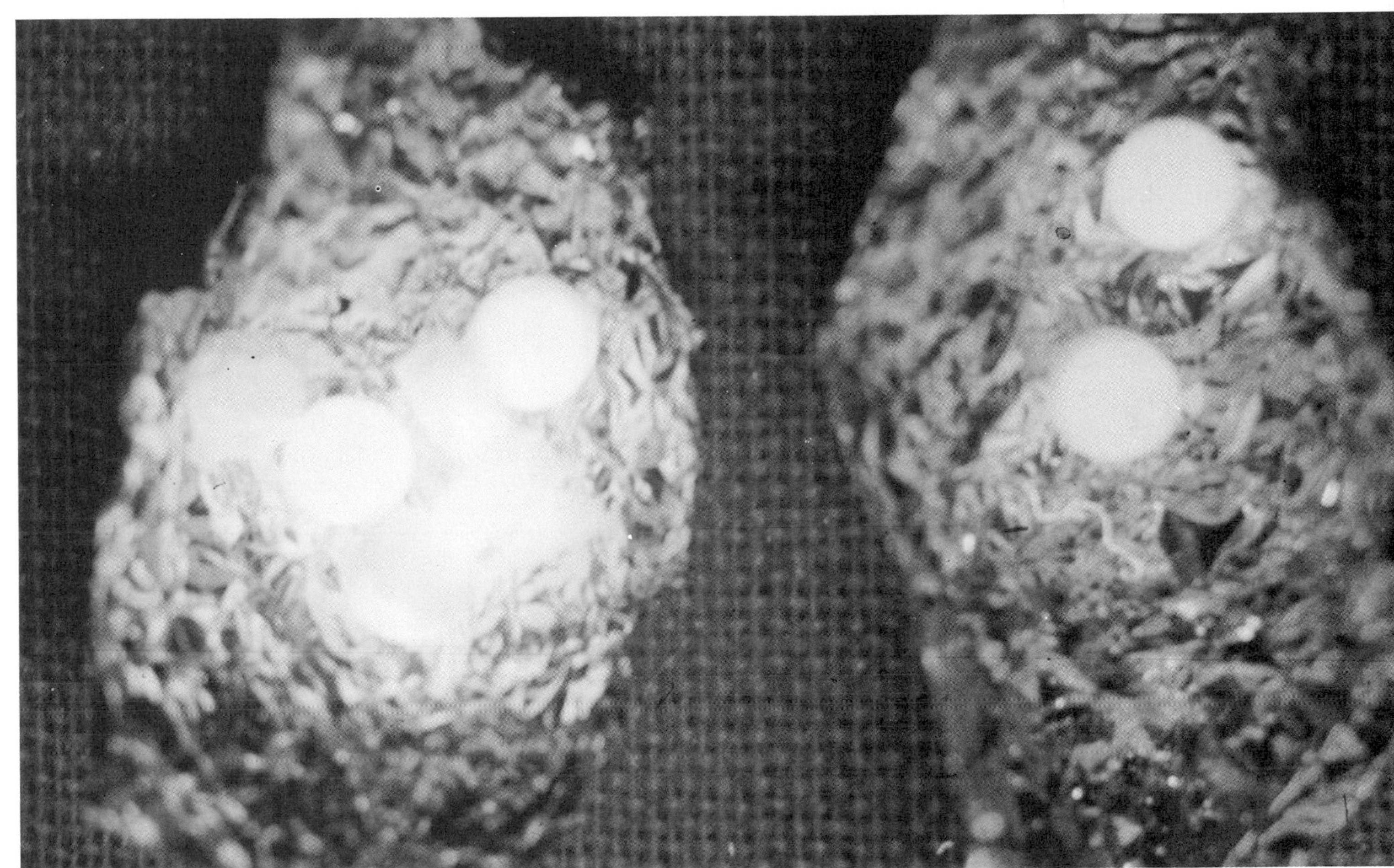

Above: *The first recorded death from an overdose of LSD. These saccharin tablets coated with the drug were smuggled to a prisoner in London's Brixton prison. The packet opened in his stomach, releasing a massive dose.*

Death of a 'mule'

During a Sabena flight from Brussels to London in November 1992, a woman passenger suddenly became violently ill. Cabin staff applied their first aid training to make her as comfortable as possible, while the aircraft requested priority clearance to land. On arrival, the by now comatose passenger – a housewife from Nigeria – was rushed to hospital, where she later died. During her treatment, doctors removed over a hundred condoms containing 17 ounces of cocaine with a street value around $75,000 from her stomach. The cause of death was from a massive overdose following the rupture of one or more of the 'parcels'. Mrs Ehirobo was the third Nigerian woman in a month to die in this way while trying to smuggle drugs into the United Kingdom.

With increasingly severe penalties for drug smuggling being adopted worldwide, traffickers are turning more and more to poverty-stricken third world 'mules', willing to carry potentially lethal cargoes in their bodies across international borders for often less than $1500. In most cases they are semi-literate and usually quite unaware of both the mortal and legal risks they are taking. Such cases present the forensic investigator with a combined example of the two main elements of his profession – narcotic abuse and the effects of toxic poisoning.

THE BARROW GANG

Bonnie and Clyde ranged through the mid-West. They brought bloodshed to the towns they descended on.

TIME, aided by the Hollywood film cameras, has given Bonnie and Clyde an aura of glamour. As many myths surround them as surround Robin Hood. The legend of Bonnie and Clyde projects them as underdogs and social protesters, fighting for their rights at the time of the great American Depression.

The truth is that they were a couple of small-time crooks who robbed purely for personal gain, and murdered either to avoid capture or out of the hatred of the police common to most low-grade criminals. Public Enemy Number One, John Dillinger, voiced the view of top gangsters when he heard of their death. "They were kill-crazy punks and clodhoppers, bad news to decent bank robbers," he said. "They gave us a bad name."

Great passions

Clyde Chestnut Barrow, sixth of the eight children of a poor Texas farmer, was born on March 24, 1909. He was irascible, quick-tempered, and a latent homosexual with two great passions in life – guns and automobiles. He also had a strong streak of sadism. Childhood friends and neighbours say he enjoyed wringing a chicken's neck almost to the point of death, then watching its agony, or breaking a bird's wings and laughing at its attempts to fly.

Bonnie, the girl who would one day grow into a tough, cigar-smoking killer and nymphomaniac, was 18 months younger than Clyde and a cut above him socially. She was the daughter of a bricklayer who died when she was four. Her family, devout Baptists, then moved to Cement City, near Dallas, Texas. Clyde was already living in West Dallas, where his father had settled down to the slightly more lucrative job of running a filling station after giving up his farm.

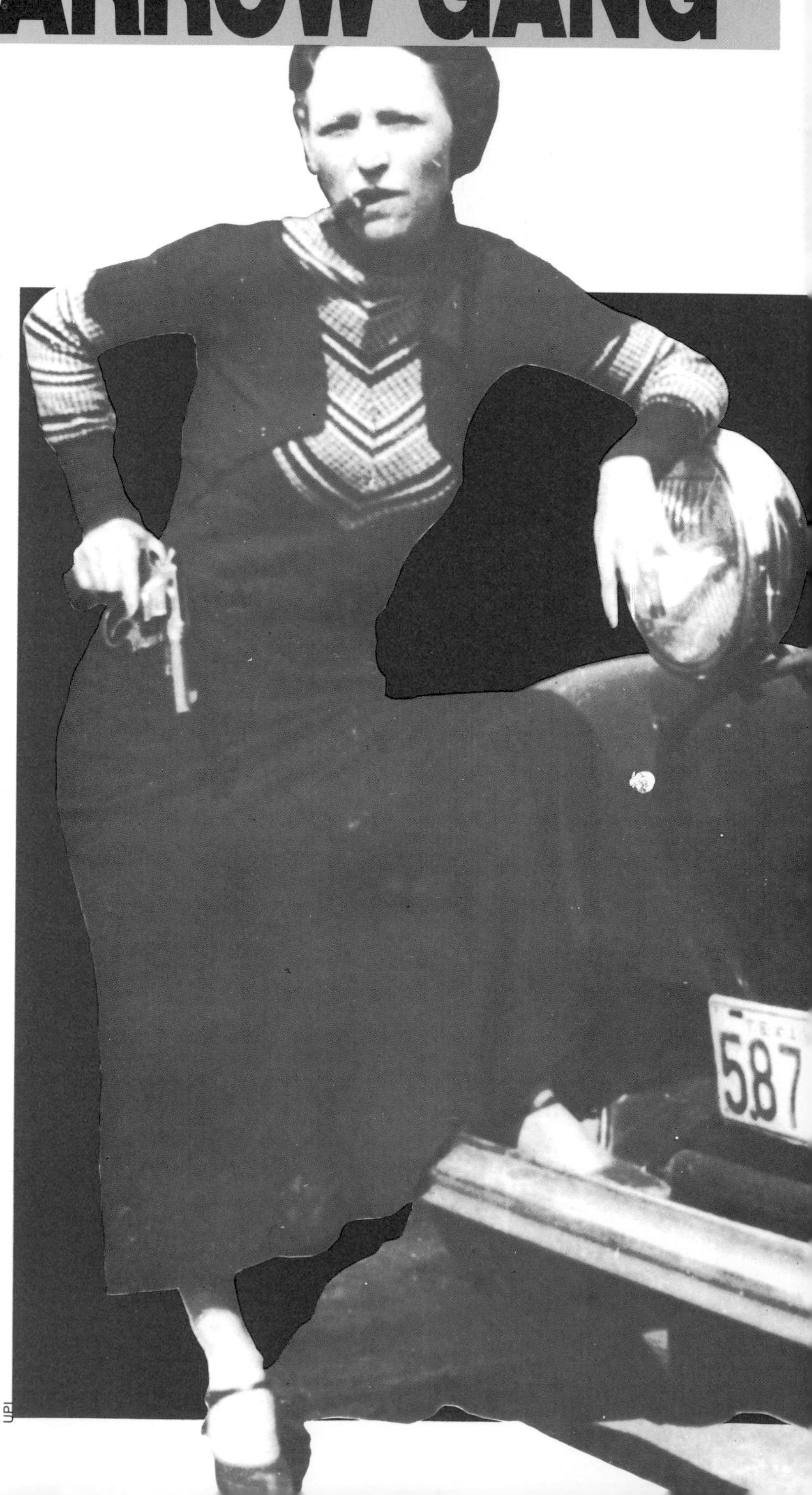

MERCILESS killers incapable of any feeling of remorse, Bonnie Parker and Clyde Barrow nevertheless managed to capture the public imagination. Their very lawlessness seemed to appeal to a society hemmed in by restrictive rules.

UPI

587-9

How the couple actually met is, like the number of murders and robberies they committed, a matter of conjecture. The most likely theory is that their paths crossed when a mutual friend in West Dallas broke an arm and Bonnie went to look after her. That is the way that Bonnie's mother, Mrs. Parker, told it. The time was January, 1930. Clyde was nearly 21, Bonnie just past her nineteenth birthday.

Clyde fell at once for the petite (under 5 ft. tall), fair-haired girl with the bright blue eyes and impudent red mouth. Bonnie fell for him, too, despite his "snake eyes" and somewhat effeminate looks.

The night after Bonnie arrived back in Cement City from looking after her friend, Clyde turned up as well and stayed so late that Mrs. Parker let him sleep on a couch in the living-room. "I was glad," she explained later, "that she had become interested in another man and stopped grieving over Roy."

Criminal activities

Roy was Roy Thornton, a childhood sweetheart Bonnie had married when only 16. Mother-in-law trouble had caused the break-up of the marriage. To both Bonnie and Clyde, the most important people in the world would always be their mothers. Even at the height of their career of terror, with the police of several states hunting them, they were always slipping home to see Ma.

Clyde was still asleep on the couch on the morning after that first visit when the police came for him. He was wanted on seven charges of car theft and burglary. He faced the prospect of 14 years in prison. But, after pleading guilty to three of the offences, he was let off with a light sentence of two years' jail.

Bonnie had hysterics when Clyde was taken away. "It was such a shock to learn the truth about him," said her mother. But Clyde had never made any secret of his criminal activities, and Bonnie was merely suffering from rage and frustration at having the new man in her life forcibly removed from her.

It didn't take her long, however, to set him free again. The girl who, according to her mother, "had never been mixed up with crime or criminals before in her whole life", calmly smuggled a gun to Clyde in jail. He broke out with two other prisoners, only to be recaptured a few days later after robbing a railway office at Middletown, Ohio, at gunpoint. Now he was sentenced to the full term of 14 years.

"It was his experiences in prison that changed Clyde," asserted his sister. "Before that he was wild but loving. Prison made him hardened and bitter."

Certainly life in a Texas prison of the period was no picnic. Convicts had to work all day in the hot cotton fields, and were beaten if they slacked or complained. At night they had to run all the way back to the jail, herded by warders on horseback. Again they were beaten if they lagged behind.

BROTHER Buck Barrow – also a member of the gang – poses with the tools of his trade: car and weapons.

First murder

It was a common practice for prisoners to sever their heel tendons to make themselves unfit for work. Clyde went even further. He persuaded a fellow-convict to chop two of the toes off his left foot with an axe.

He was still on crutches when, in February 1932, he was released under a general parole granted by the woman governor of Texas, "Ma" Ferguson. Mrs. Parker was not exactly pleased to see him. "Please try to go straight from now on for Bonnie's sake," she pleaded when he appeared at her home.

"I'll try," Clyde promised. "But," he added realistically, "it won't be easy. Nobody will give me a job, and the cops will be after me every time there's an unsolved robbery."

He made one attempt at an ordinary job. The husband of one of his sister's friends was working with a construction company in Massachusetts, and promised to get him fixed up. But Massachusetts was on the other side of the country, farther than he had ever been away from home before.

He stood the "isolation" for a fortnight. Then, homesick and lonely, and still in fear of the police, he returned to West Dallas. "If I've got to hide from the law all my life," he explained, "I want to be where I can slip back sometimes and see my folks."

Three days later, Bonnie left home. She told her mother: "I've got a job demonstrating cosmetics at a store in Houston." It was a lie. She had gone off with Clyde to start the campaign of stick-ups and murders that would – even if Dillinger was unimpressed – earn "The Barrow gang" the accolade of Public Enemies No. 1 in the south-west of the United States for the next two years.

This was March, 1932. The Barrow gang's first murder was committed on April 17, when they gunned down a jeweller named John W. Bucher in Hillsboro, Texas, and got away with $40. Clyde later claimed that two confederates – whom he refused to name – had done the shooting, and he had merely driven the get-away car.

Bonnie was in jail at the time, having been picked up for questioning about a

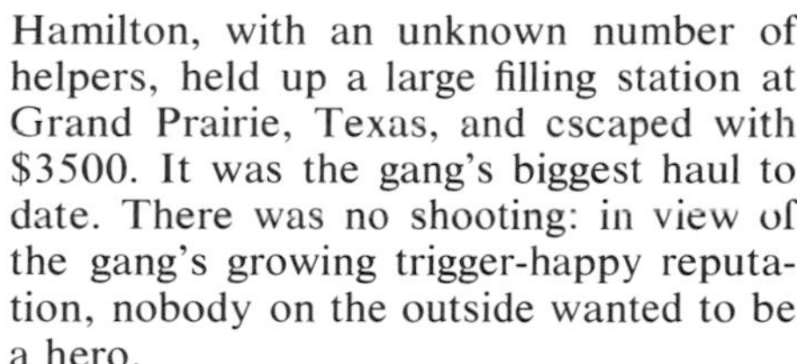

stolen car. She was released after three months without being charged. In the meantime, Clyde, a new associate named Ray Hamilton, and two other unidentified companions, had shot and killed Sheriff Maxwell and Deputy-Sheriff Moore in the little town of Atoka, Oklahoma.

The shooting took place outside a dancehall. One account says that Clyde and his friends had been drinking heavily. When one of them took out a bottle of whisky and started drinking from it, Maxwell, who was keeping watch on the dancehall with his deputy, said: "Cut that out. We don't permit that kind of thing here."

It was a reasonable request with Prohibition still in force. The guns barked at once, however. Moore, shot through the head and heart, died instantly, and Maxwell slumped to the pavement, fatally wounded.

With Bonnie out of jail, Clyde and Hamilton, with an unknown number of helpers, held up a large filling station at Grand Prairie, Texas, and escaped with $3500. It was the gang's biggest haul to date. There was no shooting: in view of the gang's growing trigger-happy reputation, nobody on the outside wanted to be a hero.

The mob celebrated their success by driving Hamilton up to Michigan to visit his father. For Hamilton it proved an unhappy trip. He drank too much and talked too much, with the result that he was arrested, taken back to Texas, and sentenced to 263 years in jail after being convicted of a string of robberies—plus the Hillsboro murder, in which he hadn't, in fact, been involved.

Insatiable desire

Meanwhile, Bonnie and Clyde were enjoying a leisurely motoring tour of Michigan, Kansas, and Missouri—which took up most of September and October. They stayed at good hotels, patronized good restaurants, and splashed out on new clothes. Both, reacting to their underprivileged childhood, were fussy and immaculate dressers. Bonnie regularly visited hairdressing salons and beauty parlours.

In no time they had less than $2 between them, and the robberies had to start again. Howard Hall, a 67-year-old butcher from Sherman, Texas was robbed after "a blond girl"—later identified as Bonnie—had shot him three times in the stomach. There were more stick-ups in Missouri, including a bank in Carthage. Nearly all of them had a spur-of-the-moment air.

The "take" from the Carthage bank was a miserable $80. A disappointed Bonnie and Clyde set out to improve their finances by robbing a second bank—only to find on arriving there that it had closed down four days earlier.

The next murder in which they were involved had a similarly casual aura. They had been joined by William Daniel Jones, a 16-year-old boy who had grown up in the same West Dallas semi-slum as Clyde, and hero-worshipped him. According to one account, Clyde allowed Jones to join the gang only because—with Hamilton in jail—he needed help in coping with Bonnie's insatiable desire for sex.

Whatever the reason, while the three of them were trying to steal a car in Temple, Texas, Doyle Johnson, the son of the car's owner, was shot dead. As Bonnie said later: "Johnson grabbed Jones by the wrist and Jones shot him. Clyde was furious at Jones for making a murder case out of it."

The date was December 5, 1932. Police believed that it was, in fact, Clyde who had fired the shot. There wasn't any doubt about his next killing, however. On January 6 the following year, he shot and killed Deputy Sheriff Malcolm Davis after he and Bonnie had accidentally walked into a trap at Dallas, Texas, set for another bank robber, Odell Chandless.

It is impossible to list the number of robberies and killings the couple committed between January 1933 and May 1934—when they were to die in a bullet-riddled car. Stick-ups had become their way of making a living; murder the automatic reflex when they were in danger of being caught.

Hunted animals

That their career lasted so long was partly the result of the ineptitude of the police of several States, partly the fact that the same police were facing an unprecedented crime wave arising out of the Depression.

But there were several "almost caughts". In March 1933, Bonnie, Clyde and Jones hid out in a rented apartment in Joplin, Missouri. They were joined by Clyde's brother, Buck, and his sister-in-law, Blanche. The neighbourhood was too respectable. One nervous resident reported to the police that the occupants were "darting in and out of the living quarters like frightened animals".

The police sent two squad cars to investigate. In the resulting shoot-out, the gang escaped, although both Clyde and Jones had minor bullet wounds. But two policemen were shot dead, and another seriously injured.

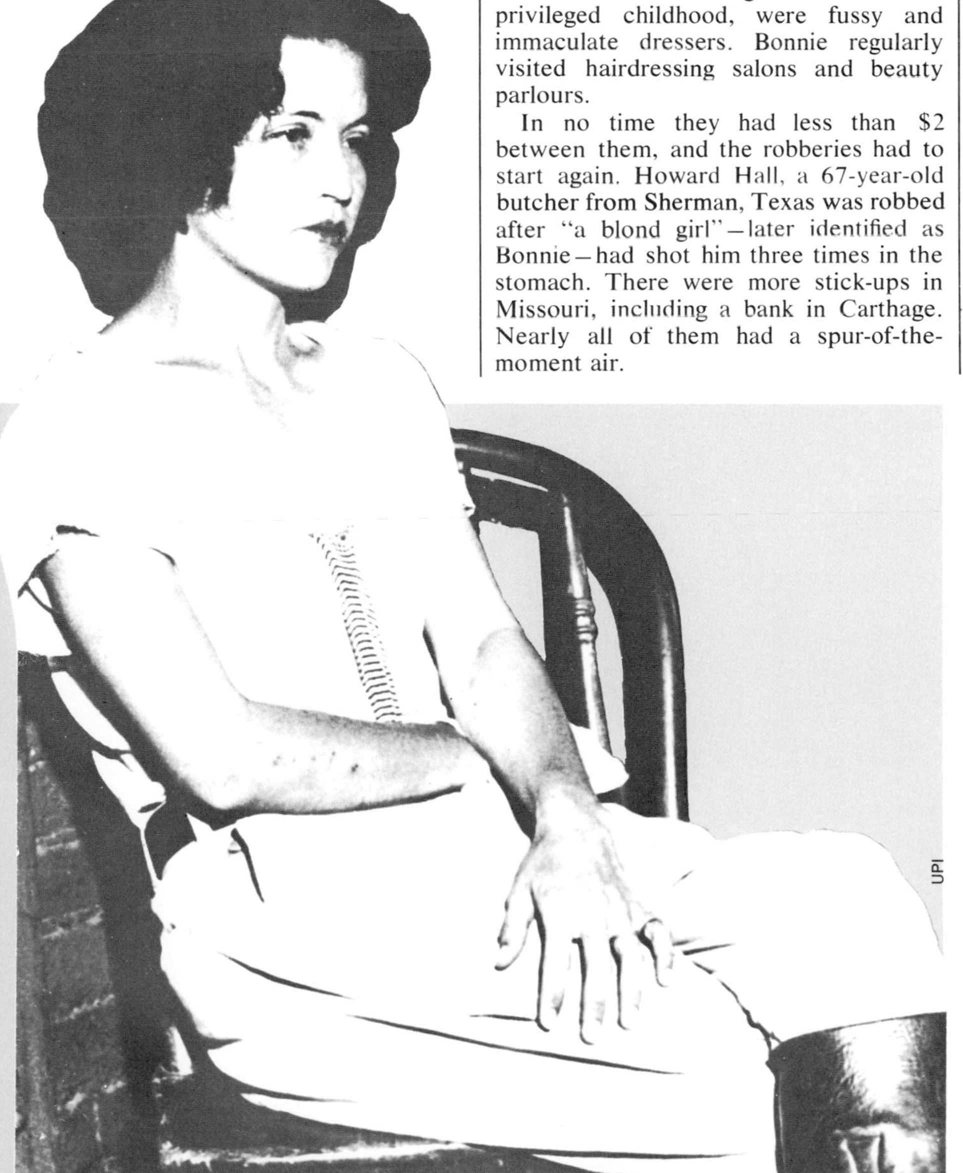

UPI

WIFE'S DUTY is to stay with her husband! This was the argument used by Blanche (left) to defend her life-style!

In the next month the fugitives were reported in half-a-dozen places in Louisiana, Oklahoma, Minnesota, and Iowa. In each place there was a robbery. The whole of the south-west went in terror of them—but the heat was on.

It was no longer safe for them to stay in tourist camps, let alone rent an apartment. They were forced to sleep in the cars they stole. When one car broke down, they stole another.

But their greatest concern was to keep themselves clean and tidy. They would leave their laundry in some small country town, and come back a few days later to collect it. The two men used barbers in the same towns to get a shave, one waiting in the car outside to sound a warning signal.

It appeared that, for a time at least, they bore crooks' luck. "It can't be long now before they get us," Bonnie reasoned on one occasion. "I want to see my mother once more before I die." But it would be nearly a year before she and Clyde said their final and bloody goodbye.

RIDDLED with bullet holes, the last car driven by Bonnie and Clyde (right and far right) finally comes to a stop. For two years the couple had robbed and murdered almost at will until the fatal ambush on the Gibsland road. The band of officers responsible for mowing down the number one public enemies are pictured below. Strangely, the public mourned.

All pictures AP

In the meantime, Clyde, driving their car at 70 m.p.h., failed to notice that a bridge over a gorge near Wellington, Texas, had collapsed. The automobile plunged to the bottom, turning over twice in mid-air, throwing Clyde clear but pinning Bonnie underneath. Then it caught fire.

Near death

"Shoot me if you can't get me clear," she pleaded with Clyde, after he had rescued Jones and their precious armoury of machine guns and revolvers. With the aid of a farmer, Stener Pritchard, and one of his hands – who had seen the accident – the badly-burned Bonnie was finally freed. The Pritchards gave them sanctuary, but quickly became suspicious about their house guests and tipped off the police. Bonnie, Clyde and Jones escaped at gunpoint.

After linking up with brother Buck and his wife, Blanche, they risked booking into a double cabin in a tourist camp near Fort Smith, Arkansas. Bonnie was delirious and near death. Clyde put the story about that she had been injured by the explosion of an oil stove while they were camping. However, even with every lawman in the territory looking for them, they managed to persuade a doctor to treat her who, when she refused to go to hospital, arranged for a nurse to tend her.

That all took money. Accordingly the gang robbed a nearby bank and two Piggly-Wiggly stores. In the process, they shot dead Henry Humphrey, a newly-elected marshal, and made their getaway in his car. During July they drove through Iowa, staging a new stick-up whenever money was running low, and finally fetched up at a tourist camp near Platte City, Missouri.

But there was little rest now. The way they sneaked in and out, and kept the curtains of their two cabins drawn, soon caused new suspicions. Police surrounded the cabins and they had to shoot their way free. The terrible trio – as they could be called – escaped unhurt. Buck, however, suffered three bullet wounds in the head – one bullet going through one temple and out the other, while Blanche was temporarily blinded by splinters of glass from a shattered window.

Chicken dinners

They were in a desperate way, hungry and thirsty, with Buck dying and both Bonnie and Blanche in agony and in need of medical attention and drugs. One of them went to buy five take-away chicken dinners, while the rest made camp in thick woods near a river at Dexter, Iowa. With the whole territory buzzing with talk of the Barrow gang, the sale of the chicken dinners was enough to bring a posse of some 200 police down on them.

Buck was shot again in the hip, shoulder, and back. Police found Blanche crouched over him, sobbing: "Don't die, Daddy, don't die." Buck and Blanche had been unlucky. Buck had just been paroled from prison, and had resolved to go straight until he became involved in the Joplin shoot-out. Blanche had stuck with him out of love.

Six days after the Dexter Park ambush, a delirious Buck died in hospital. Blanche was not at his side. She was in prison awaiting the trial that would bring her a 10-year sentence. Meantime, the Bonnie and Clyde saga still wasn't over. They and Jones escaped through the fusillade of bullets, waded the river, and were soon on their journey to nowhere again in yet another stolen car.

Jones had a slight head wound, Clyde had been shot four times in one arm. When the wounds had healed, Jones left them and Bonnie and Clyde made their way back to Dallas. They spent most of October, November, December and January there, sleeping in a succession of stolen automobiles, meeting their families at secret rendezvous in the country, and setting out to rob stores and petrol stations in the surrounding territory.

Two blondes

It was largely through Bonnie that they managed to escape detention. She had the bright idea of getting a blond wig for Clyde and dressing him up as a woman. "The police are looking for a man and a blonde, not two blondes," she pointed out. Her ruse worked.

On January 16, 1934, they departed from their normal pattern of crime by freeing Ray Hamilton from his 263 years in Huntsville Prison. Bonnie drove the getaway car, while Clyde hid automatics in bushes near the field where the prisoners were working, and also covered the escape with a machine-gun. One warder was shot dead and, in addition to Hamilton, four other convicts got away.

Hamilton promptly embarked upon a series of bank raids. Despite his denials, Clyde was alleged to be in on them. In fact, he and Bonnie were blamed for practically every crime committed anywhere in the south-west.

On Sunday, April 1, Bonnie, Clyde and Henry Methvin – one of the convicts who had escaped from Huntsville with Hamilton – were trapped by two highway patrolmen in Grapevine, near Dallas. They opened up with machine-guns, killing both officers. Five days later, near Miami, Oklahoma, Clyde shot dead another policeman, Constable Cal Campbell, who had gone to investigate a report that "a Ford with a girl and two men in it is stuck in a ditch".

By now, however, the police of Texas, Oklahoma, Louisiana, Arkansas and Kansas were determined to get the gang. It was generally supposed that it was Henry Methvin's father, Ivan, who put the finger on them in the hope of doing a deal with the police that would allow his son to go free.

Admiring strangers

On the morning of May 23, 1934, six officers waited in bushes by the side of a road eight miles from Gibsland, Louisiana. Shortly after nine o'clock, Bonnie and Clyde appeared in a Ford V-8 sedan. The police guns chattered. In all, 167 shots were fired. At least fifty of these struck Bonnie and Clyde between them, and they died almost immediately. Said one of the policemen: "We just shot the hell out of them, that's all . . . they were just a smear of wet rags."

The couple were taken home to Dallas for burial. Already the legend had started to grow. Many of the flowers for their funerals came from admiring strangers, to whom they were a folk hero and heroine. Onlookers snatched the roses, peonies, and gladioli from the coffins for souvenirs. The crush was so bad at the cemetery that Clyde's sister couldn't get within 40 feet of the gravesides.

Clyde was 25, Bonnie 23, when their saga ended in the way Bonnie had predicted in her poem, *The Story of Bonnie and Clyde:*

Some day they'll go down together,
They'll bury them side by side,
To a few it'll be grief – to the law a relief –
But it's death to Bonnie and Clyde.

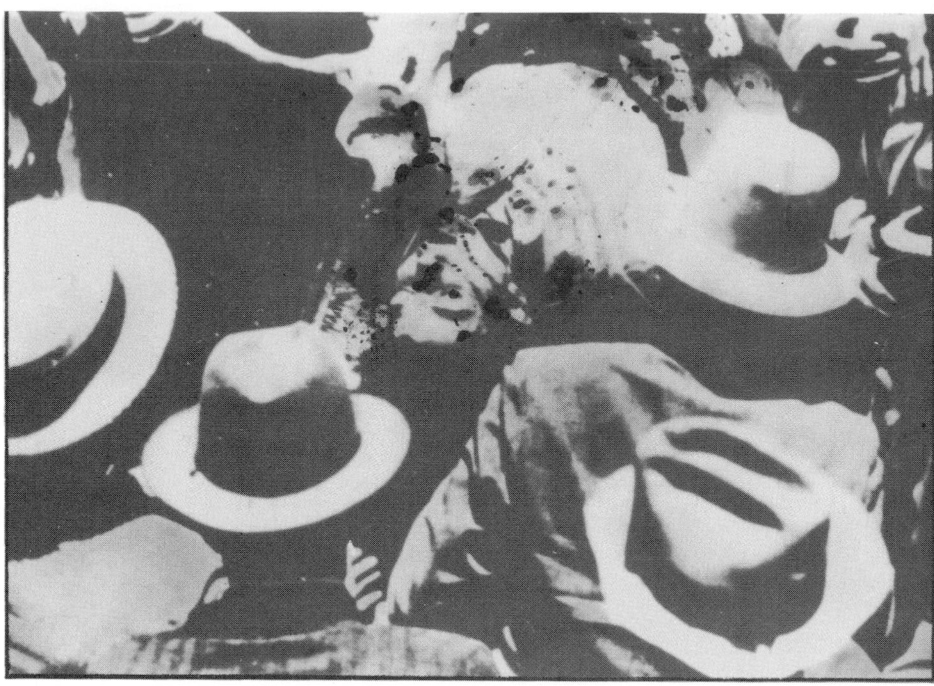

WET RAGS . . . That was how one of the officers who took part in the ambush described the dead bodies of Clyde (above) and Bonnie (below). It was the end that both knew awaited them and the beginning of the legend that was to come.

AP/Quartet

THE PETTICOAT PIRATE

Piracy was a man's game. Plunder, pillage and wholesale murder were not, even in the Caribbean, considered to be occupations for a woman. Unless you were sensual, passionate, a skilled fighter . . . and vicious.

Radio Times Hulton

AROUND THE candle-lit table, six pirate chiefs had come to a decision after a rum-soaked discussion which had lasted an hour. They had tried an agent named Collins, a man who sold their plunder for them but who, they believed, had subsequently betrayed one of their colleagues to the authorities. Five of the faces lit by the flickering candles were bearded and harsh; all five were turned on the sixth, that of a beautiful woman with tawny red hair.

"I agree," she said, "that in the interest of our safety Collins should die. Yet he is a gentleman, and should be accorded some consideration. I would not like him to be clubbed on the head and roughly dumped into the sea."

"Perhaps you'd like to kiss him to death," smirked one of the bearded men.

"Perhaps." Anne Bonny smiled. "Leave the execution to me."

That night she sought out Collins, a middle-aged, unattractive man, and blatantly invited him to bed with her. According to one account: "Anne removed certain garments and revealed her rich flesh, then lay on the bed, and Collins flung himself upon her in a frenzy. At the very point of love's climax, she held a pistol to his side and shot him dead." Anne laconically reported the "execution" to her colleagues the next day. "He died happy," she said. Sex and violence were part of Anne Bonny's life from the beginning. She was the illegitimate daughter of an Irish lawyer. William Cormac, who fled to Charleston, South Carolina, from his native Cork shortly after Anne's birth, taking her and her mother, and a servant girl named Peg Brennan, with him. The thriving sea-port proved ideal for a lawyer, and Cormac quickly made himself a comfortable fortune; little Anne was educated as a lady, but showed a tendency to tomboyishness at an early age.

Sexually aggressive

Her father's gamekeeper was an Indian named Charlie Fourfeathers, who took over her education where her French, music, and dancing teachers left off, so that by the time she was ten Anne could manage a musket and handle a clumsy flintlock—which fired an ounce ball—with the skill and accuracy of most men. Charlie also taught her to throw knives and hatchets, and later, in her career of piracy, she "swore in" her crew on an axe head rather than a Bible—an Indian habit picked up from Charlie. The only orthodox lessons she enjoyed were those given by her fencing teacher, and she added brilliance with a rapier to her other deadly accomplishments—a talent which was to save her life on more than one occasion.

In 1713, when Anne was thirteen, two important events took place; she met her first pirates, and she killed her first human being. At that time piracy was a crime, to most people, in name only; English trade and tax laws forced even "respectable" American colonists to trade with pirates and smugglers, and they were tolerated in much the same way as bootleggers or black marketeers were tolerated in the twentieth century.

Mansell

FEMINISM? There was certainly no discrimination against Anne Bonny (left). Even the formidable Blackbeard (opposite) 'recognized' her as a pirate.

Pirates even set up offices and warehouses on the waterfront in which to meet agents who bought their plunder, and much of William Cormac's business was conducted in such places. Anne was enthralled by their tales of adventure, but her behaviour was not enhanced by their influence; she had a quick and savage temper, and took to using obscenities which profoundly shocked her mother, who was by this time in delicate health.

In one of these rages, Anne stabbed her mother's maid, who had drawn a knife on her. Luckily for Anne the servant had a history of violence, and a coroner's court brought in a verdict of self-defence—but from that day on Anne became more wilful than ever.

By the time she was fifteen, she had grown to her full height, a tall girl with red-gold hair, flashing eyes, and handsome features. Her figure, too, had filled out, and she was shapely, if a little Junoesque; her breasts were described as being "of the size and strength of melons". Unlike most women of the day she was sexually aggressive and took lovers when she wanted them, rather than the other way about. Captain Paul Raynor, thirty years her senior, was one of them, and later wrote:

"She was a minx but a strapping one, with strength and vigour of mind as well as body. I could not hold her; nor do I believe could any man."

For all her aggression, however, she was capable of tenderness, usually aroused by weak men whom she mothered. The first such character to come into her life was a sickly seaman named James Bonny—an informer, pirate, and petty smuggler with an ingratiating manner. Although he lasted in her affections for only a very short time, Bonny must have had some charm, for Anne married him shortly after her sixteenth birthday; it was a fateful decision.

Wanted criminal

She had rowed violently with both her father and mother when she expressed her intention to marry Bonny. When news of the ceremony reached the Cormac household, the formerly robust Peg Brennan died of shock, and Cormac, who had been devoted to her, was wild with grief. Anne tried to talk to him, which led to another row. She then smashed the windows of her former home because her father had locked the door on her, and he called the militia. Anne was a wanted criminal for the first time in her life.

Mansell

F. Wilkinson

Mary Evans

Luckily for her she had many criminal friends, among them a small-time pirate and smuggler named Con Kesby. It was Kesby who suggested that Anne and her husband—with whom she was already growing disenchanted—should sail with him for New Providence, in the Bahamas. The place was a commune of pirates, thieves, whores and murderers where, said Kesby, the couple would be safe from the law. Bonny was horrified, but the idea appealed to Anne at once, and in the summer of 1716 she arrived at the "hellhole" with her reluctant husband.

She made a spectacular entry into the town, simultaneously impressing the inhabitants with her ruthlessness and establishing herself as their equal. On the way from the harbour, her path was blocked by a big, scar-faced man with one ear; he waved a mug of wine at her and demanded that she drink with him before he would let her past. Quite calmly, Anne drew a pistol from beneath her gown.

"I drink with whom I choose," she said, and blasted off the man's remaining ear. "Good God," she remarked, blowing the smoke from her weapon, "is that a head? I thought I was shooting the handle off a mug."

The crowd which had followed her, Kesby, and Bonny from the harbour roared with delight, and within hours her fame had spread throughout the island. Captain Henry Jennings, the uncrowned "king" of New Providence, took her under his wing and introduced her to his fellow captains—men such as the Falstaffian Benjamin Hornigold, the ferocious Sam Bellamy, and Captain Richard Turnley, a renegade "gentleman". Anne was immediately accepted by them as an equal.

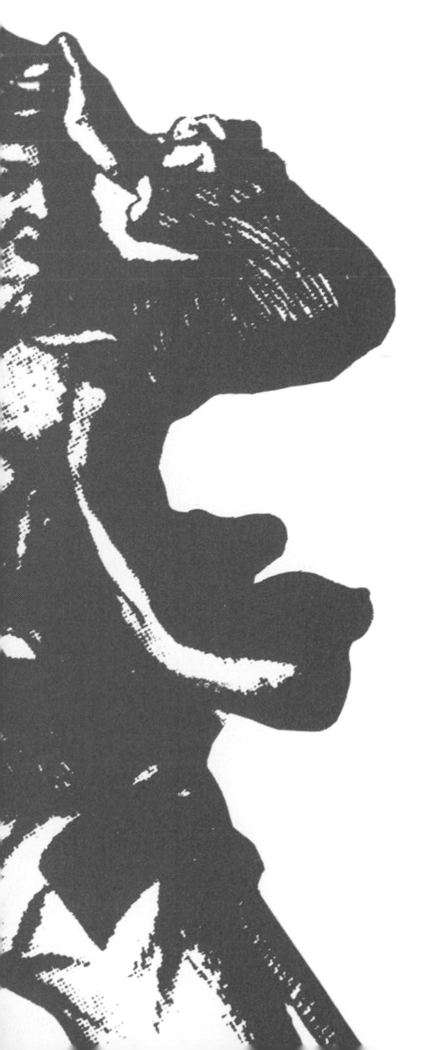

Willowy Frenchman

Although a bawdy and boisterous lot, the pirates of New Providence were not, with a few exceptions, inherently bad. Many of them—such as Jennings and Hornigold—had been officers in the British Royal Navy who had committed some breach of the rigorous laws of the time, and been forced to flee from punishment. Others had been official privateers, or "licenced" pirates, who had plundered enemy shipping on behalf of the Government before becoming tired of handing over their spoils. Their crews had taken to the buccaneering life for similar reasons; the existence of a sailor before the mast in the eighteenth century was at best a hard one, and more often than not brutally cruel.

"Far better," wrote one man, "to sail as pyrate and free, than to serve the Crown, when the noose or death in bloody battle is the ultimate end of both ways."

Often, when a pirate ship captured a prize, the crew of the ship taken would be invited to join the captors, and a considerable number of men grasped the opportunity. Life as a pirate was frequently short, but usually merry. Pirate captains were elected by free vote, and although they had supreme command at sea, ashore they moved among their men as equals. There were no floggings in pirate vessels—the usual punishment for disobedience being death at the hand of the captain. But most crews worked together smoothly. Prize money was shared more or less equally, and ashore, in the haven of New Providence, or in the pirate towns on Cuba and Hispaniola, drink, food, and women were plentiful.

Many pirates, curiously enough, were homosexuals—a fact which may account for the colourful outfits adopted by corsairs of the time. One of the best known was Captain Pierre Bousquet, alias Pierre Delvain, a close friend of Anne Bonny. Besides enjoying a highly successful career at sea—at one period under Anne's command—the willowy Frenchman also ran a coffee shop-cum-haberdashery and hair-dressing salon in New Providence. At sea he dressed in a close-fitting suit of black velvet set off with crisp white lace, and his ships sported crimson sails and a gaudily painted hull.

CHILDHOOD IN CHARLESTON was not exactly orthodox for the young Miss Bonny. The brash sea-port (opposite) was where she met her first pirates, and learned about their life style. The pistols (above) were said to be hers.

On at least one occasion, with typical homosexual humour, he flew an outsize pair of lady's bloomers from the mainmast when going into battle. Like most of his 'gay' colleagues, Bosquet had been forced by the restrictive laws of the period to take up his life of crime—for sodomy, whether on shore or at sea, was punishable by death.

Among this roustabout gang and their attendant retinue of pimps, whores, cutthroats, and beggars, Anne Bonny settled as to the manner born. Soon after arriving in New Providence she had realized that to survive she would need the support of a man much stronger than her weakling husband James. She settled for the wealthiest agent on the island, a man named Chidley Bayard, who dressed in the impeccable manner of a gentleman and spoke with the Cockney accent of his origins. Born Albert Backhouse, "Bayard" had served as a London shipping clerk in his youth, and after stealing money from his employers, and running away to New England, had put his knowledge to good use by setting up as a pirates' agent.

Cut to ribbons

When Anne met him she realized that, despite his unprepossessing appearance, his great house and grand life style were just what she wanted. For his part, Bayard lusted after the red-haired beauty from the moment he saw her. The only drawback was his current mistress—a tempestuous Spanish-Cuban named Maria Vargas, who was almost as striking in appearance as Anne, and who invariably went around armed with a cutlass. Maria saw that Anne had a potentially willing victim in Chidley Bayard, and decided to defend her position in the only way she knew.

The resulting duel—Maria armed with her cutlass, Anne wielding a slender rapier—took place in a tavern named "The House of Lords", and lasted for more than an hour. Despite a slight wound in the shoulder, Anne put her early fencing lessons to good account, and literally cut Maria to ribbons before killing her. That same day she moved into Bayard's mansion.

One of Bayard's principal "clients" was the infamous "Blackbeard"—Captain Edward Teach, a former officer in the Royal Navy of Queen Anne. Blackbeard was a keen student of psychological warfare; physically he was a giant, with the deafening voice common to most eighteenth-century naval officers used to hailing the topmast in a howling gale. To add

Radio Times Hulton

to his naturally intimidating appearance, he painted black circles around his eyes, braided his hair and beard in spikey plaits, and threaded long sulphur matches around the brim of his large floppy hat; at night he lit them, illuminating his features in a hellish glow.

Where most pirates of the time used small fast ships—sloops or brigs—Blackbeard commanded a large, forty-gun French-Guineaman, the sails and battle-flag dyed black. From its bowsprit invariably hung the mouldering head of the last unfortunate captain to cross him.

Despite his formidable reputation and appearance, Blackbeard was helpless in the hands of women. It was said of him that the "lowest whore could turn his heart with a tear", and naturally enough he fell madly under Anne Bonny's spell. There was a major barrier to the consummation of his passion. It was his proud boast that he had not taken a bath in fifteen years, except for being caught in the rain or accidentally falling overboard. "He stank," wrote a contemporary, "like a herd of hogs."

BONNY BATTLE . . . Anne was a beautiful and sensuous woman but she was also feared throughout the West Indies. Seen here, she leads a mid-ocean attack.

Anne, while expressing "mighty interest" in the famous character, was in the habit of bathing daily and could not bring herself to go to bed with him. However, she enjoyed his friendship, and he ogled her like a schoolboy; most important, he considered her worthy to take to sea with him. It was her apprenticeship in the trade, and soon she was leaving Chidley Bayard behind more and more for the thrill of battle.

Romantic rig-out

She took as deep a sexual delight in a clash of arms at sea as she did in a romp in bed, and during the following months enjoyed one lover after another. After Chidley Bayard, she seduced the dapper and gentlemanly Major Stede Bonnett, a poet and former Army officer who was, she said "the tenderest love of her life", and who was executed just before his friend Blackbeard in 1718. Next came Captain Charles Vane, one of the most skilled corsairs operating in the Straits of Florida; and finally John Rackham, otherwise known as "Calico Jack".

When at sea with Blackbeard or Bonnett, Anne wore a romantic rig-out, designed by her friend Pierre Bousquet, consisting of velvet trousers and scarlet silk blouse. Her long red hair was tied back with a black ribbon, and around her waist she wore a broad belt holding a pair of pistols. In battle she carried a feather-light rapier although—as her later saviour, Woodes Rogers, remarked—the sight of her bosom, as much as her flashing sword blade, must have unbalanced her adversaries.

Bold plan

Captain Woodes Rogers, an ex-privateer turned explorer and diplomat, came into Anne Bonny's life in July 1718 and was an important influence on her. Although her attitude to him at first was one of antagonism, he was to help save her from the gallows.

By the beginning of that year, the Caribbean pirates had become a positive nuisance to the government of George I in London. For a long time they were tolerated for their usefulness in harassing French and Spanish shipping. But some—such as Blackbeard, who had a personal grudge against Britain—had taken to attacking British and American trading vessels as well. Admiral Sir William Whetstone, commander of the British West Indies Fleet, was summoned to London to give advice on how best to curb the marauders.

Whetstone's daughter was married to Woodes Rogers—who had, incidentally, rescued Alexander Selkirk, the marooned Scottish seaman who was later immortalized by Daniel Defoe as "Robinson

Crusoe". Whetstone suggested that his son-in-law, who had operated as a privateer himself, probably understood the pirates as well as any. Rogers, recommended Whetstone, should be made Governor of the Bahamas, and sent to New Providence with authority to grant free pardons for all who would lay down their arms within a specified time.

It was a bold plan and ultimately it worked—although there was a small body of opposition to Rogers at first. This faction was led by Anne Bonny, Captain Vane, Pierre Bousquet, and Vane's quartermaster, "Calico Jack" Rackham—who by now was Anne's steady lover.

Pregnant

Captain Hornigold, Henry Jennings, and the majority of New Providence "society" welcomed the news of the pardon; all of them had realized that, between the cannonball, the noose, and the watery grave, a pirate could not expect to die in bed. But Captain Vane distrusted Rogers; Bousquet could not surrender because the pardon did not cover punishment for his known sexual leanings; and Anne and Jack Rackham had their own reasons for refusing to settle down.

Chidley Bayard was still a powerful man, and Rackham had stolen not only his mistress but, through burglary, a considerable amount of his ready money. There was the added complication that Anne was pregnant. Vane's sloop was made ready and, as Rogers sailed in on the night of July 26, the little vessel left the harbour of New Providence and set a course for Cuba—where at least two lawless refuges, those of Zagoa and Coxon's Hole, were open to them.

Only a few days later, when the ship put into port, she turned the crew against Vane and suggested an election, putting up Calico Jack for captain. Vane was voted out, took the news calmly, and put to sea in a longboat, with a handful of armed followers; soon he was flourishing again as a pirate.

The decision meant that, effectively, Anne Bonny was finally in command of her own ship; Calico Jack had taken to drink, and the crew knew that although he was captain in name, Anne was the ruling force behind him. She made a spirited start, for by November she had captured at least two lucrative prizes, and had almost accomplished the daring rescue of her old friend Stede Bonnett from his prison in Charleston. But Bonnett was hanged; "Blackbeard" Teach was captured and beheaded aboard his own ship; and, in New Providence, Rogers had won over most of the old pirate chiefs. On December 10, nine of them who reneged on their pardon agreement were hanged.

The free-booting days seemed to be over and when, in January 1719, Anne's premature baby girl died shortly after birth, she decided to return to New Providence. Ben Hornigold, who was again flying the British flag as a lieutenant of Governor Rogers, had sent her news that the free pardon would be extended for a year.

Her "retirement", however, was destined to last for only six months. James Bonny, her almost forgotten husband, had her and Rackham arrested on the then serious charge of adultery. Rogers, who liked Anne, let her off with a caution—apparently impressed by her glorious *dishabille* when she was dragged before him in her night-clothes. Later he wrote: "A more delectable doxy I have never seen—nor for that matter, a more brazen one."

But Anne was characteristically furious. If she could not live in peace, then she would go back to open war. Gathering her old crew, she first burned Bonny's newly acquired homestead and boatyard to the ground. Then she stole a sloop and escaped into the open sea. For almost a year she roamed the shipping lanes from Trinidad to Virginia, and it was at this period that she made her greatest name—not only among her contemporaries, but in the maritime annals of the world.

One of the crew members who joined her in New Providence was a young "man" named Mark Read—one of the 600 pirates pardoned under the Rogers' amnesty. After putting out to sea again under Anne Bonny's command, Read revealed to "his" captain that "he" wasn't in fact a man at all; the boyish-looking coxwain was a former Bristol barmaid named Mary Read. The knowledge that two women pirates were sailing under the same flag enhanced Anne's reputation.

ROUGH JUSTICE was meted out to a pirate who transgressed the ship's law. Blindfolded and bound to prevent him from swimming (below) he walks the plank.

Mary Evans

But she now had only a few months of her career left to run. In October, 1720, a Royal Navy sloop under Captain Charles Barnet set out from Jamaica and captured the *Queen Royal* almost without a fight. With the exception of Anne, Mary Read, and another sailor, Mary's lover Tom Deane, the crew were helplessly drunk. Almost simultaneously Vane was captured nearby, and on November 15, 1720, the buccaneers were brought to trial before Governor Lawes. It looked, finally, as if Anne Bonny would end as predicted, upon the gallows.

Three principal factors saved her. Michael Ratcliffe, who had been put ashore after his rescue and had no criminal charges to answer, got a lawyer for Anne. Governor Woodes Rogers, hearing the news, wrote a strong report to Lawes recommending mercy. And Anne herself produced a bombshell. Both she and Mary Read were pregnant—Anne by Ratcliffe, and Mary by Deane, who had been killed in the capture of her ship. Governor Lawes adjourned the trials of the two women, but carried on with the others. On November 28 Vane, Rackham, and six of their companions were hanged at Port Royal, Jamaica.

Happily married

On December 4, Mary Read died of cold in her cell, along with her unborn child. Anne was heartbroken, and public opinion began to swing towards leniency. To add impetus to Governor Lawes' deliberations, an echo of Anne's old days came in a letter from Captain Bartholomew Roberts—the most feared pirate of the day, who had never met her.

"If Anne Bonny is not instantly released," he threatened, "every port in Jamaica shall feel the thunder of my guns."

It was not a statement to be taken lightly. Ratcliffe pleaded again with Lawes, and finally the Governor, at a meeting with Ratcliffe and Anne on Christmas Eve, 1720, extracted a promise from them that they would leave the West Indies and cause him "no further embarrassment". A few weeks later the couple, happily married, landed at Norfolk, Virginia, and made their way with a waggon train into the interior of the newly-expanding continent.

Anne was twenty years old and already passing into history as one of the most notorious female criminals of all time. During the next few years she doubtless heard numerous tales of herself as the frontier moved slowly westward, but she never revealed her identity.

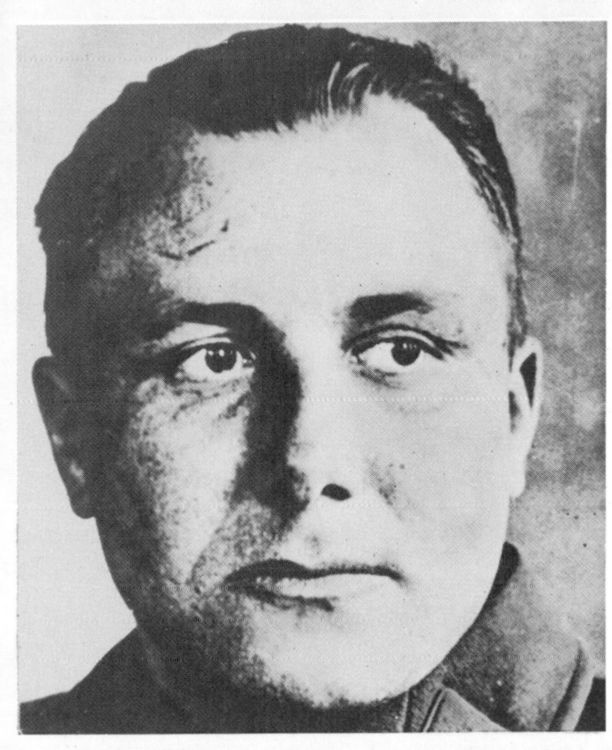

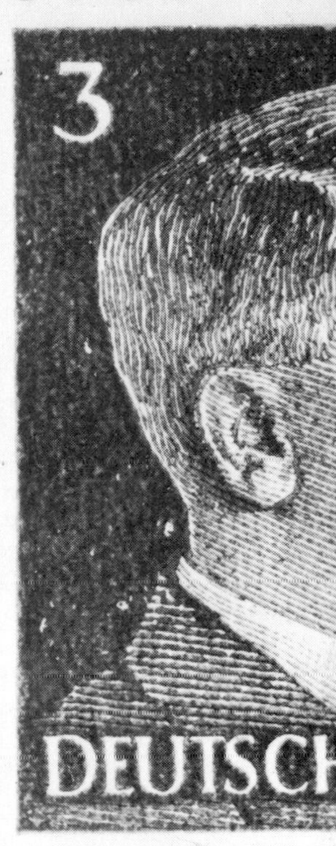

HITLER'S EVIL SPIRIT

Of all the ruthless and often sycophantic figures who made up the High Command of the Third Reich, Martin Bormann was undoubtedly the most unsavoury. He wormed his way to the top through rank obsequiousness and low cunning until his wealth, power and dementedness came second only to that of the Führer himself. Even his own colleagues envied and loathed him . . .

OF THE motley collection of henchmen who surrounded the German Nazi dictator, Adolf Hitler, none was quite so sinister as Martin Bormann, the party functionary who achieved the greatest power in the Third Reich after the Führer himself. Even his Nazi chieftain colleagues, none of whom displayed any great sensitivity about their fellow-men, called him "Hitler's evil spirit"; he was, indeed, the supreme political thug.

Two things appealed most to Bormann: power and money. And the Nazi hierarchy, wherein men lived the self-indulgent lives of medieval princes, satisfied both those ambitions – allowing him to exercise every whim of brutality and, at the same time, to provide himself with an income that was reputed to exceed £250,000 a year, and which soon turned him into a millionaire.

Martin Bormann was born in 1900, and in the unsettled Germany, writhing in its defeat in the First World War, he found a tailor-made place for himself in the fascist street-fighting groups. He was convicted of murder, sent to prison, and on his release he joined the budding Nazi party – accepting the primitive racial and strong-arm policies that Hitler proclaimed so hypnotically.

At first he served as a clerk in local party offices. But, by adopting a completely self-effacing subservience to his immediate bosses, he worked his way steadily to the top ranks of the Nazis. Then, with Hitler at last in power in Germany, he became secretary to the Führer's deputy, Rudolph Hess. He possessed infinite cunning and, on his way up, had impressed Hitler as the architect of a series of money-making projects.

One of his earliest successes was to set up a compulsory accident insurance scheme for all party members with the happy result, as Hitler himself later recalled, that "we took in far more money than we paid out, and the surplus was very useful for other party purposes". Bormann saw to it that one of those "purposes" was to top up the Führer's personal bank account, and this service did not go unnoticed.

After the Nazis had taken complete control of the state, all German stamps bore Hitler's picture; the ever-vigilant Bormann conceived the idea that his master should receive a small royalty on each reproduction. Totalled up from all the millions of stamps sold, the royalties added considerably to Hitler's income – and Bormann, having put himself in charge of the book-keeping, siphoned off comfortable bonuses for himself. Industrialists were "invited" to contribute to an Adolf Hitler Endowment Fund of German Industry; this, too, was a Bormann brain child.

Polite blackmail

Unlike some of the more flamboyant Nazi leaders, of whom Goering was the outstanding example, Bormann believed that his most certain approach to ultimate power was one of quiet stealth. He was careful to ensure that "grants" were made out of the endowment fund, and other revenue sources, to some of his prominent colleagues. This put them in his debt, and conferred upon himself power far greater than his actual party office warranted. It was partly this foxiness and polite blackmail which led even greedy Nazi comrades privately to detest the pudgy-faced Bormann, with his boxer-like frame which doubled up obsequiously in Hitler's presence.

For Bormann was also astute enough to observe that, behind his austere public image, Hitler was a foolishly vain man, who preferred sycophants to independently minded associates. So when Hitler gathered his admiring courtiers together, and lectured them for endless exhausting hours on his philosophy of world-dominance, Bormann would sit like a dutiful scholar, religiously noting down every demented thought.

Bormann's great leap forward in the Nazi empire came in 1941 when Rudolph Hess took off in a Luftwaffe fighter plane and flew to Britain on a wildly irrational peace mission. Hitler learned the incredible news at his mountain retreat in Berchtesgaden. His immediate thought was to turn to Bormann who, as always, was hovering nearby. "Bormann, come at once!" Hitler shrieked. "Get hold of Goering, Ribbentrop, Goebbels, and Himmler as quick as you can."

When the Nazi leaders arrived they learned that Bormann had been appointed Party Chancellor and was taking over Hess's duties. From that moment he assumed the role of Hitler's grey eminence, sharing his most intimate confidences and gradually, as the tide of war turned against Germany, emerging as one of the few Nazi chiefs who had ready access to Hitler.

Camera Press

Black Star

GOOD TIMES were to be had – not for one and all – just for Hitler, Eva his lover (above) and a few select Nazis who were honoured with an invitation to the Führer's "villa" (top). Life was rather different in the underground bunker in Berlin where the couple (right) were finally married with Bormann as witness.

Real power was coming his way, too. As Hitler became increasingly obsessed with the disasters of his attack upon the Soviet Union, Bormann began to formulate many of the bloodletting decrees that flowed out under the Führer's signature. The annihilation of the Jews, medical experiments on concentration camp prisoners, the persecution of the Church, and many of the other brutal and premeditated campaigns, bore the stamp of Bormann's dark mind. While Europe's familiar sound was the screaming of the tortured and dying, Bormann sat in his own quiet room thumbing through the account books of his personal fortune.

He allowed himself his occasional moments of freedom from the tedium of attending upon his master, and favoured a variety of women with his attentions. He justified this by the assertion that German women needed to breed more prolifically in order to help the nation replace the men being wiped out on the Eastern Front. One proposal which he had hoped to have accepted was that every member of the S.S. – the élite Nazi bullyboy corps – could have three wives.

Bormann, who was married to the daughter of the Nazi party's chief justice, and had sired seven children in wedlock, put his theory into practice by taking on several "unofficial" wives, and indulging in a cosy correspondence about them with his legal wife. To that wife he wrote on one occasion: "You thought M. must be a very unusual girl. No, sweetie, she is not an unusual girl, but I am an incredible rascal. I fell madly in love with her and took her despite her protests."

Frau Bormann, entering fully into the spirit of her husband's patriotic mode of life, replied: "You must see that she gets a child in a year and that next year I must have one so that you will always have one wife who feels up to it."

Greedy struggle

But Bormann's service to the Third Reich by helping to raise its birthrate did not for one moment deflect him from the major ambition of his life: to make himself as powerful as Hitler. Against all odds – and in competition with such Nazi luminaries as Goering and Himmler, who were far better known to the public – he succeeded. He had so far achieved the right to sign instructions on behalf of the Führer so that when, in April 1943, he drew up a memorandum appointing himself "Secretary to the Führer", Hitler signed it without giving it a second thought. To him it was just another title.

But the assumption by the other Nazi bosses was, as Bormann had intended, that the "secretary" could now take official action, independently, and that his decrees would have to be obeyed. Very soon, few of the top Nazi brass were able to transmit proposals on domestic policy directly to Hitler. These had first to be vetted by Bormann. If there were any that he thought might add to the power of his party rivals, he rejected them in the Führer's name. Whenever he felt that Hitler was not exercising sufficient vigour in the terror campaigns against the Jews and other "undesirables", he personally issued his own, harsher orders.

From time to time some of the Nazi leaders who particularly hated Bormann – including the armaments minister, Albert Speer – tried to encourage Goering to use his influence with Hitler to break the "secretary's" power. But the wily

Keystone

Camera Press

Keystone

HITLER'S RIGHT HAND . . . Bormann is captured (left) conversing with his chief. His obsequious pose sums up perfectly the relationship between them.

Camera Press

Bormann countered those moves by making Goering a gift of six million marks from the Adolf Hitler industrial fund.

Bormann understood the weaknesses of Hitler's courtiers: it was in that understanding, and the use he made of it, that so much of his strength lay.

The plotting among individuals, the personal rivalries, the greedy struggle for the remnants of power, continued into the twilight of Hitler's empire—when the Russian armies were hammering at the door of Berlin, and the Americans and British were sweeping onwards in the west. But, as ever, Bormann stayed close to his master's side, and followed Hitler to his last hideaway in the bunker beneath the Berlin chancellery.

There, in that fetid, underground cavern, shaken continuously by the Soviet shells raining upon the capital, the oily Bormann hovered like a dark shadow, his mind already beginning to concentrate on the bizarre possibilities of a new lease of supremacy when death removed Hitler. The Führer had only three unswerving allies still left: little Goebbels, his sinister deviser of Nazi propaganda, his mistress Eva Braun, and Bormann. Goering and the S.S. leader, Heinrich Himmler—whose former prestige he had created, and in whom he had once had so much faith—had been found guilty of treason for secret attempts to negotiate with the enemy, and expelled from the party.

Bormann had played a direct, personal role in Goering's downfall from the moment, on April 23, 1945, when a telegram from the once-proud head of Germany's air force reached the Führerbunker. "My Führer!" it read. "In view of your decision to remain at your post in the fortress of Berlin, do you agree that I take over, at once, the total leadership of the Reich, with freedom of action at home and abroad as your deputy?

"If no reply is received by 10 o'clock

tonight, I shall take it for granted that you have lost your freedom of action . . . and shall act for the best interests of our country and our people. You know what I feel for you in this gravest hour of my life. Words fail me to express myself. May God protect you and speed you quickly here in spite of all. Your loyal, Hermann Goering."

At first Hitler – who was so shattered by the events of the war that he had aged visibly, and could not control the trembling of his body – found it difficult to realize that his "dear Hermann" was already writing him off. But it was Bormann who was quick to point out the deeper implications of the telegram. "You will notice, my Führer," he stated, "that Goering demands a reply by 10 o'clock. He dares to issue an ultimatum to you! He wishes to usurp your power as leader of the German people!"

Hitler flew into a rage and screamed: "I've known it all along. I know that Goering is lazy. He let the air force go to pot. He was corrupt. His example created corruption in our state. Besides, he's been a drug addict for years. I've known it all along." Bormann began to urge again, this time for death. Goering, he advised, should pay the supreme penalty. But for once Hitler displayed an unfamiliar streak of mercy. He ordered Bormann to telegraph to Goering, in Obersalzburg, telling him that the punishment for high treason was death, but that his life would be spared if he immediately resigned from all state and party offices. Bormann duly despatched the message, but, privately, telegrammed the Obersalzburg S.S. leaders to arrest Goering and his staff.

Half an hour later a reply to Hitler's message was received from Goering stating that he would make a public announcement that he had suffered a severe heart attack and was abdicating all his powers. For whatever real value it might have – at a time when Germany was falling like a rotten oak – it was the moment of supreme triumph for Bormann. He was plunged into a variety of half-witted masquerades that marked Hitler's ludicrous final hours. With Goebbels he acted as a witness at the Führer's marriage in the bunker to Eva Braun on April 29, and toasted the "happy couple"

Bacchanalian litter

Hitler had already announced that he and Eva Braun would commit suicide, and the loyal Goebbels had agreed that he and his wife would also end their lives after poisoning their six children. But Bormann had no intention of joining in these Valkyrian rites. As soon as there was no longer a Führer to serve, he was determined to save his own skin and make his way towards whatever life his personal fortune might offer.

Keystone

SATISFYING . . . but hardly edifying. Hitler and Eva (above) feasted regally on the fruits of power while Jewish prisoners (left) fed on nothing but hope.

At around 3.30 p.m. on April 30, Hitler and Eva Braun carried out their suicide pact. Martin Bormann was one of the four men who wrapped the bodies in blankets, and carried them up the 39 steps to the armoured door of the bunker and out into the chancellery garden. Petrol was poured over them and ignited in one of history's most welcome funeral pyres.

A kind of hysteria gripped most of the hangers-on left in the bunker, as though they were relieved to be free at last of their tyrannical lord. Some hastily changed out of their uniforms into civilian escape clothes amid falsely shrill laughter and empty banter. Two generals sat down to drain all the bottles of wines and spirits they could lay their hands upon, and then shot themselves with their own pistols – the shattered heads crashing forward on to the table among the bacchanalian litter.

But still Bormann's mind slithered on in its serpentine way. His first move was to send a telegram to the navy chief, Grand Admiral Doenitz: "In place of the former Reich-Marshal Goering, the Führer appoints you, Herr Grand Admiral, as his successor. You will immediately take all such measures as the situation requires. – Bormann."

The telegram made no mention of the fact that Hitler was already dead – the reason probably being that Bormann hoped to escape and personally take the news to Doenitz. In that event he might be ready to lay claim, on the spot, to power in whatever post-Nazi regime would accept him. But Goebbels, unwavering in his plans to kill himself and his family, had no further intrigues to pursue. The following day he sent his own telegram to Doenitz announcing the Führer's death. "Bormann," he added, "intends to go to you today and inform you of the situation."

It was then that Bormann entered the realms of mystery which have fascinated countless investigators ever since. He called together the various minor party officials, soldiers and women secretaries left in the bunker and appointed himself commander of a mass escape from the Russians – who were now swarming above ground in the area.

Last testament

This, he told the officials, was what they would do: they would form into small parties and make their way through a series of tunnels under the chancellery to the underground railway station in the nearby Wilhelmsplatz. From there they would walk along the railway tracks a short distance eastwards, and come to the surface through the Friedrichstrasse underground station. Once in the open, they would pass through the remnants of the German forces staging a last-ditch defence against the Russians, and try to get away to Schleswig-Holstein, in northern Germany, where Admiral Doenitz had his headquarters.

At about 10 in the evening of May 1 the escapers began to move out of the bunker, one by one. Bormann was in a group with four other men, including the Hitler Youth leader, Artur Axmann, Hitler's doctor, Stumpfegger, and Hitler's personal driver, Kempka. In his pocket Bormann carried a copy of the Führer's last testament – a polemic in which the dead dictator had attempted to justify the war and make a final farewell attack on the Jews.

Bormann's group succeeded in reaching the Friedrichstrasse station without difficulty but when they emerged into the open they found the night air filled with the hail of bursting Russian shells and bullets. Cautiously, they crept forward, throwing themselves flat every few yards as shells screamed over them. After a long struggle they reached the banks of the river Spree, which bisects Berlin, and its Weidendammer Bridge.

What happened to Bormann from then on is a matter of speculation and conflicting eye-witness accounts. At the Nuremberg war crimes tribunal, Kempka, the chauffeur, declared: "German tanks began to move across the bridge, following the lead tank. Bormann walked behind the lead tank and this was hit and exploded. Where Bormann had stood there was a darting flame."

Dozen cases

But the Youth leader, Axmann, later reported: "The German Tiger tank, which carried a lot of ammunition, blew up. . . . There were several men there, including Bormann, but they were all unhurt." Then, he said, the party made its way back to the Friedrichstrasse station, and from there crossed the Spree by a railway bridge. Bormann and Dr. Stumpfegger then went on alone, with Axmann and the others following a few minutes later.

Axmann described what happened next: "Near the bridge, as we came up, we found two men lying on the ground. We knelt down next to them. Perhaps we could help them. They were Martin Bormann and Dr. Stumpfegger. An error is impossible. Their faces were visible. They were lying on their backs, arms and legs spread out, I touched Bormann. No reaction. I bent over him. No breath. I saw no wounds or blood. The shooting continued. We had to go on."

There were other eye-witness accounts, and after the battle of Berlin had ended, Bormann's diary was found—lying on the ground according to some reports, and in a dead man's pocket according to others. But this was not necessarily proof that the dead man was Bormann, for, as Dr. Simon Weisenthal—the famous and relentless hunter of Nazi criminals—said: "I could mention a dozen cases in which prominent Nazis put their own identity papers into the pockets of dead men, hoping that this would prove that they, the prominent Nazis, were dead."

But no one, it seemed, could produce sufficient evidence to convince the Allied authorities, and the subsequent post-war German governments, that Bormann had died in that attempted flight from Berlin. In view of the lack of absolute proof, the Nuremberg war crimes tribunal assumed that Bormann was still alive and sentenced him to death, *in absentia,* along with others who had been his leading comrades.

But, as the world slowly recovered from the Nazi convulsion, the game of I-spy-Bormann provided newspapers and magazines with millions of exciting words and an unending crop of apparently plausible accounts of the man having been seen in many countries—but mainly in South American states. It was known that some lesser Nazi lights had made their way to such refuges, and it seemed logical that Bormann would be among them.

Remote haven

It was thought that he had salted much of his fortune away, under assumed names, in South American and Swiss banks. Therefore, if he *had* escaped as Germany collapsed, he could be living royally in a distant haven.

He was reported as living under the "new" name of José Perez in Argentina, and one man claimed to have been a neighbour of his for 10 years in a riverside colony of Nazi survivors. The colony was said to be known under the German title *Kolonie 555*—and 555 had been Bormann's number as a member of the SS.

One man, among several who came under suspicion, was a Juan Falero Martinez, arrested by police in Guatemala in 1967. His fingerprints were sent to the

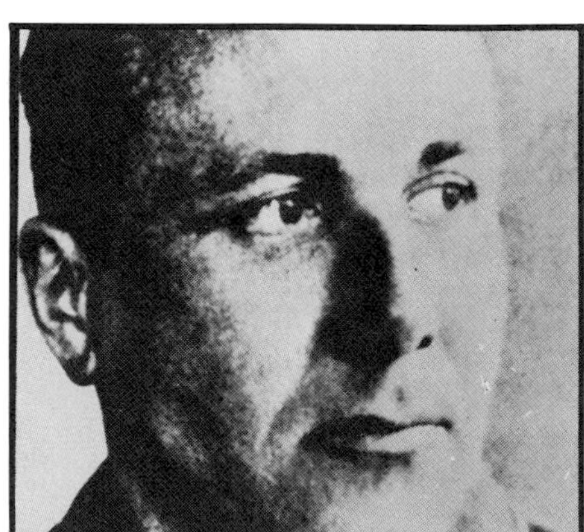

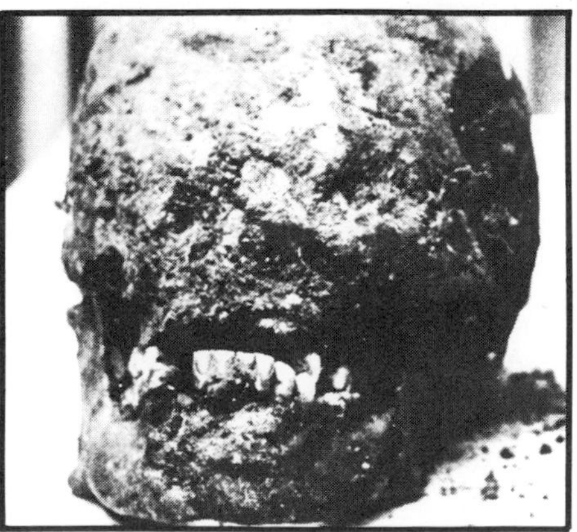

BORMANN'S SKULL? Experts seem satisfied that the notorious Nazi did die while attempting to escape from Berlin.

Both Keystone

Both Camera Press

SHATTERED and blazing furiously, Berlin suffers (left and above) the dying agonies of the war. The city was devastated in the Allies' final push.

West German Federal Investigation Office and compared with Bormann's own prints – but they failed to match. An Israeli investigator declared there was "no doubt" that Bormann had lived in the Argentine colony, at least for a time, and in 1973 British and American newspapers published the most categorical of all the I-saw-Bormann stories.

However in the same year a skeleton discovered in Berlin was examined by the then West German authorities, who declared themselves satisfied that it was that of Hitler's deputy, and the file was closed.

The mystery of Martin Bormann's disappearance continues to make headlines to this day. In 1993, fresh doubt was cast on the German conclusions by newly discovered secret files from Paraguay. *Noticias*, a leading Paraguay newspaper, printed photocopies of what it claimed was a 1961 report prepared by an Interior Ministry agent, Pedro Prokopchuk. The report from police files stated that Bormann entered the country in 1956 and died of stomach cancer on February 15 1959 and was buried in Hohenau, a small town 220 miles south of Asunción, the capital.

CRIME FILE

EICHMANN

IT WAS just the end of another working day for clerical supervisor Ricardo Klement. He left his office at the Mercedes-Benz plant near Buenos Aires, attended a staff meeting for an hour, and then caught the yellow and green workers' bus into the city. As he did so, an attractive olive-skinned girl walked briskly from the main factory gate and over to a pay telephone. She dialled a number, then said crisply, "He's on his way!"

In the bus Klement – mild-looking, balding, with prominent ears – relaxed contentedly. Soon he would be home where only his wife, Veronika, knew who he really was and what his major life's work had been. That he was Adolf Eichmann, the man responsible for the death of six million Jews in the gas chambers and furnaces of Dachau, Auschwitz, and Belsen.

For fifteen years, since the end of the Second World War, he had been sought by the police of the world. Always he had avoided exposure and capture. Then, in 1959, a team of top Israeli intelligence agents had launched Operation Eichmann, and had traced his progress across Europe to South America and the Argentine. The girl who made the phone call was one of the operatives. So was the man dressed in workman's overalls who sat behind him in the bus. So were the men in the two cars trailing the yellow-and-green vehicle in the direction of Liniares Avenue, Buenos Aires, on Wednesday, May 11, 1960.

There "Klement" left the bus and glanced up at the overcast sky. It had been dull and drizzling for most of the day, but the rain had stopped now. There was time to buy some cigarettes before catching the next bus which took him to the suburb of San Fernando, and his crude concrete house on Calle Garibaldi. The 54-year-old former Nazi was proud of the home which he had built with the help of two of his growing sons. There was a small chicken farm attached to it, which provided him and his family with delicious fresh eggs. They ate especially well on Sundays, when "Ricardo" would play

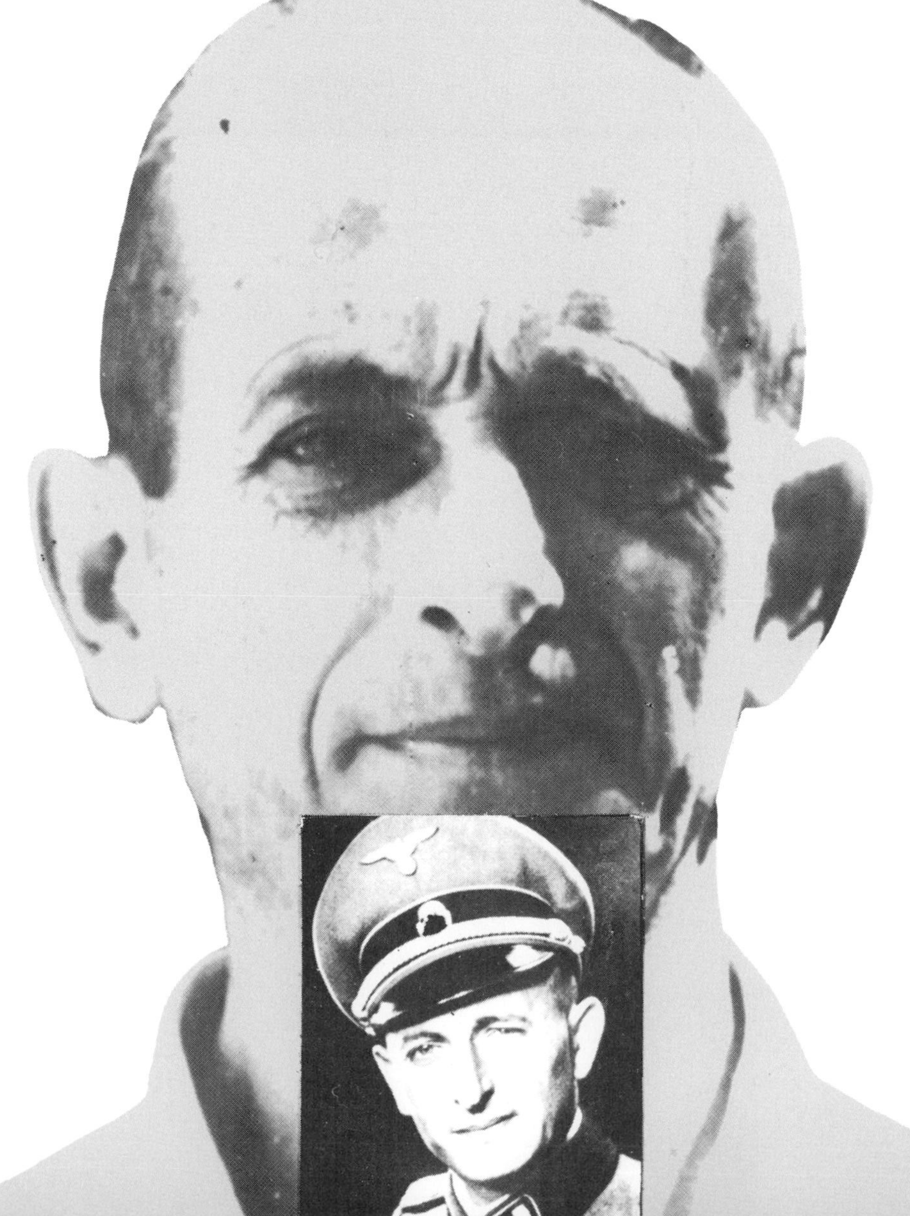

CAPTIVE KILLER Karl Adolph Eichmann stares stonily into the camera from a prison "somewhere in Israel". (Inset) Eichmann in Nazi uniform – the S.S. officer who was responsible for the deaths of over six million Jews in the gas chambers and furnaces of Dachau, Auschwitz and the other infamous death camps of the Third Reich.

Popperfoto

his violin while Veronika was busy in the kitchen.

Leaving the tobacconist's, "Klement" wandered back to the bus stop. There was nothing about the street scene to alarm or disturb him. A few housewives chatting about the price of groceries. The usual loiterer or two. A number of workers—as ordinary-seeming and inconspicuous as himself—on their way home to dutiful wives, hot meals, and noisy children. Then the black sedan came in view, cruising along the gutter like a prowl car. It drew level with him and only then, as the car stopped, did Adolf Eichmann feel that his hour may have come; that the long pursuit of him was over.

The nearside door of the sedan opened, and four men jumped out and grabbed him. Too startled to try to run or put up any resistance, "Klement" spoke to his captors in Spanish. "Who are you? What do you want?" he asked. The answer came in German: "Good evening, *Herr Obersturmbannführer*!" With that, Eichmann was bundled into the car, the door slammed closed, and the driver nosed cautiously off into the city, making sure he obeyed the speed limit and the traffic code. A blow over the head had rendered the Jew-killer unconscious, and he had no knowledge of being eased through the packed main streets, past the city centre, and on to a secluded villa in a quiet suburb.

Held by the armpits, he was hustled into the house and taken upstairs to a tiny, low-ceilinged bedroom. He was laid on the narrow bed and, as he came-to, told to undress. He did so fearfully, gazing with apprehension at the grim-faced men who surrounded him, the cheap, sparse furnishings, the stains and cracks that disfigured the walls. Bare from the waist up, he was ordered to raise his left arm. The men leant forward and peered at the scar which Eichmann had kept hidden from his friends and colleagues. They looked at each other and nodded their heads in agreement: the tattoo mark that was the "stamp" of every SS commander had been removed.

An SS cap was then put on the prisoner's head, and the effect was compared with a photograph taken of Eichmann at the time when he had successfully "disposed of" some 450,000 Austrian Jews. Again the men nodded silently. Later, to clinch the identification, a doctor entered the room holding two X-ray plates. With skilled, knowing fingers he felt Eichmann's skull and collarbone. "There are fractures here," he said matter-of-factly. "They match the breaks shown on the X-rays."

The leader of the captors then turned coldly to the man half-naked and trembling on the bed. "You are Karl Adolf Eichmann," he intoned. "We arrest you and charge you with committing crimes against the Jewish people. What we must now decide is whether we assassinate you out of hand, or take you back to Israel to stand trial. Much of our decision depends upon you. If you cooperate, and sign a full confession, we shall spare your life and let the law deal with you as it will."

Eichmann looked up hopefully. More than 15 years had gone by since most of his crimes had taken place – when the millions of men, women and children had been shot, gassed, tortured, experimented upon, and burned. Surely the present generation of Jews would forgive him his old sins. Besides, he had only been following orders. If he had failed to fill the chambers and furnaces, then his own life would have been forfeited. People would appreciate that, understand, and forgive. "All right," he agreed. "I'll sign."

For the next few days Eichmann was kept hidden in the house. No one in Buenos Aires—not even his wife—was told what had happened to him. The statement containing his confession (". . . I will do everything possible to give an explanation of the facts of my last years of service in Germany, in order that a true picture of the facts will be described for the coming generation . . .") was made known to the authorities in Tel Aviv—where Prime Minister David Ben-Gurion eagerly awaited news of Operation Eichmann. Then at midnight on May 20, during celebrations of the 150th anniversary of the deposition of the Viceroy, Eichmann was driven to Buenos Aires airport and smuggled aboard an El Al turbo jet bound for Israel.

The flight between Tel Aviv and the Argentine had been inaugurated only two days before—ostensibly to meet the demands of Israeli businessmen. The four-engined Bristol Britannia had been at the airport for less than seven hours when it took off again, bearing Eichmann to the "fair and unbiased" trial he had been promised. Probably only to his surprise, his defence of "orders are orders" did not impress the court.

He was found guilty as charged and was hanged at Israel's Ramle Prison on May 31, 1962. By his standards it was a humane death.

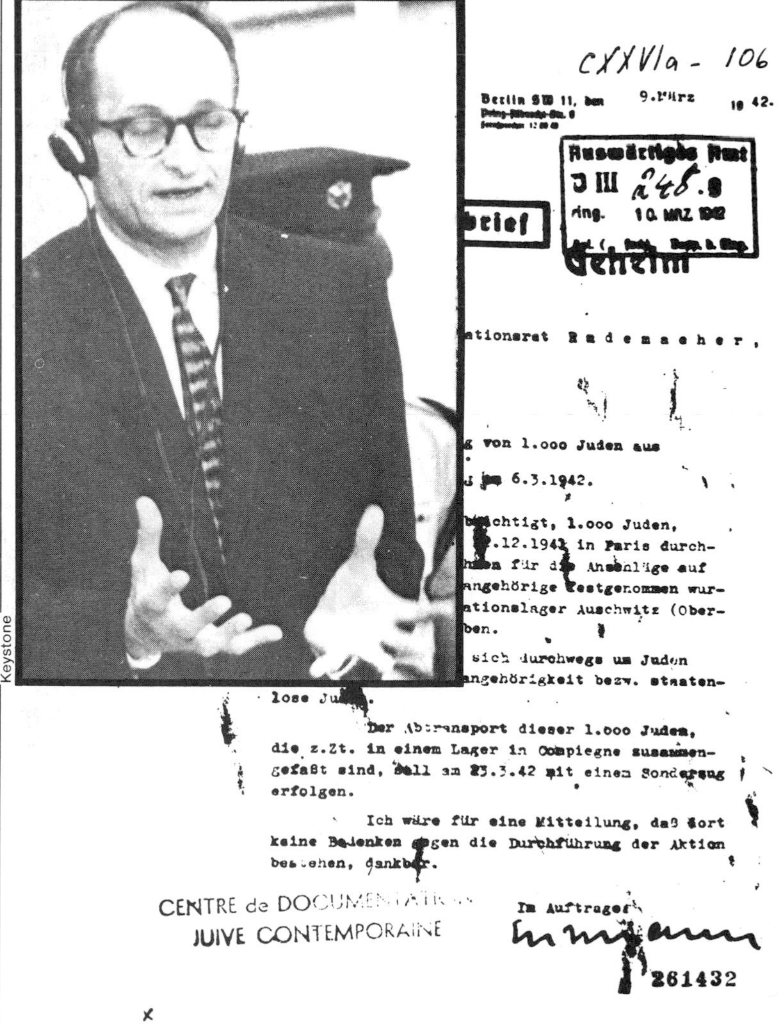

CXXVIa - 106

Berlin SW 11, den 9.März 1942.

Auswärtiges Amt
D III 248.g
Eing. 10. MÄRZ 1942

...brief

Geheim

...ationsrat Rademacher,

...g von 1.000 Juden aus

... am 6.3.1942.

...chtigt, 1.000 Juden,
....12.1941 in Paris durch-
...n für die Anschläge auf
...angehörige festgenommen wur-
...ationslager Auschwitz (Ober-
...ben.

... sich durchwegs um Juden
...angehörigkeit bezw. staaten-
lose Juden.

Der Abtransport dieser 1.000 Juden, die z.Zt. in einem Lager in Compiegne zusammengefaßt sind, soll am 23.3.42 mit einem Sonderzug erfolgen.

Ich wäre für eine Mitteilung, daß dort keine Bedenken gegen die Durchführung der Aktion bestehen, dankbar.

CENTRE de DOCUMENTATION JUIVE CONTEMPORAINE

Im Auftrage:
Eichmann

261432

Keystone

Popperfoto

BULLET-PROOF EVIDENCE . . . Eichmann (inset) in court, shielded by his "glass box". Right, document signed by Eichmann authorizing deportation of Jews.

THE WAKING NIGHTMARE

When he woke up, the face of a girl was etched vividly on his mind. Something had happened during the night. A body had to be disposed of. Three days later, they found her . . . in a field, near Lovers' Lane.

Essex Chronicle

NEW Year's Eve. Outside, people were going to parties. There was the sound of singing and distant laughter. Staff-Sergeant Willis Eugene Boshears was lonely. His wife was away with their three children at the home of her parents. He should have been with them. In fact, he would have been with them if his leave had not been cancelled at the last minute. He needed a drink. Just a little vodka at first. Only a glass or two. Then just a little more....

Late the following morning he awoke in his flat at Dunmow, Essex, England, near the Wethersfield American Air Force base, with a hangover and the pervading memory of a nightmare. The face of a dead girl was etched vividly on his mind, and there was a confused connection between her and the spare bedroom. He went into the next room and there, neatly laid on the floor by the bed, was the corpse of a beautiful girl. She had been strangled.

For two days, in a torment of panic and bewilderment, he kept the body in his flat. Dimly at first, and then more clearly, he began to remember how he had hacked off her lovely, long brown hair in a pathetic attempt to disguise her. Then eventually he dumped her in a ditch six miles away. Those events led to one of the most remarkable murder cases in British legal history. They also led to the crew-cut Boshears—known as Little Mac because of his smallness—being recognized as a Sleep-Walking Slayer.

Boshears, at the age of 29, was an American hero. He had three rows of medals and there were 49 combat missions in Korea to his credit. When the American authorities realized he was to face a murder charge they asked Britain to hand him over—so that he could be tried at a court martial. However, the Director of Public Prosecutions refused. In February, 1961, Boshears appeared at the assize court in Chelmsford, England—pleading not guilty to murder before a jury of 11 men and a woman.

Essex Chronicle

THE KOREAN-WAR HERO . . . whose fate was snatched from the United States by the arm of Britain's law.

Quiet and respectable

His duties with the 20th Field Maintenance Squadron were as a jet-engine fitter, and he had eight months to serve before completing his second three-year tour of duty in Britain. He and his Scots wife, Jean, were a happily married couple whose youngest child, a boy called George, was born two weeks before Christmas, 1960. Jean had gone to her parents' pre-fab home at Ayr, Scotland, with the two older children for the birth of George and had stayed on there to recuperate. So, on the last day of December, Boshears, who came from Michigan, was alone in their flat. He got up shortly after 6 a.m. and went to the Wethersfield base to draw his pay.

He stayed there for about five hours and had a meal at the N.C.O.s' club. He had just had a number of teeth out so he ate only one egg. Before leaving the base he had a few drinks and then bought a 40 oz. bottle of vodka to take home. But, without the family around him, the flat seemed intolerably empty. He began to feel bored and restless and he thought of all the people outside enjoying themselves. So he decided to join the noisy, cheerful crowds in the local pubs.

At about the same time a 20-year-old girl called Jean Constable was also on her way to the pubs to seek lively company. She worked in a nearby plastics factory and had a reputation as a good-time girl who "liked G.I.s". One of her favourite evening places was the Wethersfield base where she often went dancing and, according to one of her closest girlfriends, she "was always asking people to give her lifts there".

Despite this, she felt that her parents, a quiet and respectable couple, might not altogether approve so she often kept her activities a secret from them. They could hardly fail to know that she often spent complete nights away from their neat rented house in Halstead, Essex. But they assumed she was safely at the home of a girl friend.

As she left the house on New Year's Eve, wearing the black-and-white fur coat of which she was so proud, she told her parents she was going to a party in London with some girl friends—but did not mention the names of those friends. Mr. and Mrs. Constable never saw their daughter alive again.

Meanwhile, Jean tried, as she had done so often before, to find an American serviceman who would take her to the base. One of them later told the police: "She asked several of us but most of the guys had girls with them already."

In the Nags Head public house at Braintree, after failing with the Americans, she "picked-up" a 20-year-old English apprentice engineer called David Sault. They shared a few drinks before moving on to the Bell Hotel. Boshears was in the bar at the Bell, quietly drinking on his own. He was delighted when Jean and Sault arrived, for he had known her casually for some three months, and it was good to see a familiar face.

Jiving to a jukebox

"Hey! It's great to see you!" he cried. "Come and have a drink!" Jean gladly accepted the invitation—which was the first step towards her death. "I'd love a vodka and tonic," she replied, and introduced Sault to the sergeant. So the three of them had a lively evening, drinking round after round of vodka and jiving to jukebox records. When it was time for the pub to close, Boshears suggested that they should return to his flat for more drinking and dancing.

There they played records so loudly that the people living above and below complained. But still the party went on. Boshears, after dancing with Jean, left the sitting-room for a while and Sault had intercourse with her on a rug. He claimed afterwards that she had made the initial advances. Then Boshears returned and, after a few more drinks, he offered—according to Sault—to show them round.

All three went into a bedroom where, once again, Boshears left them alone. "We were left together in the bedroom and we had intercourse again on the bed," said Sault. Boshears, he added, "more or less disturbed" them, and shortly after midnight he asked the couple if they were planning to stay the night. They said that they were, and Boshears placed a mattress and some blankets in front of the sitting-room fire. The trio sat by the fire for a

Press Association

Both AP

while. Then Jean undressed in front of both men before curling herself up in blankets and going to sleep.

Boshears lay on blankets by the side of the mattress and, a few minutes later, Sault undressed and settled down on the mattress beside Jean. After a while he changed his mind, decided to go home, and got dressed. The girl was then "drowsy and pretty well asleep". But Boshears, who told Sault where to get a taxi, was – according to Sault – "sober as far as I could say". So Sault left the flat somewhere between 12.30 and 1 a.m. Later, at around 1 a.m., Mrs. Clara Miller, wife of a United States Air Force sergeant, in the flat above, heard a girl crying.

"It was like sobbing and I heard something which sounded like either 'You love me' or 'You don't love me', but it was muffled as though she was holding a handkerchief," she said.

Experts later believed that it was more likely that the indistinct words heard by Mrs. Miller carried a far more sinister message. "You're hurting me", perhaps. Or even: "You're choking me." During the day Mrs. Miller challenged Boshears about the crying, but he made no reply.

Boshears' own memory of the evening was not as clear as Sault's. He remembered showing Sault and the girl to the main bedroom and placing a mattress on the floor for himself. There was nothing particularly unusual in that as he had put people up in that manner before. Then he remembered Jean falling asleep on the mattress where she had been sitting.

"The other fellow and I had a couple more drinks and I must have fell asleep – not fell asleep but passed out," he said. "The next thing I remember was the fellow waking me up and asking me where he could get a taxi."

Lay down beside her

When Sault had gone Boshears lay down on the edge of the mattress. "Jean was asleep and I lay down beside her," he said. "The next thing I remember was something scratching and pulling at my mouth. I opened my eyes and Jean was lying there under me and I had my hands round her throat. She was dead then. That sort of sobered me up. I got scared and did not know what to do."

So, his brain stupefied by terror and by alcohol, he panicked. He had to disguise her. He had to make sure that no one could recognize her. Her hair! Yes, that was it! He had heard people say what lovely hair she had – that would make her easy to identify.

So he hacked off her hair until it was almost as crew-cut as his own, and then he burned it. The body had to be cleaned. Yes, that was the next move. He picked up the dead girl and carried her into the bathroom. He placed the body in the bath and thoroughly washed it. The next thing was to dress her – or partially dress her – and place her on the floor of the spare bedroom.

Then, after tidying the sitting-room, he returned to the mattress and collapsed into sleep. When he awoke, suffering from a severe hangover, he had the strange half-memory of something having happened during the night . . . something – very unpleasant . . . and yet . . .

"I decided that it had been a dream, but I went to check and I saw clothes in the bathroom and Jean in the spare bedroom," he said "I wanted to go to the police but I was scared. I figured out how to get rid of the body and I washed the sheets and blankets."

Her fur coat was too distinctive. Too many people—particularly men at the base—could hardly fail to recognize it. It had to be destroyed. He burned the coat. Then, continuing his pathetic attempt to hide his crime, he stripped Jean of her watch and ring and disposed of her handbag. But the body was still there. For two days, dreading the approaching return of his wife and children, he lived with it—puzzling how to get rid of it in safety.

That must be a Yank

Then one evening, shortly before midnight, he wrapped up the body in some of his own heavy winter clothing, carried it downstairs over his shoulder, and placed it in the back of his car. He drove through the night until he came to a lonely country spot, about five miles from his base, which was known locally as "Lovers' Lay-by". There, four yards inside a field, he pitched Jean head-first into a ditch which was partly screened by a wild rose bush. A lorry driver called Sidney Ambrose found her there on January 3 and, in view of Jean's friendships with servicemen, the American Air Force police were asked to help the team of British detectives.

A murder headquarters was set up at the Wethersfield base, and around-the-clock interrogation of scores of servicemen began. The following evening Boshears was detained and taken to Braintree police station by Chief Detective-Superintendent Ernest Barkway, and Chief Inspector Harry Burden There he was charged with murder. Strangely enough, his wife Jean saw him being arrested, while watching television—but did not realize it was him.

THE WIFE WHO WENT HOME for the Christmas holidays. A wedding-day smile is transformed into stunned horror . . . "My head spun. I screamed. I collapsed." And the man whose testimony was vital to the defence . . . David Sault had made love to Jean Constable that same night.

Essex Chronicle

She was at her parents' home when, only half-listening, she heard a newscaster say: "A man at Wethersfield American Air Force base has been arrested for murder . . ." She looked up and saw pictures of a man being escorted from the base with his head covered by a cape. She said casually to her brother: "That must be a Yank they've arrested." Then came a knock at the door. The local police were there to tell her that the man under the cape was her husband. "Horror took my breath away," she said later. "My head spun. I screamed. I collapsed."

Boshears spent the night in Brixton Prison, in South London. The following day he had to wait in a police cell at Braintree for five hours while urgent calls went out to assemble an unexpected magistrates' court hearing at the 800-year-old village of Castle Hedingham. A clerk had to be hurriedly brought from a court in a different part of the county and Lady Beatrice Plummer, chairman of the magistrates, had to be summoned from London.

Eventually Boshears, wearing a fur-lined parka, green combat suit, and boots, was standing rigidly to attention in the little courtroom—which was heated by a roaring coal fire—while the Americans argued for the right to try him by court martial. Major Carl B. Prestin of the United States Judge Advocate's Department asked that Boshears be remanded to a U.S. detention centre. This plea, made under the Visiting Forces Act, was vigorously opposed by the police and was subsequently rejected by Sir Theobald Mathew, the Director of Public Prosecutions. A U.S.A.F. spokesman explained the application:

"Under the terms of the N.A.T.O. status of forces agreement, the British authorities have primary jurisdiction to try this man. But, under the agreement, we are required to ask that we shall receive jurisdiction, which would mean an air force court-martial. The British authorities have the right to refuse our request and to try the man in their Courts and that is what they are doing."

N.A.T.O. observers and U.S.A.F. officers were in the crowded courtroom at Essex Assizes, Chelmsford, when the trial formally began and Boshears pleaded not guilty to murder. Boshears spoke in a low voice which, at times, was difficult to hear. He told the jury that he did not know how Jean Constable died and added: "There was no quarrel or argument. At no time did I make any overtures or sexual advances to her, nor did I have any desire to kill her or harm her in any way."

He then said: "I cannot throw any light on how I came to have marks on my face. I have no more knowledge of how Jean met her death than I have told the police and the jury." Initially, when questioned by the police, he had stated: "Jean and her boy friend came into my flat. It might have been around 11 p.m. We had a few drinks in the living-room and I passed out. We were there an hour or two before that. I could not be sure."

Jean Constable and her "boy friend" had left the flat but he did not know at what time. Under cross-examination by Mr. Stanley Rees, prosecuting, he admitted that, at first, he had told lies to the police—but had done so because he had been scared. He had been sober when he threw the body in the ditch, and had not been telling the truth when he informed the police that he did not know why he had done so.

Less intense struggle

Mr. Rees: "It is a lie because you knew exactly why you took the body to the ditch?"

"Yes, sir."

"And in a sober and determined attempt to cover up what had happened you carried her body into the bathroom and then into the bedroom. This was a calculated attempt to hide the crime?"

"Yes, sir."

"What crime did you think you had committed?"

"The logical one."

"What did you think was the logical one?"

"I had killed someone."

"But you didn't think it was a crime to kill someone when you were fast asleep?"

"I thought to kill any way was a crime."

The eminent pathologist Dr. Francis Camps was then asked: "On the findings which you made on that body did you think it is possible that he could have killed her while asleep in that way?"

"I should think it is certainly within the bounds of improbability," said Dr. Camps. "My reason, from my findings, is this process would take a certain amount of time and during that period the person would go through certain phases of movement and, from the description given of finding her suddenly dead like that, I don't think it fits in with that type of crime."

When Dr. Camps was cross-examined by the defending counsel, he agreed that marks on Jean Constable's elbow and wrist were nothing to do with the activity of the death night. This indicated that the struggle could have been less intense than had earlier been supposed. The defence made great play of this statement—and of

AP

SISTER AND MOTHER of the victim arrive at the headline – making trial. When it was all over, Staff-Sergeant Boshears was surrounded by a horde of women . . . some booing, some cheering. He had to be rescued by the police.

the fact that Dr. Camps had said he would not go as far as to say that it was "impossible" for a man, while asleep, to strangle someone.

Mr. Justice Glyn-Jones, summing up, said the jury might think that, in putting his hands on the girl's neck and applying pressure for such a length of time, the strangler intended to cause grievous bodily harm or death. "He must have known what would be the result of what he was doing," he said.

He explained to the jury that there were only two verdicts possible – guilty of murder or not guilty of anything at all. "There is no lesser alternative verdict open to you," he stressed. The judge apparently had not studied the earlier cases of sleep-walking slayers, for he asked: "Have you ever heard of a man strangling a woman while he was sound asleep?" "We have no medical evidence that there exists any record in all the records of the medical profession that such a thing has happened." Dr. Camps had said that this might be possible. The judge paused and looked sternly at the members of the jury. "You use your common sense and decide whether it happened," he instructed.

Was it within the bounds of possibility that Boshears could have moved from his position beside the girl, taken the covering from her and then, straddling himself across her, seized her throat in his hands and applied pressure resulting in unconsciousness, convulsion and death – without him being awakened by his own exertions?

That was the vital question. And, again, it was the duty of the jury to use its common sense. During his 22-minute summing-up the judge also stressed that if Boshears had strangled while he was asleep, it was not a voluntary act and he was entitled to be acquitted. If the jury were in any doubt about whether or not he was asleep he was also entitled to be acquitted. The jury retired for one hour and 50 minutes. When they returned and gave a "Not Guilty" verdict, there were incredulous shouts from the public gallery.

Six weeks of hell

Fantastic scenes took place outside the court following the acquittal. As Boshears walked out a free man there was a barrage of booing and cheering. Hordes of women, hoping to catch a glimpse of him, disrupted the rush-hour traffic. The handful of U.S.A.F. officers surrounding him could not carve a way through the crowds. Finally a squad of policemen rescued Boshears, and formed a protective circle around him as he walked 400 yards through the main streets to an Air Force car. The hearing had lasted two days, and Boshears commented:

BRENTWOOD, MALDON, BILLERICAY, LAINDON ED

THE ESSEX
Chronicle

Telephone: Chelmsford 4631/2
SALES NOW EXCEED 37,000 WEEKLY
PRICE THREEPEN
196th YEAR
FRIDAY, JANUARY 6th, 1961
No. 10,241

For Properties
Businesses
Smallholdings
IN ESSEX OR BORDERS consult . . . .
EVERSHEDS
SURVEYORS and ESTATE AGENTS
122 King's Road, Brentwood
Telephone: 322617 Evenings 1721

JEAN: STA
SERGEA
IN COU

This is JEAN CONSTABLE, the murdered girl, as her American friends knew her . . . gay, party-loving, high spirited.

COMMENT COLUMN

is handed over this week to one of our regular readers. We are unable to improve on his remarks! He says:—

A HIGH STANDARD

TO THE EDITOR

SIR, — I have pleasure of renewing my 'Essex Chronicle' subscription for 1961 and thank you for the prompt despatch of your newspapers throughout the year.

May I once again compliment you upon the high standards of reporting and "Comment" which you maintain, so valuable in these days when so much that is vulgar and cheap is foist upon the public.

My mother, who is now in her eighty-fifth year, values your paper which still serves as a link with Braintree and Coggeshall, which she left nearly 30 years ago to come here.

May 1961 be happy and prosperous for you all.

With every good wish,

Yours sincerely,

NORMAN G. CRESSWELL
24 Court Drive
Croydon

SEE BACK PAGE

Frederick Home, of Fairfield Road, Chelmsford, was fined £1 at Chelmsford yesterday for leaving his car outside his house without lights.

Press Association

"It has been six weeks of hell. I'm still in a daze. I cannot believe it's true that I am a free man. British justice? It's wonderful. My wife has forgiven me. She came to see me in prison while I was awaiting trial to tell me so. I am longing to see my kids again. I kept a picture of them in my cell."

But the real torment which his wife had experienced was described more evocatively by her. She told how she felt living with the knowledge that the girl Jean Constable had been in her flat and had died there.

"The most terrible moment was when I had to return to the flat at Dunmow where it all happened," she said. "I had vowed I would never set foot in it again. But a month after Bill's arrest I had to go back to pick up our belongings. My knees were shaking and my hand trembled so much I could scarcely get the door key into the lock. The place was in a terrible shambles.

"The police had turned out the kitchen fire in search of clues. In the bathroom the ceiling plaster had fallen. I walked down the long hall to our living-room. This is where the girl had died. I pushed open the door. I could see the mattress by the fire. The bloodstains on the carpet. I turned and ran. I remembered all my hopes and all my disappointments. I wept."

"I REMEMBERED all my hopes and disappointments. My knees were shaking. My hand trembled." . . . "My wife has forgiven me. I'm longing to see the kids."

Twenty-four hours after being cleared of the murder, Boshears, re-united with his family, was at the Wethersfield base – preparing to go on leave. Then in July of that year – after returning to America – Boshears was dismissed from the army. The official statement said that his dismissal was "under other than honourable conditions"

BATHTUB BIGAMIST

The notorious bigamist who preyed on lonely, unsuspecting women. He married them, took their money . . . then he drowned them.

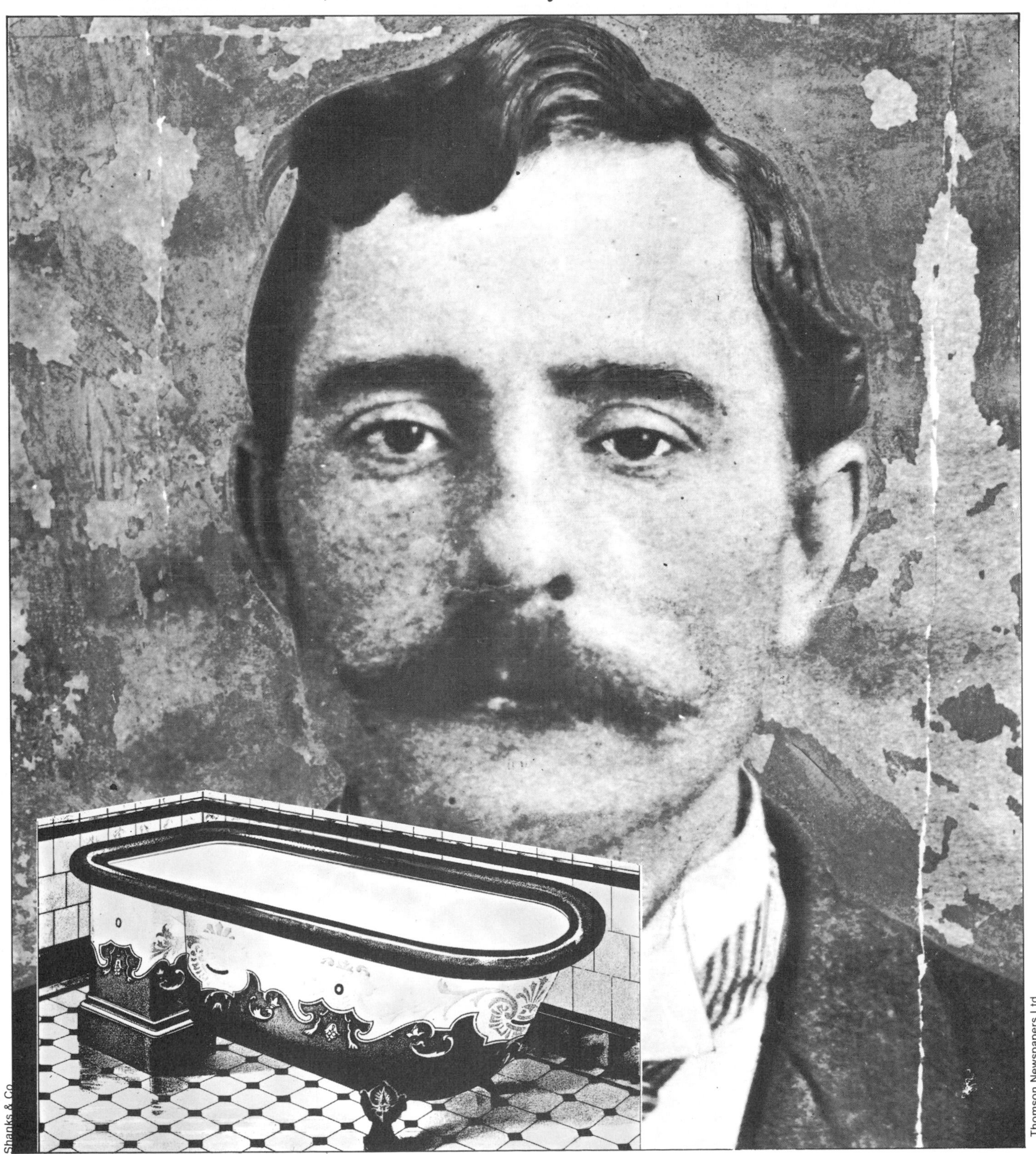

Shanks & Co

Thomson Newspapers Ltd

MUSTACHIOED MURDERER George Joseph Smith (right) was a skilful seducer. Women found him irresistible and gave up not only themselves but their money in response to his charm. He drowned three of his wives in the bath. Below, the two who escaped: Caroline Thornhill (top), Edith Pegler.

Syndication International

Popperfoto

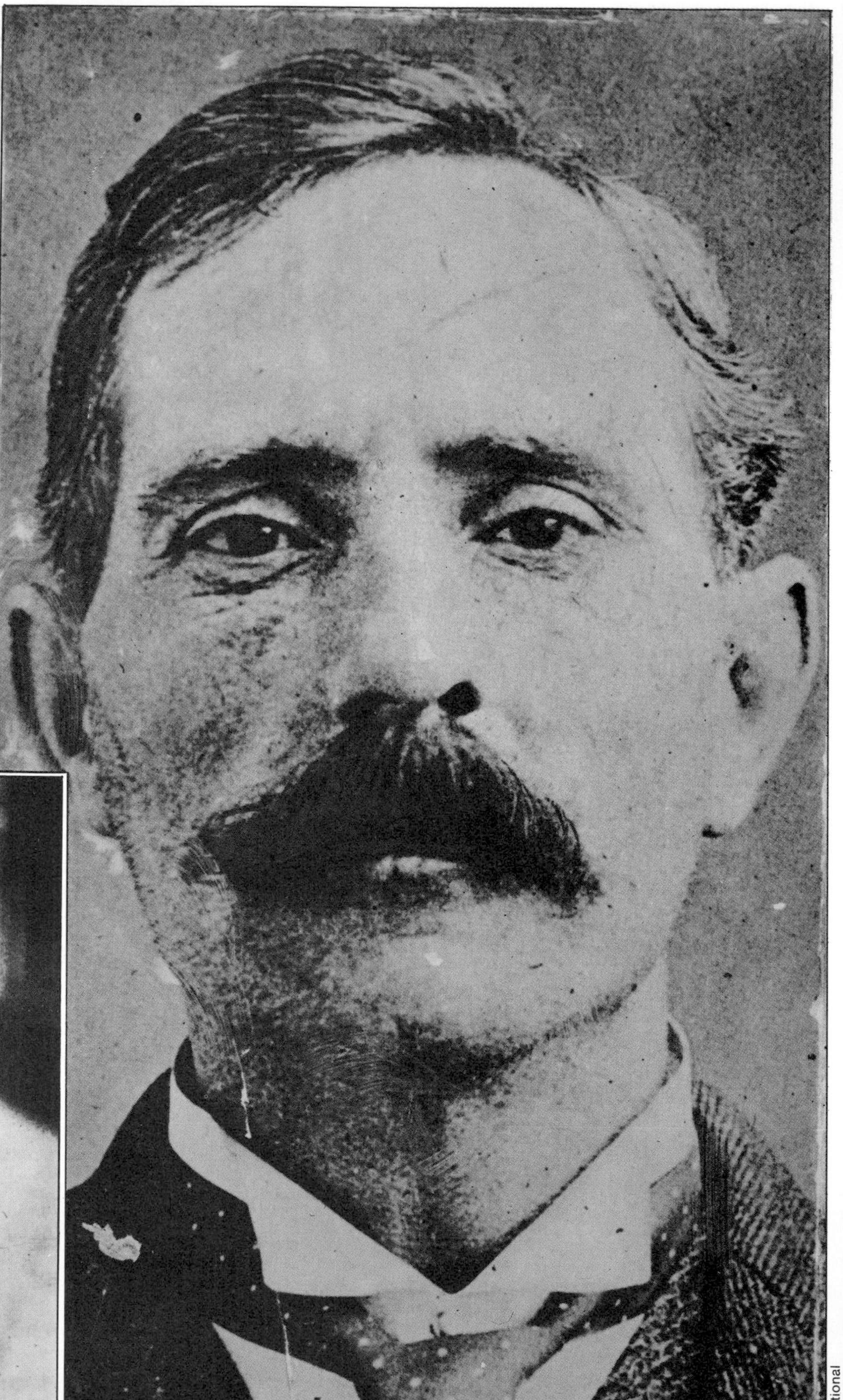

Syndication International

FOR NINE days during the summer of 1915 the attention of the British public was temporarily diverted from the bloody trench warfare in France to an amazing murder trial which took place in London's Central Criminal Court, the Old Bailey. The accused whom the police brought into the dock on June 22, 1915, was a 43-year-old criminal adventurer charged under his real name of George Joseph Smith—although he had employed a number of aliases in the course of his unsavoury sexual and criminal career.

As a youngster he had been sent to a reformatory and later went to prison twice for stealing. From an early age, in spite of a certain talent for drawing and playing the piano, he was the despair of his respectable mother—who prophesied with remarkable accuracy that he would die with his boots on. He had tried his hand at a variety of occupations: gymnasium instructor in the army, music hall songwriter, baker, junk shop owner, and finally dealer in antiques.

Lonely women

However, his principal occupation was preying upon lonely and unsuspecting women who, unfortunately for them, found him most attractive. It was one of these women, Bessie Mundy—whom he had "married" bigamously as Henry Williams in 1910—that he was tried for murdering two years later. She died while taking a bath at the lodgings where they lived together in Herne Bay, on the English south coast.

The presiding judge at the trial was the great commercial lawyer Mr. Justice Scrutton. The prosecution was led by the senior prosecuting counsel Mr. (later Sir) Archibald Bodkin, afterwards Director of Public Prosecutions. Smith was defended by Sir Edward Marshall Hall, the most popular and successful criminal advocate of his day and then at the height of his powers. As Smith had no money, Marshall Hall provided his services for £3 5s. 6d.—the maximum fee allowed defence counsel by the Poor Prisoners' Defence Act.

After Smith had formally pleaded not guilty, Mr. Bodkin began his opening speech for the prosecution. In outlining the prisoner's career to the jury, the prosecutor drew particular attention to the fact that the accused—under the assumed name of George Oliver Love—had married Caroline Beatrice Thornhill at Leicester in 1898. A year or two later she left him, but she remained his legal wife and was alive at the time of the trial. In 1908, Smith met a young woman named Edith Pegler in Bristol and "married" her under his own name. They lived together from time to time, and though he would leave her for long periods, he always returned to her in the end. In fact he had done so after the death of Bessie Mundy.

On August 26, 1910, the prisoner went through a ceremony of marriage, posing as Henry Williams, with 31-year-old Beatrice ("Bessie") Constance Annie Mundy in Weymouth Registry Office. She had a small fortune of £2,500 left by her late father, who had been a bank manager. She could not touch the capital sum, which was held in trust for her, but she was paid £8 a month from the trust, which she allowed to accumulate.

By September 1910 the accumulated balance amounted to £138, and this Smith obtained by applying for it to the trust solicitor in his "wife's" name. As soon as he received it, he made off, leaving her without a penny. He subsequently wrote to her explaining that his health had become "terribly impaired" as the result of an "infectious disease" which he claimed she had given him, and that a long cure was necessary before he could return.

Meanwhile, Bessie went to live in lodgings with a friend in Weston-super-Mare. There, by an extraordinary coincidence, while walking along the esplanade one day in March 1912, she spotted her errant "husband". Instead of running away or calling the police, she spoke to him and again fell completely under his charm. She immediately left her lodgings to spend the night with him, not even taking her nightdress. The reunited couple then moved together to lodgings in Herne Bay.

There was no bath in the new house, but Smith bought one secondhand and installed it in an empty room in the lodgings. This was on July 6, 1912. Next day they both made wills, the unfortunate Bessie appointing her "husband" sole executor and legatee. Four days later the couple called on a local doctor named French. Smith said that his wife had shown signs of epilepsy—although the lady described herself as being perfectly well except for occasional headaches.

Completely submerged

On the morning of July 13, Dr. French received a note from Smith: "Do come at once. I am afraid my wife is dead." When the doctor arrived at the lodgings, he found that this was so, the woman's body being completely submerged in the bath water. In one hand she clutched a piece of soap.

At the coroner's inquest, Dr. French stated that in his opinion the woman drowned as the result of a fit of epilepsy in the bath. In these circumstances it was not surprising that the jury returned a verdict of death by misadventure—"the cause of death being that while taking a bath she had an epileptic seizure causing her to fall back into the water and be drowned".

The dead woman's estate was proved at £2,571, and under the terms of her will her "husband" inherited all of it. He first invested the proceeds in house property, and after selling out at a considerable loss, used the £1,300 that was left to buy an annuity which brought him an income of £76 a year. Clearly George Joseph Smith had an expectation of a long life.

"This case is of a very grave character," said the prosecutor after he had told the jury how Bessie Mundy had died, "and one to which you will give the most earnest attention in the interests not only of the prisoner, but also of the public." Counsel paused dramatically for a few moments. He then turned to the judge and said that he had an important point of law concerning the admissibility of certain evidence to put to him. Mr. Justice Scrutton accordingly directed the jury to retire while it was being argued.

Virtually doomed

This was a move which Marshall Hall had feared, since he knew from the documents in his brief that there was evidence that his client had "married" two other women, that the two had likewise died in their baths, and that they had previously both executed wills making the prisoner sole beneficiary. Hall realized that if once this evidence was admitted his client was virtually doomed.

Mr. Bodkin's point was that the prosecution was entitled to call evidence of any character tending to prove that this was a case of killing by deliberate design and not by accident—and that the accused in causing the death of Bessie Mundy was operating a "system". In reply Marshall Hall submitted that evidence of "system" was only admissible where it was necessary for the defence to set up a denial of intent. It was not necessary in this case, he said, since as yet the prosecution had not put forward sufficient evidence to displace the primary presumption of innocence in the prisoner.

It was a gallant effort on the lawyer's part, but it proved of no avail. The judge ruled that such evidence *was* admissible. However, he warned the jury that they must not use it to infer that the prisoner was a man of bad character and infamous acts, but only to help them to decide whether Miss Mundy's death was the result of an accident or had been deliberately engineered by Smith.

The prosecutor then proceeded to outline the facts of the two additional murders for which he suggested that the prisoner was responsible. In 1913 Smith had bigamously married a buxom young nurse named Alice Burnham whom he had seen praying in a Wesleyan-Methodist chapel in Southsea. Her father, a fruitgrower in Buckinghamshire, had been keeping a sum of £104 for her, and when Smith wrote to Mr. Burnham demanding that it should be handed over, Mr. Burnham

FIRST VICTIM . . . Bessie Mundy pictured with Smith after their "marriage". Two years later she lay in her grave (right). At the inquest the jury gave a verdict of "misadventure". Smith's luck did not last.

Syndication International

BUXOM BRIDE number four, Alice Burnham. Smith collected £500 insurance.

Popperfoto

replied in a letter in which he asked some questions about his son-in-law's family background. To his letter he received the following astonishing postcard:

> Sir, – In answer to your application regarding my parentage, my mother was a bus-horse, my father a cab-driver, my sister a roughrider over the Arctic regions. My brothers were all gallant sailors on a steam-roller. This is the only information I can give to those who are not entitled to ask such questions contained in the letter I received on the 24th inst.
>
> Your despised son-in-law,
> G. SMITH

In the end Smith got Alice Burnham's £104 through a solicitor. He also saw to it that she took out an insurance policy of £500 on her life, as well as making a will leaving everything she had to him. Together they visited Blackpool and stayed in lodgings – where the landlady saw water coming through the ceiling one evening when Alice was taking a bath. She was afterwards found drowned in the bath. Much to the landlady's surprise, Mr. Smith had the body put in a plain deal coffin and given a pauper's funeral. "When they are dead, they are done with," he remarked callously. The coroner's jury brought in a verdict of accidental death.

Insurance money

Shortly afterwards Smith received the £500 insurance money on Alice Burnham's life, which he prudently handed back to the insurance company in order to increase his annuity by some £30 a year. He spent Christmas with one of his former "wives", Edith Pegler, and her family in Bristol, saying he had just returned from a profitable antique dealing visit to Spain.

About a year later, under the name of John Lloyd, he contracted another bigamous marriage, this time in Highgate to a clergyman's daughter named Margaret Lofty. She was the most highly born as well as the most short-lived of his brides. She likewise made a will the day after their "marriage", and later the same evening the sound of splashing was heard coming from the bathroom, followed by the slapping of wet hands on flesh, and finally a sigh.

A short while later the landlady heard the mournful strains of the hymn "Nearer my God to Thee" being played on the harmonium in the Lloyds' sitting-room. Then she heard the slamming of the front door. Before long the male lodger returned and knocked at the landlady's door. He asked about the key which she had given him, but which he had forgotten, and added: "I have bought some tomatoes for Mrs. Lloyd's supper."

A third coroner's jury exonerated Mr. Lloyd, who showed great emotion. "We were only married on Thursday," he said. Being a Friday evening the incident attracted the attention of the national press, and on the following Sunday the *News of the World* headlined the story of a "Bride's Tragic Fate on Day after Wedding".

Under observation

Among those who read the story was the late Alice Burnham's father, and also another landlady who later turned Mr. Lloyd away when he came to engage lodgings. He could not provide a satisfactory reference after he had been shown the bath which he had complained was very small—although as an afterthought he murmured: "I daresay it is large enough for someone to lie in." Both the landlady and Mr. Burnham got in touch with the police, and as a result Mr. Lloyd was kept under observation. He was arrested on February 1, 1915, when about to enter a solicitor's office in Shepherd's Bush, London, with a view to proving the late Margaret Lofty's will.

He was first charged with causing a false entry to be made at his bigamous marriage to his third victim. Then after he had been identified by Mr. Burnham, he was remanded in custody for further police inquiries. Two months later he was charged with the murder of Bessie Mundy, Alice Burnham, and Margaret Lofty—although he was only indicted for killing the first named.

"In each case you get the simulated marriage," said Mr. Bodkin in concluding his speech to the jury. "In each case all the ready money the woman had is realised. In each case the woman made a will in the prisoner's favour. In each case the property could only be got at through the woman's death . . . In each case there were inquiries about the bathroom. In each case the prisoner is the first to discover the death. In each case the prisoner is the person in immediate association with each woman before her death. In each case the bathroom doors are either unfastenable or unfastened . . . In each case there is the immediate disappearance of the prisoner."

The only one of Smith's "brides" to testify was Edith Pegler, the only one whom he loved enough neither to desert, to rob, nor to kill. On the whole, she said, the prisoner had been kind to her. But she added a curious fact when she stated that Smith had once warned her of the danger of baths to women. "I should advise you to be careful about these things," she stated he had told her, "as it is known that women often lose their lives through weak hearts and fainting in a bath." While she was giving her evidence, the prisoner showed some signs of distress.

When a police inspector took the stand, Smith lost all control. "He is a scoundrel!" he shouted as he jumped up from his seat in the dock. "He ought to be in this dock. He will be one day!"

"Sit down," said the judge. "You are doing yourself no good." But the prisoner refused to be pacified and he banged his fist on the ledge in front of him, his face white with fury. "I don't care tuppence what you say," he roared back at Mr. Justice Scrutton, "you can't sentence me to death. I have done no murder!"

The police inspector described how he had induced a woman friend, who was a strong swimmer, to don a bathing costume and subject herself to an experiment in one of the baths, which had been filled with water. The inspector pulled up her legs at the narrow end so that her head fell under water. She immediately lost consciousness and there was considerable difficulty in bringing her round.

This testimony was corroborated by the celebrated pathologist Sir Bernard Spilsbury, who was called for the prosecution after the three baths had been brought into court as exhibits. "If a woman of the stature of Miss Mundy was in the bath in which she died," said Sir Bernard, "the first onset of an epileptic fit would stiffen and extend the body. In view of her height, 5 feet 7 inches, and the length of the bath, 5 feet, I do not think her head would be submerged during that stage of the fit . . .

Limp body

"After the seizure has passed the state of the body is that of relaxation. The body would probably be limp and unconscious. Bearing in mind the length of the body and the size of the bath, I do not think she would be likely to be immersed during the state of relaxation . . . Dr. French has described the legs straight out from the hips and the feet up against the end of the bath, out of the water. I cannot give any explanation of how a woman—assuming she had had an epileptic seizure—could get into that position by herself. *If the feet at the narrow end were lifted out of the water, that might allow the trunk and head to slide down the bath.*"

Defence counsel could do little with this formidable witness in cross-examination. However, Marshall Hall tried his best, as always. He endeavoured to get the witness to say that clutching a piece of soap lent support to the theory of epilepsy.

"It is not impossible," was as far as Spilsbury would go, "not very likely," he concluded cautiously.

When the case for the prosecution was closed—no less than 112 witnesses had been called and 264 incriminating exhibits put in—Marshall Hall rose and announced briefly: "I do not call any evidence." This gave him the last word with the jury, and again he exerted all his great rhetorical skill with the scanty material at his disposal.

ONE DAY was all Margaret Lofty (above) lasted—just enough time to sign her will in Smith's favour. Opposite, Smith listens calmly to the overwhelming evidence presented against him. But he frequently interrupted the trial with passionate outbursts. Far right, Sir Archibald Bodkin, prosecuting counsel (top) and the famous Sir Edward Marshall Hall who used all his celebrated verbal skill in a vain attempt to get Smith acquitted of the ghastly charges.

The gist of his defence argument was that no act of violence had been proven, and that it would have been impossible for his client to have killed Bessie Mundy without leaving marks of violence and evidence of a struggle. "If you tried to drown a kitten, it would scratch you, and do you think a woman would not scratch?"

Popperfoto

Syndication International

Syndication International

Popperfoto

WATERTIGHT EVIDENCE . . . Home Office pathologist Sir Bernard Spilsbury arrives at the Old Bailey clutching vital evidence. It was his testimony which tied up the case against Smith. The whole trial was a fascinating and lurid diversion for Londoners accustomed to a diet of gloomy war news.
Above, crowds jostle and push at the doors of the Old Bailey on the last day of the trial in tense anticipation of the verdict being pronounced.

As evidence of Smith's humanity he stressed the mutual affection between the prisoner and Edith Pegler, adding that the crimes of which Smith had been accused were outside the orbit of sane humanity.

Most dramatic moment

"Let me with all the solemnity I can," he besought the jury, "and with all the power of conviction I can put into words say to you: be fair to yourselves, be fair to the prisoner, be just to justice itself before you decide the fate of this man by saying that this terrible accusation against him has been proved."

Mr. Justice Scrutton summed up largely against the prisoner, as he was obliged by the evidence to do. With great effect he compared the knocking at the landlady's door by Smith – shortly after Margaret Lofty had died – to the knocking at the gate just after the murder of Duncan in *Macbeth* – "The most dramatic moment in English poetry," the judge called it.

"You may as well hang me at once, the way you are going on," the prisoner shouted from the dock. "It is a disgrace to a Christian country, that is. I am not a murderer, though I may be a bit peculiar."

It took the jury only twenty minutes to find Smith guilty. Before sentencing him to death by hanging, Mr. Justice Scrutton observed sternly: "Judges sometimes use this occasion to warn the public against the repetition of such crimes – they sometimes use such occasions to exhort the prisoner to repentance. I propose to take neither of these courses. I do not believe there is another man in England who needs to be warned against the commission of such a crime, and I think that exhortation to repentance would be wasted on you."

An appeal was lodged challenging the evidence of the other murders, but the Court of Criminal Appeal held that this evidence of "system" had been rightly admitted, and the appeal was dismissed. The Home Secretary refused a reprieve and the law took its course.

Holy Communion

Smith protested his innocence to the last. On the morning of his execution in Maidstone Prison, in Kent, he partook of Holy Communion. To the prison chaplain who administered the sacrament he said: "I beg of you to believe me when I say I am innocent. No one else does, except my wife. I don't care now. I shall soon be in the presence of God, and I declare before Him I am innocent."

As the hangman put the cap over his head and adjusted the noose, he again declared, "I am innocent." Then the trap-door fell and the pinioned figure disappeared into the pit below the scaffold. George Joseph Smith died like his three lonely-hearts brides – by suffocation.